An Elementary
ETHICS

PRENTICE-HALL PHILOSOPHY SERIES

Arthur E. Murphy, Ph.D., Editor

An Elementary
ETHICS

ALBUREY CASTELL

Department of Philosophy
University of Oregon

New York   PRENTICE-HALL, INC.   1954

for Carsten, Matthew
and Adelaide
when they are old enough

Preface

I should like to preface this book by a brief excursion into autobiography. I enrolled as a freshman for a course in ethics, or, as it was called, "moral philosophy," back in the early 1920's. I can still recall the first meeting of the class. It was exciting. It was given over to attempts on the part of the class to answer the question: "In what different senses of the word 'good' do we speak of things as being 'good'?" At the end of twenty minutes I felt the ground shifting out from under my feet. In many ways that ethics course made a deeper impression upon me than any other course which I had in college. I have been puzzled many times since then to explain to myself just why that was so. Perhaps the word "impressed" does not best convey the point. Perhaps some such words as "entangled," "enmeshed," "frustrated," "exasperated" come nearer to it.

Some years later, it was my business to teach an ethics course. I came in time to feel somewhat uneasy about it; began, indeed, to see it as something of a "problem-child" in the department's relations with its customers. I found that this worry was shared by others. The course was, I discovered, frequently disliked by those who found themselves teaching it. The text-books frequently had a reputation for being dull or edifying or strident or just plain confusing. You soon found, after the first few sessions of the course, that you were trafficking in platitudes, or dealing with the arbitrary, or sliding into outright skepticism. Except by luck or by definition there seemed no way to get any matters settled; and all too frequently your luck gave out or you couldn't get anyone to accept your definitions. Too often also such masterful enterprises as psychology on the one side, and politics on the other, had an awkward habit of stealing the show.

For a number of years I shied away from teaching ethics. I took up with logic and epistemology, learning to bounce p's off q's and to talk austerely about the redness of the cherry, the flatness of the penny, and the relation between implication and inference. Much of this was good business. No moralist is worth his salt unless he can put on the gloves with the local logicians. But after a while it ceased to pay off. From being invigorated with its austerities, I became bored with its aridities. Meanwhile, my interest in the ethics course began to revive. I had some experiences which left me skeptical about being skeptical in matters pertaining to right and wrong. I encountered men who were men of bad will in any linguistic usage that I cared to authorize. I found also that I was constrained to say of myself upon occasion, "*Video meliora proboque, deteriora sequor.*" In short, I began to authorize moral judgments. Now, any man who is willing to make moral judgments, about himself or anyone else, is already committed to a moral philosophy; for a moral philosophy is a statement of the principles and presuppositions upon which, when pushed to it, we rest our moral judgments. The function of an ethics course is to enable a person to figure out the principles and presuppositions upon which he criticizes and revises his attempts to do what is right and to avoid doing what is wrong. I believe now, what I did not believe some years ago, that the *onus probandi* rests with the person who says that this can't be done, or is not worth doing.

A. C.

Table of Contents

Summary of Contents

Chapter I draws attention to the distinction between judgment and principle, thesis and hypo-thesis. Traditional ethical theory asks what principle underlies moral judgments. The judgments are theses. What is their hypo-thesis? Chapter II presents three traditional ethical theories, three attempts to formulate the principle which underlies moral judgments. Chapter III presents three recent alternatives to traditional ethical theory. These alternatives repudiate the question which generated traditional ethical theory. Chapter IV argues that moral judgments presuppose free will; it attempts to disprove the claim that this presupposition cannot be granted. Chapter V argues that a good society is one which expresses the wills of good men; and that it does this, in great part, by laws which provide legislative definition for its major institutions. The reader is invited to propose legislative definition for one major institution (marriage). No society is infallible in devising these legislative definitions; in addition, great power is required for their enactment. Lest this power be abused, J. S. Mill is quoted as urging that as far as possible society allow the individual to think and act for himself.

An Elementary
ETHICS

I. Moral Judgment and Ethical Theory

1. THE STUDENT LOOKS FOR DATA

An ethical theory is a set of principles by which a person attempts to do what is right and avoid doing what is wrong. Any person who tries to do what is right and avoid doing what is wrong has an ethical theory. He may not know this fact about himself. His ethical theory may be implicit in his efforts without being explicit in his thinking about those efforts. To the extent that this is so, he is not fully aware of what he is doing and why he is doing it. He is, in a philosophical sense, naive; that is, ignorant of the principles upon which he thinks and acts. It is the function of philosophy to dispel the naivete with which each generation begins its life, to provide it with a grasp of first principles and a sharpened sense of their presence in thought and action. Where philosophy is understood and respected, it contributes heavily toward producing that alert and criticized mind which is an essential ingredient in civilized living. It is the function of moral philosophy, in particular, to do this for people's efforts to do what is right and avoid doing what is wrong. One of the world's great moralists is reported to have said, "The unexamined life is not worth living."

The Central Question. The reader is invited to put this question to himself: By what principles do I attempt to do what is right and avoid doing what is wrong? That is the central question. When you ask that question you are asking for self-knowledge, you are seeking to get better acquainted with yourself;

1

and that is a slow and difficult business. Many people are strangers to themselves, or at best bowing acquaintances. If you doubt this, try your question on someone whom you know reasonably well as a person. Say to him: "By what principles do you attempt to do what is right and avoid doing what is wrong?"

You have here a question of universal human concern. Do you know anyone of whom you would be prepared to say: "He never at any time attempts to do what is right and avoid doing what is wrong"? Anyone of whom you would be prepared to say: "He never criticizes and revises his attempts to do what is right and avoid doing what is wrong"? Anyone of whom you would be prepared to say: "There are no principles involved in his attempts or in his criticisms and revisions of his attempts to do what is right and avoid doing what is wrong"?

It may not be amiss to comment briefly on the key words that are used to state the central question. What is a principle? The question refers to principles, in the plural. Is that perhaps a mistake? The question speaks of attempting to do what is right and avoid doing what is wrong. Why the modest word "attempt"? Is it always only an attempt, and never a resounding success? If so, is the explanation to be sought in the character of rightness and wrongness, or in the character of persons? In speaking of attempts, the question suggests the possibility of failure. Where failure occurs, criticism and revision are in order. Indeed, you could amplify the original question thus: "By what principles do I criticize and revise my attempts to do what is right and avoid doing what is wrong?" What is a criticism? Wherein does it differ, say, from a description? And what is a revision? Wherein does it differ from, say, mere change?

In that revised form the question asks after principles by which you criticize and revise your conduct. That seems clear enough. There is you, there is your conduct, and there are your principles. You use the principles in criticizing and revising the conduct. That, however, is not an end of the matter. Nothing has been said, thus far, of criticizing and revising one's principles. We have spoken only of criticizing and revising one's conduct, and of using one's principles to do that. And yet, the further step, namely criticizing and revising one's principles, is not only possible: it may even be necessary. A person may indeed find himself driven to criticize and revise his principles. That raises new questions altogether. When do principles themselves need criticism and revision? And how does one go about criticizing and revising them?

Moral Judgment and Moral Principle. When we are not acting thoughtlessly, our action embodies a judgment; and the judgment embodies a principle. Suppose you owe money. You judge that it would be right to repay it and wrong not to repay it. What principle is involved here? You can get at it by asking yourself why it would be right to repay and wrong not to repay; that is, give a reason for your judgment. Your first answer may not carry you directly from the judgment to the principle. Your soliloquy might run along these lines: Why would it be wrong not to repay the debt? "Because the money is his; he merely lent it to me." But why is it wrong not to give a man what is his? "Because it will distress him." Why is it wrong to distress him? "Because he might refuse to help me at some later time." Why is it wrong to risk future trouble for yourself? "Because such trouble when it arrived would distress me." Why is it wrong for you to bring about distress for yourself? "Because such distress would reduce my happiness." Why is it wrong for you to reduce your happiness? "Why, you say?" Yes, why. "I don't know how to answer that. That's as far as I go. Any act of mine is wrong if it reduces my happiness. That's the principle, upon which, ultimately, I judge any act of mine to be wrong." If this imaginary soliloquy did move along those lines and did reach a dead end at that point, the original judgment would have been traced back to its principle. It is unlikely that it would have moved along those lines or reached a dead end at that point, but that fact does not spoil it as an illustration. The analysis began with a moral judgment and regressed in search of a moral principle. In calling the outcome by that name, "principle," two things are intended: first, the regressive analysis could be carried no further; second, similar analyses, taking off from other moral judgments, would also arrive at that same principle.

We need to confront ourselves with some moral judgments which we would authorize. Unless we would authorize them, they would not be our judgments. The following cases provide opportunities to make particular moral judgments, judgments declaring that it would be right (or wrong) for a particular person to perform a particular act under these particular circumstances.

CASE I. Mr. X is dying slowly of a painful and incurable disease. Medical advisers agree that he may linger on for months, in increasing torment and possible loss of sanity. Knowing these things, and knowing too that the hospital expenses are a severe drain upon his limited financial resources, Mr. X decides that he would rather die than continue to live under these circumstances. His physician will not run the professional risk of providing him with the necessary suicide drug. There is only his friend, Mr. Y, to whom he can turn. Should Mr. X revise his initial decision, and decide instead that, under these circumstances, he would rather continue to live than to die? If he holds by his initial decision, should he appeal to his friend, Mr. Y, to get him the suicide drug? Should Mr. Y procure that drug for his sick friend? If news of this business reached the ears of the physician, should he intervene and put a stop to it? These questions are representative.

CASE II. A psychiatrist has reason to believe that Mrs. M is suffering from a serious nervous disorder caused by a suppressed passion for a friend of her husband. None of the parties concerned know what is probably the cause of her trouble. Put yourself in the shoes of the psychiatrist. Should any of these three persons be told? Which? What advice should you give, after having told what you take to be the facts of the case? You can extend your questions by shifting from the psychiatrist to the three persons concerned.

CASE III. Mr. A. comes of poor but devout parents, who, at great sacrifice to themselves, have seen him through high-school and college because they desire him to become a clergyman. Thanks to denominational scholarships and fellowships, he was able to spend the required years of post-graduate studies in a theological seminary. He was placed in charge of a church in his home town. Here he has won the respect and devotion of a large circle of men and women who have grown to look to him for help and guidance in matters of faith and morals. He is married to a girl to whom their way of life means a great deal. His parents feel amply repaid for all that they have done. His alma mater is known to be considering him for an appointment to the teaching staff of the college. Gradually, however, Mr. A has begun to lose his faith, until finally he has ceased to believe in most of the teachings which it is his duty to expound. What should Mr. A do?

CASE IV. The son of a wealthy man is kidnapped and threatened with death unless ransom is paid. The terms of the ransom are that the numbers of the bills be withheld from the G men. Ought the boy's father to pay the ransom? Ought he to turn the bill numbers over to the federal authorities if he has agreed not to?

CASE V. As I make out the grades for a logic class, I am tolerably sure of the following facts. Student No. 1 will not get into law school next fall unless he receives a B. He has earned a C. To miss entering in the fall means having to wait another entire year. Student No. 2 will be dropped from college by the dean if he fails to get a C in each of his courses. He has earned a D. The logic course was not in any sense necessary to him in his future work; he registered for it because he had heard that it was interesting and not too difficult. Student No. 3 will be able to graduate if he receives merely a D. If he receives an F, he will not. He has earned an F. His low mark was probably due to a combination of laziness and indifference. What ought I to do in each case?

CASE VI. Did Brutus do right or wrong in bringing about the assassination of Caesar? Caesar had been Brutus' personal friend and benefactor. Caesar had done great things for the Roman people, had extended their territory, had made their army the most efficient fighting machine in the ancient world, had laid the foundations of the great "Pax Romana" by conquering and imposing peace upon multitudes of warring peoples in the Mediterranean world. On the other hand, he was inaugurating a one-man control of public affairs. He was introducing "Caesarism" into the Republican tradition of Roman politics. He was converting the partially democratic and senatorial administration into a bureaucratic autocracy.

CASE VII. In 399 B.C. the Athenian people executed Socrates on the charge of introducing the worship of false gods and corrupting the youth of Athens. There had been more to it than that. Socrates had, it is true, dealt skeptically and critically with traditional Greek polytheism and had raised doubts in the minds of the younger generation. He had also set himself up as a critic of the follies and extravagances of the political democracy which governed Athens; and this at a time when the city was fighting for its life against the aristocratically-minded Spartans, who sought to suppress the "democratic spirit" wherever it appeared. Furthermore, the Athenians had given Socrates a chance to leave Athens and go into exile, if he chose. But rather than overlook corruption in politics and obscurantism in religion or be exiled from his native land, Socrates chose death. Who was in the right in these matters? Should Socrates have kept his "gadfly" views to himself? Should he have ceased expressing them once he was warned? Should he have chosen exile? Should the Athenian people have put up with him?

Many of the questions raised by the cases cited above would be diagnostic of a moralist's concern. Their answers would be moral judgments. From the fact that a man was raising these questions, and expressing concern over them, you could infer that he was a moralist. Questions might arise out of our cases which would, however, not be diagnostic of a moralist's concern. In the case of Socrates you might ask: How reliable are the primary historical documents upon which we base our knowledge of his life and teaching? In the case of the kidnappers you might ask: In what year was the law passed which they have violated? In the case of the man contemplating suicide you might ask: What was the name and chemical composition of the drug he wanted? To sharpen this matter, you might contrast a moralist's concern with an artist's concern, or a scientist's concern, or an historian's concern. A moralist's concern is defined by questions having to do with the right and wrong of a situation. His characteristic first-round question is, "Under the circumstances, what would be the right thing to do?" His characteristic first-round statement is, "Under the circumstances, the right thing to do is this." Where the word "right" is used in the sense of "morally right," such a question is not artistic or scientific or historical. A moralist's concern in human affairs is one which requires for its expression such distinctions as right–wrong, good–evil, ought–ought not, rights–duties, virtue–vice. Judgments using such distinctions are moral judgments.

General Moral Judgments. When you reflect upon those cases, or others which they might suggest to you, and endeavor to answer the moral questions which they raise, you have begun to produce data for an ethical theory. This search can be pushed a step further, namely, from particular moral judgments to general moral judgments. This next step is controlled by the following unfinished sentence: "Under assignable circumstances, it is wrong to. . . ." Lead off with that statement, and proceed to enumerate the actions which, under assignable circumstances, you would consider it wrong to do. The going will be easy at first. Under assignable circumstances, you will probably find yourself saying, it is wrong to lie, to steal, to slander, to kill, to kidnap, to commit suicide, to cheat, to bully, to gossip, to gamble, to boast, to swindle, to drink, to betray, to take drugs. There are fifteen items to start with. They are a beginning. If, to quote a recent theologian, humanity is a huge enterprise in sin, the list of "wrong to" will be considerably longer and more imaginative than that. No moralist worth his keep is brought to a stop this side of fifty items. Provoke your mind to range widely and burrow deeply in what an American moralist has called "the kingdom of evil." Your answers to this question are data. If the question, "What are the things which under assignable circumstances you consider it wrong to do?" finds you or leaves you skeptical, finds you or leaves you unable to make *any* answers, then you will be lacking in valuable data needed to enable you to think out a moral philosophy. In these matters a beginning cannot be made with total skepticism or ignorance on the part of the philosopher with regard to what he thinks.

Summary. This section is called "The Student Looks for Data." The idea in that title is that a person must have some data before he can have an ethical theory. The theory is about those data. To the extent that the theory is to be *his,* the data must be his too. He must authorize the data. Now, moral judgments are the data for an ethical theory. It is a theory about them. The purpose of this section is to enable the reader to provide himself with some moral judgments. To that end he was presented with some situations which invite moral judgment. These might be called particular moral judgments, since they referred to particular cases. To that end, also, he was asked to indicate what actions he considers it, under assignable circumstances, wrong to do. These might be called general moral judgments, since they referred to types of actions, not particular cases. To the extent that he has been clearheaded and sincere, he has already provided himself with some data. The job of the next section is to show that, given such data, it is possible to raise certain relatively abstract problems.

2. THE DATA RAISE PROBLEMS

In the preceding section the reader was given two exercises in self-knowledge. There is no point to proceeding further until they have been worked at. And only the reader can provide the answers. The first exercise was a set of situations inviting particular moral judgments. The second was the unfinished statement "Under assignable circumstances, it is wrong to . . ." inviting general moral judgments. If the reader's list is representative of his insight into wrongdoing and sufficiently imaginative to do justice to man's capacity for bad will, the exercise will have served its purpose. It will have thrown him into a mood of reflection. It will have put him into a position to ask himself some questions which will lead from moral judgment to ethical theory.

As you keep working at the list of actions which, under assignable circumstances, you consider it wrong to do, the following question might occur to you: Is it possible that, under assignable circumstances, any action, no matter what, is wrong to do? Could it be that the real problem is in assigning the circumstances, rather than in ascribing the "wrong"? If, under assignable circumstances, any action can be a wrong action, then the center of concern seems to shift from "wrong" to "circumstances."

Reflection might move along that line. Let me suggest another. As you made out your list of the things which, under assignable circumstances, it is wrong to do, some item might catch your eye and incline you to ask, "What have assignable circumstances to do with the wrongness of this sort of action? This sort of action would be wrong under any circumstances." This line of reflection, together with the one suggested in the preceding paragraph, raise the question: Is wrongness relative to circumstances or independent of circumstances? Do circumstances make all the difference, or some difference, or no difference, when you want to ascribe wrongness to an act? The matter might be put this way: Are there any acts which are always wrong, regardless of circumstances? Are there any acts which are never wrong, regardless of circumstances? Can anything be said, in principle, about the "assignable circumstances"? The title for this section is "The Data Raise Problems." You have here an example.

As a consequence of working out completions for the unfinished sentence "Under assignable circumstances, it is wrong to . . ." you have a miscellaneous list. Can you do anything to get rid of this miscellaneous character? One way would be to arrange the items in alphabetical order. Such a list would be ordered. But the principle of order would not be diagnostic of a moralist's concern. Suppose, however, that you try ordering your items so that those you consider worst come at the top, and the others taper down until they represent what you regard as venial, not very wrong. The resulting series might not be continuous: it might show gaps. But it would be a qualitatively changing series, moving from very wrong to not so very wrong, from monstrous to trivial. Items at the top would have more of wrongness in them than items occurring lower down in the series. The problem, then, is: Can wrongdoings be ordered in such a series? This leads immediately to another problem.

Suppose you have arranged the items in your list in such a manner that those you consider worst come at the top, and the others taper down until they represent what you regard as venial, not very wrong. Select an item from the "very wrong" group, say murder or betrayal. Consider a particular instance, occurring at a particular time and place. Project your mind as vividly and intimately as you can into the circumstances of the case. Recreate the act in all of its uniqueness and detail. Build up the situation. Make every effort to "feel" for the wrongdoer. Put yourself in his place. Take stock of his world as he saw it, his urgencies as he felt them. You must exert your mind at this task of recreating the supposed actual in all of its multitudinous particularity. Here is the question: "You being what you were, the circumstances being what they were, could you have done otherwise that you did do?" You have been trying to project yourself into another man's life. Ask the question about him: He being what he was, the circumstances being what they were, could he have done otherwise than he did do? If you answer "Yes," you are affirming his free will. If you answer "No," you are denying his free will. You have here a problem of major proportions, a problem of long standing, a problem to which no moralist can afford to be indifferent. Many persons have affirmed their disbelief in man's free will, and have sought to give reasons to justify their affirmation. The question has ramifications. If you say, of the hypothetical person who committed your very wrong act, "He did wrong, but he could not have done otherwise," are you willing also, and therefore, to add "He should not be blamed"? Also, and therefore, "He should not be punished"? In calling an act wrong do you presuppose that the person could have done otherwise? This question asks whether free will is a presupposition of moral judgment. Is free will a fact about human nature? If a theory says, "Free will is a fact about human nature," is the theory true? It is one thing to ask whether moral judgment presupposes something about human nature; it is another to ask whether the presupposition is true.

Your list of wrong actions is good for another problem leading from moral judgment to ethical theory. Keeping that list before your mind's eye, consider this question: "Is there any fact, common to all your cases of wrongdoing, which is your reason for calling them cases of wrongdoing?" The question invites you to ask yourself, for each item, "What is my reason for including that one?" In doing this, do you find any fact common to all your items, which is your reason for including each item? This is an important exercise in self-knowledge. If you do not know your own mind very well, you will be unable to arrive easily at an answer. If your use of the term "wrong" is vague or obscure, you will find this question hard to answer clearly. If your use of the term "wrong" is ambiguous, you will find yourself coming out with two or more answers. If you don't know what you mean by the term "wrong," you will find yourself unable to get any answer. This last possibility would be curious, because you have your list of items: if you didn't know what you were looking for, it is difficult to see how you got that list. And, presumably, your list could be arranged to show a qualitatively changing scale from "very wrong" to "not so very wrong," from "monstrous" to "trivial"; suggesting, therefore, that you do have a working insight into what you understand by wrong. The question, stated impersonally, is this: What fact, common to all cases of wrongdoing, is the reason for calling them cases of wrongdoing?

3. EVERY MAN HIS OWN MORALIST

Autonomy, Not Authority. The term "ethical theory" refers to principles and presuppositions which are implied in our moral judgments but usually left implicit. Ethical theory is about moral judgments; moral judgments are about actions, or about character as expressed in actions. The purpose of this book is to incite you to render explicit principles and presuppositions which your judgments imply and your actions embody. To speak strictly, no one can do this for you. You must do it for yourself. You are trying to clarify and extend your self-knowledge. To think of having someone instruct you is to misunderstand the character of the enterprise. There are no "authorities" in philosophy, in the popular sense of the word authority. There are, it is true, moralists who in their writings give evidence of having thought more clearly and more persistently than most of their readers. These are the classical moralists from Plato to the present. But even a classic should not be studied as an authority, because, in the end, you have to pass judgment on the classic. It is well to see the necessity of that outcome from the beginning. To repeat, in going to the classics, there is no notion of going to authorities for "answers." It is a matter of examining the work of men who know how to think and learning, by a kind of intellectual osmosis, how they spy out the land; how they uncover leads and difficulties; how they achieve clarity and coherence; and how, despite everything, their work is never final or perfect. A beginning moralist needs an opportunity to examine ways in which more mature and sophisticated minds have addressed themselves to the task. It is difficult, at first, to do the sort of thinking that is involved in formulating a moral philosophy. The mind is required to move easily and with precision from the concrete to the abstract, from judgment to principle, from thesis to hypo-thesis; and writers who have attained the status of classics are often useful as spurs to reflection.

Are questions of the sort raised in this chapter to be answered by an authority independent of and external to the person who asks them or by the individual who asks them? In the one case you have authority, in the other case you have autonomy. The man who refuses to answer these questions for himself is a man who appeals to an authority. The man who insists upon answering these questions for himself is the man who claims autonomy.

Persons who refer such questions to authority have found this authority in many different places: their parents, God, the

Bible, the Church. Or they might refer their questions to "nature" or "society" or "the state" or "the majority" or "experts." What people will accept as authority varies considerably. What a man will accept as authority makes no difference to our problem. That problem is "Authority versus Autonomy," and any authority will do in contrast to autonomy. If a man's ultimate court of appeal is some authority, then he does not exercise autonomy as that term is used here.

There is one misunderstanding that should be avoided. We may accept an authority in a provisional way, yet refuse to accept it in a final way. A man may say, "I will accept the authority of Freud," and mean merely that until need arises to question Freud he will accept him as an authority. A man may say, "I will accept the Gospels as an authority," or "I will accept Kant as an authority," and mean merely that up to a point he will accept the authority of the Gospels or Kant, but beyond that point he will insist upon judging for himself. Such a person does not illustrate the problem. To accept an authority up to a point, provisionally, subject to eventual revision by yourself, is not to accept an authority in the sense here intended. If a man says, "In ethical theory I accept authority; I do not set myself up as the final judge," and really means what he says, then no matter what authority he accepts, he illustrates the problem of authority. That problem can be given a first formulation by asking such a person why he accepts an authority in ethical theory; why he does not set himself up as judge. Presumably he has his reasons for proposing an authority in these matters. How does he defend or justify this authoritarianism?

Fortunately, we do not need to know what his reasons are. We might begin by noting that his position, provided it has reasons, contains two decisions. The first is his choice between autonomy and authority: the second is his choice between or among authorities. These choices expressed his own appraisal, his own judgment, his autonomy. He used his autonomy to choose between autonomy and authority, to decide that autonomy should be abandoned in favor of authority. We might go on to note that the authority he has chosen is not the only one in the field. He might have chosen some other book, or person, or institution, or tradition. Why did he choose this one? Provided he had any reasons for his choice, his choice expresses his own appraisal, his own judgment, his autonomy. He used his autonomy to choose a specific authority.

Our question to him would be this: If your autonomy is good enough to enable you to decide between autonomy and authority, and between one authority and another, why is it not good enough to enable you to get along without an appeal to authority at all? Any answer he gives to this question will be an expression of his autonomy.

The questions raised in these two sections are expressible in the second person singular: Upon what principle do you criticize and revise your attempts to do what is right and avoid doing what is wrong? What actions do you consider it, under assignable circumstances, wrong to do? Do you consider wrongness independent of, or relative to, circumstances? When you call an act wrong, do you presuppose that the person could have done otherwise? You being what you are, the circumstances being what they are, can you ever do other than you do? If you cannot are you blameworthy? Should you be punished? What fact common to all cases of wrongdoing is your reason for calling them cases of wrongdoing? These questions, and others like them, are goads to reflection upon right and wrong. They are as old as philosophy itself. No age in history has been content to leave them entirely alone. They are wedges to drive into the general enquiry. If you work at them and not merely trifle with them, you will find your mind beginning to gather data and raise questions upon which you can reflect, and without which your reflecting is likely to get off to an erratic start.

Every Man His Own Moralist. The phrase "Every man his own moralist" goes a long way toward indicating the intended outcome of an ethics course. The phrase might be taken to mean simply, "Every man the author of his own moral judgments," for example, that under assignable circumstances, stealing is wrong or truth-telling is right. This use of the phrase draws attention to part of the meaning of "judgment," namely, that a person must make it for himself. To speak strictly, one person cannot judge for another person. If you accept another person's judgment without making it your own, it is not your judgment, but is his. The process of taking over his judgment and making it your own will force you to go through the steps needed to make the judgment yourself. This is not peculiar to moral judgments: it holds for judgments of any kind. The phrase indicates that, in the last analysis, moral judgments can be made only by persons who can stand on their own feet. Back of every judgment must stand an individual who is responsible for the judgment, able to answer for the judgment.

The phrase might be taken to mean, "One man's moral judgments are as good as any other man's moral judgments," that moral judgments are idiosyncratic in the sense that, while a person must answer *for* his judgment, he does not have to answer *to* anyone else. This would be a mistake. That a judgment requires an individual to make it, in the sense of authorize it and be responsible for it, does not mean that in making the judgment he is irresponsible in relation to others. A judgment comes from a self, but it is always implicitly addressed to other selves. A pronouncement is not a judgment unless someone authorizes it, stands back of it. Someone must say, "I offer this as my judgment." But more is implied. It is offered also as holding *of* what it refers to, and holding *for* all persons capable of judging. A judgment has three "dimensions": it is made by someone; it is made about something; and it is implicitly addressed to other persons. No judgment is ever without these three aspects. Judgments are made by individuals and they are, implicitly, addressed to other individuals. Individuals so related constitute a community. If community were not a fact, then judgments would be idiosyncratic. A moral judgment presupposes a moral community, a community of individuals who make moral judgments which are, implicitly, addressed to each other.

The phrase "Every man his own moralist" might be taken to mean, "Every man the author of his own moral philosophy, his own ethical theory." So construed, it comes closer to indicating the intended outcome of an ethics course. It is one thing to make a moral judgment, such as, for example, "Stealing is wrong." It is another thing to make clear the moral philosophy, the ethical theory, the principles and presuppositions, implicated in the moral judgment. An ethics course invites a person to do that, to think philosophically, that is, with reference to principles and presuppositions, about his moral judgments. The phrase "Every man his own moralist" issues the same invitation. It proposes to anyone who authorizes moral judgments that he think out the ethical theory which underlies those judgments. If his moral judgments are "theses," his ethical theory will be a "hypo-thesis," where "hypo" is used in the etymological sense of "under." It will be at the basis of them. To say that his ethical theory is an hypo-thesis is not to suggest that it is held "hypothetically" (tentatively) in a way that his moral judgments are not. The notion of tentative is not, of necessity, more diagnostic of a man's moral philosophy than of his moral judgments. He may say tentatively, subject to correction, "The Athenians did wrong in executing Socrates." This means he is not sure of the truth of his judgment; more facts or more reflection might show him that he had misjudged the Athenians. But he may also say, tentatively, subject to correction, "My judgment that the Athenians did wrong rests on the principle that an act is wrong if and only if it is contrary to the will of God." More facts or more reflection might show him that his judgment did not rest on that principle but on some other principle. In one sense, the word *hypothetical* is used in contrast to *categorical*: "I say the act was wrong and I say it categorically, not hypothetically." In another, older, sense, the word *hypothesis* is used in contrast to *thesis*: "On the hypo-thesis that an act is right if and only if it makes for the greatest happiness of the greatest number, my thesis would be that this country did right in abolishing slavery." In this sense, you can say that an ethics course invites a person to formulate the hypo-theses which underlie his moral judgments. And the phrase "Every man his own moralist" invites a man to do this job for himself. If he does not do it for himself, it will not get done. To speak strictly, no one else can do it for him. In this respect a person's moral philosophy is similar to his moral judgments: to be a philosophy at all, it must first be his. "What are your theses?" is not more surely addressed to an individual than "What are your hypo-theses?"

However, the phrase "Every man his own moralist" is not intended to suggest that a man's moral philosophy is immune to criticism. If he is not immune in respect to his theses, why should he be immune in respect to his hypo-theses? Philosophizing is the activity of thinking out your hypo-theses. It is an activity in which you can encounter failure: the outcome may be error or continued ignorance. And there is nothing idiosyncratic about it.

In both of its senses, then, the phrase "Every man his own moralist" tells you something about an ethics course: the course assumes that men authorize moral judgments, and it invites them to work out the ethical theory on which those judgments rest. Men *pro*pose moral judgments; these are their theses. The philosophical question is what do they thereby *pre*suppose, what are their hypo-theses?

When you know the essential nature of something, for example, that a triangle is a plane figure bounded by three straight lines, it is said that you possess a theoretical understanding of it. When you know the essential nature of a right act, its definition in principle, you possess a theoretical understanding of it. Now, given a theoretical understanding of something, you may set yourself to construct or enact an example of it. Thus if you have a theoretical understanding of the essential nature of a triangle, you may set yourself to construct (draw) one. Here your theoretical insight guides your practical endeavor, your theory guides your practice. The result, the diagram of a triangle, embodies, as well as you can make it, your theory of the essential nature of triangularity. Similarly, if you have a theoretical understanding of the essential nature of rightness, you may set yourself to do a right act, to enact rightness. Here, too, your theoretical insight guides your practical endeavor, your theory guides your practice. The result, an act, embodies, as well as you can make it, your theory of the essential nature of rightness.

Suggested Comparison. An introduction to ethics may be compared to an introduction to logic or an introduction to aesthetics. The distinction between moral judgment and moral theory is a special case of the general distinction between judgment and theory. Logic and aesthetics would introduce comparable special cases. We speak readily enough of the distinction between aesthetic judgment ("*X* is a work of art") and aesthetic theory ("What fact common to all works of art is the reason for calling them works of art?"). We speak less readily, perhaps less handily, of the distinction between logical judgment and logical theory; but the distinction is similar, and equally genuine. Logic is concerned with the truth of statements and the validity of inferences. Thus the judgments, "*P* is a true statement" and "*X* is a valid inference," are comparable, *mutatis mutandis,* to the judgments, "*A* is a right act" and "*B* is a work of art"; and like them they involve a theory elucidating what the judgments imply. Such a theory would be a logical theory: it would set forth the conditions under which we would be justified in calling a judgment true or false, or an inference valid or invalid. Ethics has as its central question: On what principles do you criticize and revise your attempts to do what is right? Aesthetics has as its central question: On what principles do you criticize and revise your attempts to produce a work of art? Logic has as its central question: On what principles do you criticize and revise your attempts to believe truly and infer validly?

QUESTIONS

1. Which of the cases cited in this chapter do you find easiest to decide on? Why? Hardest? Why?

2. Have you ever passed from revising a line of action to revising the principles on which you revise lines of action? What brought about this shift?

3. Would you subscribe to the following sequence of statements? (*a*) A good society is one which expresses the wills of good men. (*b*) A good man is one who tries always to do what is moral and avoid doing what is immoral. (*c*) An act is moral if done because believed to be right. (*d*) An act is right if it embodies the principle "Demand of yourself what you demand of others."

4. A law is just if, and only if, it can say to those who must live under it: "I am what you ask of others. I am therefore what you ask of yourself." Would you subscribe to this statement? If not, why not?

5. Why do you hear the first of the following statements more often than the second? (*a*) "I did that because I believed it to be right, and I wanted to do what is right." (*b*) "I did that because I believed it to be wrong, and I wanted to do what is wrong."

6. It has been said: "No one ever knowingly does what he believes to be wrong." It has also been said: "I see and approve the better, but I pursue the worse." What do you say?

7. Point out what you take to be important differences between diagnosing an act as wrong and diagnosing a belief as false.

8. The following items are intended to enable you to check on your reading. Jot down a brief explanatory sentence making clear the point in each case: (*a*) the central question; (*b*) naive *vs.* sophisticated; (*c*) relation of judgment to principle; (*d*) diagnostic of a moralist's concern; (*e*) moralist contrasted with scientist and historian; (*f*) particular *vs.* general moral judgment; (*g*) unfinished sentence leading to general moral judgments; (*h*) five questions raised in section 2; (*i*) the distinction between autonomy and authority; (*j*) in what sense the classics of moral philosophy may serve as authorities; (*k*) our question to the person who professes to follow an authority in moral philosophy; (*l*) three possible meanings of the phrase "Every man his own moralist"; (*m*) the distinction between thesis and hypo-thesis; (*n*) the point of comparison between ethics and logic and aesthetics.

II. Three Ethical Theories

The present chapter will be long and perhaps difficult, but the plan is simple. There is an over-all division into three sections. Each section presents a late eighteenth-century moralist (Paley, Bentham, and Kant) who proposed an answer to the question, "What fact, common to all cases of wrongdoing, is the reason for calling them cases of wrongdoing?" These three moralists are representative of traditional ethical theory. Their answers differ; their agreement is to be sought in a common acknowledgment of the question. Paley works with the notion of the will of God; Bentham, with the notion of the happiness of man; Kant, with the notion of what reason demands. All three published within the decade 1780-1790. They would criticize and argue with one another but they would close ranks against any repudiation of their common problem.

1. PALEY

The following paragraph is quoted from a seventeenth-century moralist:

That God has given a rule whereby men should govern themselves, I think there is no one so brutish as to deny. He has a right to do it. We are His creatures. He has goodness and wisdom to direct our actions to what is best, and He has power to enforce it by rewards and punishments of infinite weight and duration in another life; for nobody can take us out of His hands. This is the only touchstone of moral rectitude, and by comparing them to this law, it is that men judge of the most considerable moral good or evil of their actions; that is, whether as duty or sins, they are like to procure them happiness or misery from the hands of the Almighty.

The following paragraph is quoted from a nineteenth-century English historian of eighteenth-century English thought. The passage does not state the historian's own beliefs. It is a paraphrase of what many eighteenth-century English moralists believed.

We ought to do good, say all moralists, and the question remains, What is meant by *ought* and *good?* Theology, so long as it was a vital belief in the world, afforded a complete and satisfactory answer to these questions. Morality was, of necessity, its handmaid. Believe in an active ruler of the universe, who reveals His will to men, who distributes rewards and punishments to the good and the evil, and we have a plain answer to most of the problems of morality. God's will, so far as known to us, determines what is good.

The following quotation is from an editorial in a popular American weekly newspaper:

Our own doctrine of natural rights, set forth in the Constitution and the Declaration of Independence, holds that each and every one of us, regardless of color, creed, or birth, has certain inalienable rights. They are inalienable for one reason only: because they are the endowment of the Creator. If the day ever comes when the men and women of our Western Civilization desert completely the historic concept of man as a child of God with free will and an immortal soul, if the day ever comes, in short, when we too go over to "scientific materialism," on that day not all our oil or gold in the ground, nor our assembly lines, nor our air forces, nor our navies, nor even our sole possession of the atomic bomb, shall save us. On that day freedom will perish in the totalitarian night of the world. Lincoln was right to remind us that it is only "under God" that this nation, or any nation, can be free.

These three quotations agree that there is a close connection between morality and theology. Each would say that all wrong actions are contrary to the will of God; and that that fact is the reason for calling them wrongdoing. They would define wrongness by reference to the will of God. Moralists who entertain a lively belief in the existence of God and ascribe to Him an interest in human affairs do, many of them, base their moral judgments upon what they believe to be His will. They argue that an act is right because it is according to the will of God and wrong because it is contrary to the will of God. They appeal to theology for their ethical theory.

This way of thinking about right and wrong is not peculiarly modern. In some form or other it is probably as old as the human race. The student of ethics cannot begin better than by giving it a sympathetic hearing. It is simple, clear-cut, and, initially, plausible. It is widely understood and perennial in its appeal. It has the advantage, too, of raising questions about itself which suggest other lines of reflection.

A good statement of this appeal to theology in ethics will be found in a book by an eighteenth-century English moralist, William Paley. The book, *Principles of Moral and Political Philosophy*, was published in 1785. The author was a Church of England clergyman. His book sold well, running through fifteen editions during the author's lifetime. It became a widely used university textbook in England and in this country, during the last years of the eighteenth century and the first quarter of the nineteenth century. One of Paley's contemporaries remarked of the book: "It may be said to be the only work on moral philosophy fitted to be understood by every class of reader." I am going to suggest a conversation between ourselves and William Paley. You would have found him an affable sort of man, easy to talk to, and a ready talker himself. You could lead off with one of the questions with which we began:

"Mr. Paley," you might begin, "would you indicate for us some actions, which, under assignable circumstances, you would consider it wrong to do?" He would accede to that request. Any moralist would. If you were to glance over the table of contents of his book you would have no difficulty in conjecturing the items that would make up his list. You could then pose our next question: Is there any one fact, common to all your cases of wrongdoing, which is the reason for calling them cases of wrongdoing? "Yes," he would say, "indeed there is. It is this: They are contrary to the will of God. And that fact is my reason for calling them wrongdoing. A wrong act is one which is contrary to the will of God. The whole duty of man may be resolved into this one injunction: Know the will of God and keep it." The next move would be up to us: "Mr. Paley, you have staked everything on one point. Everything is going to depend on whether you can discover what the will of God is. If you do not know, or cannot find out, you are not going to be able to say which acts are right and which are wrong." "Yes," he would say, "I see that; but I see no difficulty in it." "Perhaps not. But how do you discover what God wills?" "The answer is simplicity itself," he would say. "The will of God is our rule. To know that will becomes thus our first step. To obey it becomes our second step. Your question was how we know what God's will is. There are two ways. The first is by His express declarations, when they are to be had, in the Scriptures. These are your first and most authentic sources for discovering His will." "Every statement in the Scriptures, Mr. Paley, or just some?" "Not *every* statement; just those which say what the will of God is." "What you say, Mr. Paley, places a heavy burden on the Scriptures. There are many men; and each man in his lifetime does many actions. Taking all men into account, that is going to amount to a very large number of actions. In your opinion, do the Scriptures provide for all actions by all of mankind?" "I see your point," he would say. "It does amount to a large number of actions." "Yes, it does. What do you do about it?" "I have two answers to that question," he would say, "and the first one is this: The Scriptures contain rules, and these rules cover kinds of action. Whoever expects to find in the Scriptures particular directions for particular acts looks for more than he will meet with. Such a detail of particular actions would have so enlarged that sacred volume that it would have become too bulky to be read or circulated. In the Scriptures, general rules are laid down. Sometimes these rules are illustrated by parables or by reference to persons or events known to the speaker. That is the way any general matters are taught. That is the way you teach arithmetic, grammar, navigation, and the like. You lay down rules. You subjoin examples. The examples illustrate and explain the rules, and enable us to see for ourselves the methods of applying them. Do I make myself clear?" "Yes, so far so good." "My second answer carries me beyond the Scriptures to another way of coming at the will of God," Paley might continue. "Another way? What is this other way? Is it necessary? Aren't the Scriptures enough?" "You are asking two questions there, my friend, and I must insist upon separating them. To your first question, 'What is this other way?,' I have an answer. To your second question, 'Why aren't the Scriptures enough?' let me say at once that I have no answer. Let me add also that I feel no urgency about it. I did not create man. I did not write the Scriptures. In the end, therefore, I am not answerable for the facts of this matter, whatever they may be. My only point would be that man does have a way of coming at the will of God without consulting the Scriptures. Shall I proceed?" "By all means. What is this second way?" "I call it the light of nature." "Perhaps you do, Mr. Paley, but you are going to have to explain that. There are nearly two centuries between you and us. If we were to tell a man that he can discover the will of God by consulting the Scriptures, he might not believe us, but he would understand us. If we were to tell him that he could also discover the will of God by consulting the light of nature, he would not understand what we meant. That phrase has gone out of use. What do you mean by the 'light of nature'?" "I find it odd that you should not understand so simple and well-established a term." "Yes, Mr. Paley, it is odd; but it is so, just the same." "Well, God inspired men to write the Scriptures. Hence you are able to discover His will in them. But He also created nature. He did, you know. Or do I have to explain about that, too?" "Let's not argue over that. As you say, God created nature. What then?" "Well, since God created nature, it must embody His will, His intentions you might say. If a man made a watch, you could infer that he wanted to measure time, or that he wanted to enable others to measure time. Now, just as you can learn a man's intentions from what he makes, so can you study nature and learn what God intends. God's will is revealed in nature as surely as it is revealed in the Scriptures." "Have you studied nature with this point in mind, Mr. Paley?" "In a manner of speaking, yes. At least, you could say that I have observed nature and thought about what I have observed." "What general conclusions have you come to?" "I have come to this general conclusion: In creating nature, and in placing man in it, God intended the happiness of man. From what I know of nature, I would say that God wills the happiness of man. This point, next to the existence of God and the revelation of His will in the Scriptures, is the foundation of my moral philosophy. Upon it rests my second method of deciding whether an act is right or wrong. You must see that. I shall have to keep on explaining till you do." "Perhaps you had better explain a little further, Mr. Paley. Why do you infer from nature that God intends the happiness of man? That is a large inference." "Look at it this way: When God created nature and put the human species into it, either He wished their happiness, or He wished their misery, or He was indifferent to both. Are you agreed as to that?" "Proceed, Mr. Paley; the argument is in your hands." "Very well then. I shall now argue that nature presents ample evidence that God did not intend the misery of man and is not indifferent to the happiness of man, and therefore must have intended his happiness. If you agree to three possibilities, and I remove two of them, you must accept the third." "The argument is still in your hands, Mr. Paley." "Suppose God had intended the misery of men. He could, and therefore would, have done a much more thorough job. We would have been much more miserable than we are. Consider one example: He could have formed our five senses to be just so many sores and pains. He could have formed the world so that everything revealed to the senses would be repulsive and disgusting. He did neither of these things. Our senses do not hurt us when we exercise them; and what we perceive by means of them does not cause us distress. I suggest the senses as one example. You can extend this argument in many ways. It is as though I were to say of a wise and skillful physician: If he intended to put an end to me, I should not now be alive and healthy. But I am alive and healthy. Therefore, he did not intend to put an end to me. So much for my first claim: God did not intend the misery of men. My second claim was that God is not indifferent to the happiness of men. My reasoning is this. If you assume that God was and is indifferent to the happiness of man, then you must attribute what happiness we do have to the workings of sheer chance. Now, the amount of happiness that men do have, and can have, is too great to be explained by chance. Nature is such, and we are such, that we do have a great deal of happiness, and we could have a great deal more. Now, if a man wins too frequently at dice, you infer finally that his winning is not a matter of chance. When I see the amount of happiness men do possess, and the amount they could possess, I find it difficult to believe that their happiness is a matter of chance. I find it incredible. There is, actually and potentially, too much of it to explain it so. If it is not a matter of chance, it must be a matter of intention. If it is a matter of intention, then you cannot say that God is indifferent to it. Do I carry you with me?" "Mr. Paley, you missed your calling. You should have been an advocate." "In a manner of speaking, I suppose I am. Do you see now what I mean by the light of nature? Do you see now why I offer it as an alternative, or supplement, to the Scriptures? God wills the happiness of man. Therefore any man can ask of any action, does it produce, maintain, increase, the happiness of men? If it does, then since God wills the happiness of men it is according to the will of God and is therefore right. If it does not, then it is contrary to the will of God and is therefore wrong. It is as simple as that."

The essentials of Paley's argument are these: (1) An act is right if it agrees with the will of God, wrong if it is contrary thereto. (2) We discover the will of God in either of two ways: by consulting the Scriptures, or by consulting the light of nature. (3) The light of nature shows us that God wills the happiness of men. (4) We can, therefore, decide the rightness or wrongness of an act, that is, whether it agrees or disagrees with the will of God, by noting whether it makes for or against the happiness of men.

The following quotations from Paley's book should be studied carefully. They are your assignment in this section. It will be well to grasp that point now, because throughout the rest of this book each chapter or section is built around a substantial selection from some modern moralist. In each selection the author will be making his main point or expressing his characteristic thesis. Much of the book's value lies in these "invitations to read." The selections are long enough to enable you to get the flavor of the original. If you find a selection interesting, you can look up the author in your college library and read further. Wherever convenient, the passages are quoted literally. In some cases, however, the originals have been condensed or rearranged or even paraphrased. Wherever such changes occur the effort has been made to preserve intact the meaning of the original. Now, Paley, from his 1785 publication, *Principles of Moral and Political Philosophy.*

1. Moral Philosophy, Ethics, mean the same thing; namely, that science which teaches men their duty and the reasons of it. The use of such a study depends upon this, that, without it, the rules of life, by which men are ordinarily governed, oftentimes mislead them, through a defect either in the rule, or in the application.

2. In the treatises I have met with upon the subject of morals, I have remarked the following imperfections;—either the principle was erroneous, or it was indistinctly explained, or the rules deduced from it were not sufficiently adapted to real life and actual situations.

There is another fault which some moralists have not always been careful to avoid; namely, the dwelling upon verbal and elementary distinctions, with a labour and prolixity proportioned much more to the subtlety of the question than to its value and importance in the prosecution of the subject. The reader becomes impatient when he is detained by disquisitions which have no other object than the settling of terms and phrases; and, what is worse, they for whose use such books are chiefly intended will not be persuaded to read them at all.

An experience of nine years in the office of a public tutor in one of the universities, and in that department of education to which these chapters relate, afford me frequent occasions to observe, that in discoursing to young minds upon topics of morality, it required much more pains to make them perceive the difficulty than to understand the solution.

I have examined no doubts, I have discussed no obscurities, I have encountered no errors, I have adverted to no controversies, but what I have seen actually to exist. If some of the questions treated of appear to a more instructed reader minute or puerile, I desire such reader to be assured that I have found them occasions of difficulty to young minds; and what I have observed in young minds, I should expect to meet with in all who approach these subjects for the first time.

3. Virtue is "the doing good to mankind, in obedience to the will of God, and for the sake of everlasting happiness." According to which definition, "the good of mankind" is the subject; the "will of God," the rule; "and everlasting happiness," the motive, of human virtue.

A man is said to be obliged, "when he is urged by a violent motive resulting from the command of another." Let it be asked, Why am I obliged to keep my word? and the answer will be, "because I am urged to do so by a violent motive" (namely the expectation of being after this life rewarded, if I do, or punished if I do not), "resulting from the command of another" (namely of God). This solution goes to the bottom of the subject, as no further question can reasonably be asked.

When I first turned my thoughts to moral speculations, an air of mystery seemed to hang over the whole subject; which arose, I believe, from hence,—that I supposed, with many authors whom I read, that to be obliged to do a thing, was very different from being induced only to do it; and that the obligation to practice virtue, to do what is right, just, and etc. was quite another thing, and of another kind than the obligation which a soldier is under to obey his officer, a servant his master; or any of the civil and ordinary obligations of human life. Whereas, from what has been said it appears, that moral obligation is like all other obligations, and that obligation is nothing more than an inducement of sufficient strength, and resulting, in some way, from the command of another.

4. They who establish a system of morality, independent of a future state, must look out for some different idea of moral obligation, unless they can show that virtue conducts the possessor to certain happiness in this life, or to a much greater share of it than he could attain by a different behaviour.

Mr. Hume, in his *Principles of Morals,* has been pleased to complain of the scheme of uniting Ethics with Christian Theology. They who find themselves disposed to join in this complaint, will do well to observe what Mr. Hume himself has been able to make of morality without this union. And for that purpose, let them read the above essay. When they have read it over, let them consider, whether any motives there proposed are likely to be found sufficient to withhold men from the gratification of lust, revenge, envy, ambition, avarice; or to prevent the existence of these passions. Unless they rise up from this celebrated essay with stronger impressions upon their minds than it ever left upon mine, they will acknowledge the necessity of additional sanctions.

5. Whoever expects to find in the Scriptures a specific direction for every moral doubt that arises, looks for more than he will meet with. Had the same particularity, which obtains in human laws so far as they go, been attempted in the Scriptures, throughout the whole extent of morality, it is manifest that they would have been much too bulky to be either read or circulated; or rather, as St. John says, "even the world itself could not contain the books that should be written."

Morality is taught in Scripture in this wise: General rules are laid down, of piety, justice, benevolence, and purity: such as, worshipping God in spirit and in truth; doing as we would be done by; loving our neighbour as ourself; forgiving others, as we expect forgiveness from God; that mercy is better than sacrifice, that not that which entereth into a man, (nor, by parity of reason, any ceremonial pollutions,) but that which proceedeth from the heart, defileth him. These rules are occasionally illustrated, either by fictitious examples, as in the parable of the good Samaritan; or in instances which actually presented themselves, as in Christ's reproof of his disciples at the Samaritan village; or, lastly in the resolution of questions, which those who were about our Saviour proposed to him.

And this is in truth the way in which all practical sciences are taught, as Arithmetic, Grammar, Navigation, and the like.—Rules are laid down, and examples are subjoined: not that these examples are the cases, much less all the cases, which will actually occur; but by way only of explaining the principle of the rule, and as so many specimens of the method of applying it.

Besides this, the Scriptures commonly presuppose in the persons to whom they speak, a knowledge of the principles of natural justice; and are employed not so much to teach new rules of morality, as to enforce the practice of it by new sanctions, and by a greater certainity; which last seems to be the proper business of a revelation from God, and what was most wanted.

6. As the will of God is our rule; to inquire what is our duty, or what we are obliged to do, in any instance, is, in effect, to inquire what is the will of God in that instance, which consequently becomes the whole business of morality. Now there are two methods of coming at the will of God on any point: by his express declarations, when they are to be had, and which must be sought for in Scripture; by what we can discover of his designs and dispositions from his works, or, as we usually call it, the light of nature.

The method of coming at the will of God concerning any action, by the light of nature, is to inquire into "the tendency of the action to promote or diminish the general happiness." This rule proceeds upon the presumption, that God Almighty wills and wishes the happiness of his creatures; and, consequently, that those actions, which promote that will and wish, must be agreeable to him; and the contrary. As this presumption is the foundation of our whole system, it becomes necessary to explain the reasons upon which it rests.

When God created the human species, either he wished their happiness, or he wished their misery, or he was indifferent and unconcerned about both.

If he had wished our misery, he might have made sure of his purpose, by forming our senses to be so many sores and pains to us, as they are now instruments of gratification and enjoyment; or by placing us amidst objects so ill-suited to our perceptions, as to have continually offended us, instead of ministering to our refreshment and delight. He might have made for example, everything we tasted, bitter; every thing we saw, loathsome; every thing we touched, a sting; every smell, a stench; and every sound, a discord.

If he had been indifferent about our happiness or misery, we must impute to our good fortune (as all design by this supposition is excluded) both the capacity of our senses to receive pleasure, and the supply of external objects fitted to produce it. But either of these (and still more both of them) being too much to be attributed to accident, nothing remains but the first supposition, that God, when he created the human species, wished their happiness; and made for them the provision which he has made, with that view, and for that purpose.

The same argument may be proposed in different terms, thus: Contrivance proves design; and the predominant tendency of the contrivance indicates the disposition of the designer. The world abounds with contrivances: and all the contrivances which we are acquainted with, are directed to beneficial purposes. Evil, no doubt, exists; but is never, that we can perceive, the object of contrivance. Teeth are contrived to eat, not to ache; their aching now and then, is incidental to the contrivance, perhaps inseparable from it: or even, if you will, let it be called a defect in the contrivance; but it is not the object of it. This is a distinction which well deserves to be attended to. In describing implements of husbandry, you would hardly say of the sickle, that it is made to cut the reaper's fingers, though from the construction of the instrument, and the manner of using it, this mischief often happens. But if you had occasion to describe instruments of torture or execution, this engine, you would say, is to extend the sinews; this to dislocate the joints; this to break the bones; this to scorch the soles of the feet. Here, pain and misery are the very objects of the contrivance. Now, nothing of this sort is to be found in the works of nature. We never discover a train of contrivance to bring about an evil purpose. No anatomist ever discovered a system of organization calculated to produce pain and disease; or, in explaining the parts of the human body, ever said, this is to irritate; this is to inflame; this duct is to convey the gravel to the kidneys; this gland to secrete the humour which forms the gout; if by chance he come at a part of which he knows not the use, the most he can says is, that it is useless: no one ever suspects that it is put there to incommode, to annoy, or to torment. Since then

God hath called forth his consummate wisdom to contrive and provide for our happiness, and the world appears to have been constituted with this design at first; so long as this constitution is upholden by him, we must in reason suppose the same design to continue.

We conclude, therefore, that God wills and wishes the happiness of his creatures. And this conclusion being once established, we are at liberty to go on with the rule built upon it, namely, "that the method of coming at the will of God, concerning any action, by the light of nature, is to inquire into the tendency of that action to promote or diminish the general happiness."

Questions for Paley. What can the reader learn from Paley? In the imaginary conversation set forth above, Paley did most of the talking. He made a number of assertions. A good part of their importance lies in the fact that they enable us to raise certain questions. In the conduct of philosophy, the person who will make assertions almost always possesses that kind of utility. In the absence of assertions it is not possible to ask any questions; and you need questions, because they enable you to clarify your own thinking. If you reflect on what Paley has said, what questions can you raise? A beginning can be made by asking whether Paley's principle rests on any presuppositions; and if so, what these are. These presuppositions are crucial. If they are open to doubt or denial, they will infect the principle which presupposes them, and through it, they will infect the moral judgments which embody the principle.

(1) Paley's central assertion is that an act is right if, and only if, it agrees with the will of God. This presupposes that God exists. If it is doubtful that God exists, then (on Paley's principle) it is doubtful that any act is ever either right or wrong. If God does not exist, then it would follow that no act is ever either right or wrong. If you don't know whether God exists, then you don't know whether any act is ever either right or wrong. Your lack of knowledge renders the principle no longer usable.

(2) Paley's central assertion that an act is right if, and only if, it agrees with the will of God also presupposes that God has

a will. This may indeed be so, but it is an exceedingly obscure statement. Anyone who denies the obscurity of that statement has not, I submit, given much thought to its meaning. To say that a statement is obscure is not, of course, to imply that it is false or improbable. It is to say that its meaning is not clear. This obscurity in the presupposition will infect the principle and through it, the moral judgments which embody it.

(3) That an act is wrong if, and only if, it disagrees with the will of God presupposes also that our actions can disagree with the will of God. If the relation between God's will and men's wills is such that men's wills never could disagree with, be contrary to, God's will, then men's actions never could be wrong. If that were so, Paley would not need a principle for distinguishing between right and wrong, because there would never be such a thing as a wrong act. That is one horn of a dilemma. The other is this: If it is possible for a human act to be wrong, for a man to act contrary to God's will, to defy God, then God is not omnipotent, His will is not all-powerful. Can Paley call any human act wrong, unless he is willing to presuppose free will in man? If what Paley's principle presupposes about God's will is incompatible with what it presupposes about man's will, then he has a dilemma on his hands.

(4) Again, Paley's central assertion presupposes that we can get to know God's will. At this point Paley refers us to the Scriptures and to the light of nature. Why the Scriptures? Because the Scriptures themselves say so? But that is to beg the question. The question is not whether the Scriptures claim to contain the will of God; they do claim that. The question is whether that claim is true, or rather, why we should believe it to be true. When a man testifies, he does not increase the probability or credibility of his testimony by adding that it is true; for *that,* you want evidence which does not form part of his testimony. You want to be able to say, "He claims so and so, and, on grounds that do not form part of his claim, we believe his claim to be true." This is a reasonable demand, where the assertions are important and the possibility of their false-

ness is genuine. Does Paley propose that the Scriptures be declared exempt from this demand? If so, why? If not, what, outside of the Scriptures, certifies to the reliability of the Scriptures? When Paley says, "In the Scriptures you will find God's will," does he mean, among writings, *only* in the Scriptures? Why so? Why not in Plato's dialogues? Why not in the Apocrypha? Why not in the Mohammedan Koran? Why not in the Book of Mormon? Why not in *any* writings which profess to contain the will of God? Paley says "in the Scriptures." In which parts of the Scriptures? In those parts which enjoin "an eye for an eye"? Or in those parts which enjoin the golden rule? If in both, what about clashes? If in one, how choose which? Paley says "in the Scriptures." This presupposes that present-day copies of the Scriptures correspond to the originals as written down by Moses and others. Do they? The originals do not exist. What we possess are copies of copies of copies, and so on, but not originals. What reasons have we to believe that present-day copies would, if we could compare them with now lost originals, be found to agree with those originals? The difficulty here could be stated another way. Paley proposes the Scriptures as an "authority." Why accept this authority? A man must, in the last analysis, himself authorize his authority; he must choose it, assert it, follow it. If he has reasons for doing so, then those reasons fall outside of the authority and are more ultimate than it. If he has no reasons for doing so, then why does he do it? He could not criticize anyone who selected a different authority or who selected none at all.

(5) Passing to Paley's second subsidiary assertion ("the light of nature"), has he proved at all conclusively that God, in creating the world and putting man in it, intended the happiness of man? This hypothesis may account for some of the facts, but it does not account for all of them. Pessimism, the perception of the tragedy of life, may not be the whole truth, but it is not foolishness. It is true that there are many cheerful facts in nature. We know what Paley infers from these. It is also true that

there are many gloomy facts in nature. We do not know what
Paley infers from these.

(6) Paley's second subsidiary assertion, as we have said, was
that God wills the happiness of men, and that, therefore, an act
which produces more happiness than any other act possible
under the circumstances agrees with the will of God and is
right. Is this not to formulate a moral principle that swings
clear of the first subsidiary assertion, and could stand on its
own feet, without that first assertion? If so, what about cases
where the appeal to Scriptures and the appeal to happiness
appear to clash? Would any man who considers the whole of
the Scriptures and the whole of human life care to claim that
all such clashes are apparent only?

(7) Paley's central assertion is that an act is right if, and only
if, it agrees with the will of God. If, in this sense of "right," it is
claimed that some acts are right, then it is presupposed that
we know that God exists, and that He has a will, and that we
know what that will is. Now, there are such persons as honest
atheists and honest skeptics. They may be misguided, but they
are sincere. They deny (atheist) or doubt (skeptic) that God
exists. They do not, all of them, deny or doubt that some acts
are right and some wrong. You have then the spectacle of an
honest atheist or skeptic prepared to say that, under assignable
circumstances, some actions are wrong. The question is, what
will Paley have to say to such persons, and about such persons?
There is nothing paradoxical about their existence, but, from
the point of view of Paley's argument, there ought to be.

(8) Paley's central assertion, that an act is right if, and only
if, it agrees with the will of God, seems clear when you first
start to think about it. But a doubt suggests itself. Does Paley
mean (what he says) that an act is right if it agrees with God's
will? Or, does he mean that it agrees with God's will because
it is right? These two are not the same. If the latter should be
the meaning, then rightness and wrongness become logically
independent of and prior to God's will. Rightness becomes

something with which God's will agrees; and because of that agreement we would say that His will is right. The matter might be put this way: When you adopt Paley's principle as ultimate ("right = agrees with the will of God"), you overlook the possibility that God may Himself be a rational being, that is, a being who deals in reasons, and that He presumably, therefore, has some reason for willing one thing and prohibiting another. These reasons would be independent of His will. They would justify His will. If you say that God has no reasons for what He wills, you threaten His rationality. That is a high price to pay for agreeing with Paley. If you say that He does have reasons, then those reasons, whatever they are, would be the basis for distinguishing between right and wrong. Given them, you could define right and wrong in principle. It sounds fantastic, but not silly, to imagine oneself able to ask God why His will is opposed, say, to theft or murder. It sounds silly, however, to imagine that He would have no answer to such a question; or that His answer would be, "I am opposed to theft because I am opposed to theft." What, then, might His reason be?

Thus, Paley. Before moving on to our next moralist, two minor misunderstandings should be prevented. Sometimes people say: "Act rightly or God will punish you." Now, that is as may be. The point to be insisted upon, however, is that whether an act is wrong and whether it will be punished are separate questions. It is not the job of a moral philosophy to ask the question, "Which acts will be punished?" Its job is to ask, "Which acts ought to be punished?" And to insist on the answer, "Only acts which are wrong." To know that God punishes wrongdoing is no answer to the question, "When is an act wrong?" From the fact that God is rational, one would expect of Him that He would punish only wrongdoing. The wrongness would be at least part of His reason for punishing it. But that leaves untouched the question of His reason for calling it wrong to begin with.

The second is this: Sometimes people say, "If I did not believe in God, I would forget all about right and wrong. I would do just as I pleased. If men ceased to believe in God, they would give up trying to do what is right and avoid doing what is wrong." Again, this is as may be. But the person who says this is confusing two matters, namely, why he calls an act wrong, and why he refrains from performing it. There may be evidence that atheists will steal your tablespoons. There may also be evidence that God-fearing men are sometimes guilty of wrongdoing. The point is that such evidence is irrelevant to the question, "What fact, common to cases of wrongdoing, is the reason for calling them cases of wrongdoing?" The question is not why a man does or should do what is right and avoid doing what is wrong. The question is why some acts are right and others wrong.

QUESTIONS

1. Name two ways of getting to know the will of God, according to Paley.

2. Why must Paley show that God wills the happiness of men? Why can he not use the Scriptures to do this? How does he go about doing this?

3. What is Paley's point in contrasting a sickle and an instrument of torture?

4. Why is the transition from Paley to the Utilitarians an easy one?

5. Which of these statements would Paley endorse: (a) God wills a line of action because it is right; (b) A line of action is right because God wills it?

6. Mention some presuppositions of the principle that an act is right if, and only if, it is according to the will of God.

7. Use any two of those presuppositions to show how trouble at the level of presuppositions results, via the principle, in trouble at the level of judgments.

8. Suggest Paley's answer to this question: "Why does agreeing with the will of God make an act right?"

9. At which point, in your opinion, is Paley's position weakest? Why?

2. BENTHAM

From Paley to Bentham. Paley's answer to the question "When is an act right?" was "When it agrees with the will of God." His answer to the question "How do we know the will of God?" was "In two ways: by consulting the Scriptures, and by the light of nature." His answer to the question "When, according to the light of nature, does an act agree with the will of God?" was "When it makes for the happiness of men."

You have in that last claim a point of possible departure for a moral philosophy which seeks to swing free of theology, and which could therefore be described as secular. One such position, widely held and acted upon in the modern world, is best known by the name Utilitarianism. It is the claim that happiness is the only intrinsically good thing, and that an act is right if, and only if, it produces more happiness than any other act possible under the circumstances. This doctrine is sometimes called Benthamism, after Jeremy Bentham, its most famous and forceful propounder and defender. Utilitarianism is an alternative to the position set forth by Paley, and, like Paley's position, is much older than the modern world. Utilitarianism, though not original with Bentham, received its most trenchant presentation in his book, *Introduction to the Principles of Morals and Legislation,* published in 1789, just five years after Paley's *Principles of Moral and Political Philosophy.*

Bentham. Bentham was born in England in 1748. He died at the age of eighty-four in 1832, the year in which England passed its first Reform Act. As a child and youth he was precocious, entering Oxford at the age of twelve, and obtaining his B.A. at sixteen and his M.A. at eighteen. His father intended him to enter law, beginning with practice and moving on to a judgeship. Young Bentham was interested in the law, but not as a prospective barrister or judge. He decided, while yet under twenty, that he would devote himself to examining, criticizing and revising the theory of legislation, the principles and the presuppositions embodied, or believed to be embodied, in the law-making of his day. His first book on these matters, *Fragment on Government,* was published in 1776. It contained a sharp criticism of Sir William Blackstone's then recent *Commentaries on the Laws of England.* During the next five years he followed up the *Fragment on Government* with the first draft of *Introduction to the Principles of Morals and Legislation,* printed for private circulation in 1781. The book was not published, however, until 1789. Bentham delayed publication those eight years because he was not sure what reception the book would get. His friends urged him to publish. One of them wrote to him, "There is a Mr. Paley, a parson and archdeacon of Carlisle, who has written a book called *Principles of Moral and Political Philosophy* and it has gone through two editions with prodigious applause." When Bentham's book was finally published, whatever doubts the author may have had were soon dispelled. It became a storm center, and remained so for his own and the following generation. In England during the closing years of the eighteenth century and throughout the civilized world during the first thirty years of the nineteenth century, the book had a divisive effect upon its readers. They swore by it or they swore at it. It left few readers neutral. It asked one question: By what standard should men judge their customs, laws, institutions, constitutions? It proposed one answer: By their effect upon the greatest happiness of the greatest number, and by nothing else. Responsible English historians have said that no writer in England, during the century following the publication of Bentham's book, exercised a greater influence upon public opinion and legislative social reform.

The Argument. Bentham began as a student of law and became committed to a theory of morals. You can get at this matter if you ask: What fact about a law justifies its enforcement? Bentham's answer was simple: The fact that it makes for the greatest happiness of the greatest number. His own words were these: "The greatest happiness of the greatest number is the measure of right and wrong." You have here a principle which applies to more than laws. If it applies to the act of making or administering a piece of legislation, why need it stop there? What action need fall outside its scope? This extension is indicated in the title which Bentham finally gave to his book: it was to be an introduction to the principles of morals as well as of legislation.

The book contains seventeen chapters. The first four, and especially the first two, contain his statement of the principle upon which he would have men criticize and revise their attempts to do what is right and avoid doing what is wrong. The first chapter states the position, the second criticizes other positions. The two together give what is still the most terse and vigorous presentation of the utilitarian theory. Bentham had the great advantage of knowing his own mind, and of believing that what it contained was true.

The argument of the first chapter can be paraphrased as follows: Happiness is the only finally good thing, the only thing good in itself, good as an end, and not merely as a means to something else. The utility of an act is its power to produce happiness. Utilitarianism is the claim that the rightness of an act is determined by its utility, its power to produce happiness. In a given situation, only that act which would produce more happiness than any other act would be right. These are matters of first principle: they cannot be proved. You cannot prove that happiness is the only finally good thing, nor that the rightness of an act is a function of its power to produce happiness. If, however, you admit these initial claims, you can then proceed to criticize and revise attempts to do what is right and avoid doing what is wrong. If you were to ask Bentham what fact, common to cases of wrongdoing, was his reason for calling them cases of wrongdoing, he would point to Chapter I of his book and say, "The answer is there. The fact in question is that they militate against the greatest happiness of the greatest number. If they did not do that, I would not call them wrong. That is my sole reason for calling them wrong." If you fell in with Bentham at this point, you could proceed to discuss law-making, and how it can be used to create, to preserve, and to increase the greatest happiness of the greatest number.

If, however, you did not fall in with him, if you refused to admit that happiness is the only finally good thing and that the rightness of an act is determined by its power to produce happiness, you would be "dealt with" in his second chapter. If, that is, you were neither a skeptic nor a utilitarian, but held a position "adverse to the principle of utility," Bentham would set himself to show you the weakness or foolishness of your position. His problem in Chapter II is to arrive at a clear-cut way of disposing of all comers who do not agree with him.

His procedure is simple. It involves two steps. He first sets up three possibilities: (a) you define rightness in terms of happiness, in which case you are a utilitarian and on his side, or, (b) you define rightness in terms of unhappiness ("an act is right if it produces unhappiness"), in which case he refers to you by the tag "principle of asceticism"; or, (c) you define rightness without reference to either happiness or unhappiness, but in some third way which is different altogether, in which case he refers to you, for reasons stated below, by the tag "principle of sympathy-antipathy." In effect, you are clearheaded if you choose (a); wrongheaded if you choose (b); and muddleheaded if you choose (c). Bentham will have it that any opponent worth powder and shot falls into group (b) or (c).

His second step is revealing. You might expect a series of long and detailed criticisms of these alternatives to the principle of utility, leading up finally to their refutation. But it is not so. Bentham, whatever one may think of him as a moralist, is a shrewd logician. He says bluntly: There is only one criticism of any alternative to utilitarianism, and that is simply to show that it *is* different from utilitarianism. If the principle of utility defines rightness, and these others, these alternatives, differ from it, then you can say at once that *they* do not define rightness. The point is worth noting: when you assert an ultimate position you can do no more than assert it. You cannot argue for it. To do so would be to admit that you did not hold it as an ultimate position. Bentham's procedure amounts to saying this: "My primary assertion is that happiness is the only intrinsically good thing, and that the rightness of an act is determined by its power to produce happiness. This I say to begin with. This I lay down as an ultimate principle. On this rock I will build my moral philosophy." At some point, any moralist must be prepared to talk that kind of language. He must be able and willing to make his ultimate assertions and denials. And when he has done that, he can deal with those who differ only by pointing out that they do differ. This sort of forthrightness you find in Bentham.

The Text. The first two chapters of Bentham's *Introduction to the Principles of Morals and Legislation* are reproduced herewith, omitting all but two of the large mass of footnotes. These chapters should be read with care; they are a famous manifesto. They are brief and are written with clarity. It has become customary to belittle them for their dogmatic character. That is a mistake. This dogmatic character will not hurt any reader today, and it was much needed at the time they were written.

CHAPTER I

I. Nature has placed mankind under the governance of two sovereign masters, *pain* and *pleasure*. It is for them alone to point out what we ought to do, as well as to determine what we shall do. On the one hand the standard of right and wrong, on the other the chain of causes and effects, are fastened to their throne. They govern us in all we do, in all we say, in all we think: every effort we can make to throw off our subjection, will serve but to demonstrate and confirm it. In words a man may pretend to abjure their empire: but in reality he will remain subject to it all the while. The principle of utility recognizes this subjection, and assumes it for the foundation of that system, the object of which is to rear the fabric of felicity by the hands of reason and law. Systems which attempt to question it, deal in sounds instead of sense, in caprice instead of reason, in darkness instead of light.

But enough of metaphor and declamation: it is not by such means that moral science is to be improved.

II. The principle of utility is the foundation of the present work: it will be proper therefore at the outset to give an explicit and determinate account of what is meant by it. By the principle of utility is meant that principle which approves or disapproves of every action whatsoever, according to the tendency which it appears to have to augment or diminish the happiness of the party whose interest is in question: or, what is the same thing in other words, to promote or to oppose that happiness. I say of every action whatsoever; and therefore not only of every action of a private individual, but of every measure of government.

III. By utility is meant that property in any object, whereby it tends to produce benefit, advantage, pleasure, good, or happiness (all this in the present case comes to the same thing) or (what comes again to the same thing) to prevent the happening of mischief, pain, evil, or unhappiness to the party whose interest is considered: if that party be the community in general, then the happiness of the community: if a particular individual, then the happiness of that individual.

IV. The interest of the community is one of the most general expressions that can occur in the phraseology of morals: no wonder that the meaning of it is often lost. When it has a meaning, it is this. The community is a fictitious body, composed of the individual persons who are considered as constituting as it were its members. The interest of the community then, is what?—the sum of the interests of the several members who compose it.

V. It is in vain to talk of the interest of the community, without understanding what is the interest of the individual. A thing is said to promote the interest, or to be for the interest, of an individual, when it tends to add to the sum total of his pleasures: or, what comes to the same thing, to diminish the sum total of his pains.

VI. An action then may be said to be conformable to the principle of utility, or, for shortness sake, to utility, (meaning with respect to the community at large) when the tendency it has to augment the happiness of the community is greater than any it has to diminish it.

VII. A measure of government (which is but a particular kind of

action, performed by a particular person or persons) may be said
to be conformable to or dictated by the principle of utility, when in
like manner the tendency which it has to augment the happiness
of the community is greater than any which it has to diminish it.

VIII. When an action, or in particular a measure of government,
is supposed by a man to be conformable to the principle of utility,
it may be convenient, for the purposes of discourse, to imagine
a kind of law or dictate, called a law or dictate of utility; and to
speak of the action in question, as being conformable to such law
or dictate.

IX. A man may be said to be a partizan of the principle of utility,
when the approbation or disapprobation he annexes to any action,
or to any measure, is determined by and proportioned to the tendency which he conceives it to have to augment or to diminish the
happiness of the community: or in other words, to its conformity or
unconformity to the laws or dictates of utility.

X. Of an action that is conformable to the principle of utility
one may always say either that it is one that ought to be done, or
at least that it is not one that ought not to be done. One may say
also, that it is right it should be done; at least that it is not wrong
it should be done: that it is a right action; at least that it is not a
wrong action. When thus interpreted, the words *ought*, and *right*
and *wrong*, and others of that stamp, have a meaning: when otherwise, they have none.

XI. Has the rectitude of this principle been ever formally contested? It should seem that it had, by those who have not known
what they have been meaning. Is it susceptible of any direct proof?
It should seem not: for that which is used to prove everything else,
cannot itself be proved: a chain of proofs must have their com-
mencement somewhere. To give such proof is as impossible as it
is needless.

XII. Not that there is or ever has been that human creature
breathing, however stupid or perverse, who has not on many, perhaps on most occasions of his life, deferred to it. By the natural
constitution of the human frame, on most occasions of their lives
men in general embrace this principle, without thinking of it: if not
for the ordering of their own actions, yet for the trying of their
own actions, as well as of those of other men. There have been, at
the same time, not many, perhaps, even of the most intelligent, who

have been disposed to embrace it purely and without reserve. There are even few who have not taken some occasion or other to quarrel with it, either on account of their not understanding always how to apply it, or on account of some prejudice or other which they were afraid to examine into, or could not bear to part with. For such is the stuff that man is made of: in principle and in practice, in a right track and in a wrong one, the rarest of all human qualities is consistency.

XIII. When a man attempts to combat the principle of utility, it is with reasons drawn, without his being aware of it, from that very principle itself. His arguments, if they prove any thing, prove not that the principle is wrong, but that, according to the applications he supposes to be made of it, it is misapplied. Is it possible for a man to move the earth? Yes; but he must first find out another earth to stand upon.

XIV. To disprove the propriety of it by arguments is impossible; but, from the causes that have been mentioned, or from some confused or partial view of it, a man may happen to be disposed not to relish it. Where this is the case, if he thinks the settling of his opinions on such a subject worth the trouble, let him take the following steps, and at length, perhaps, he may come to reconcile himself to it.

1. Let him settle with himself, whether he would wish to discard this principle altogether; if so, let him consider what it is that all his reasonings (in matters of politics especially) can amount to?

2. If he would, let him settle with himself, whether he would judge and act without any principle, or whether there is any other he would judge and act by?

3. If there be, let him examine and satisfy himself whether the principle he thinks he has found is really any separate intelligible principle; or whether it be not a mere principle in words, a kind of phrase, which at bottom expresses neither more nor less than the mere averment of his own unfounded sentiments; that is, what in another person he might be apt to call caprice?

4. If he is inclined to think that his own approbation or disapprobation, annexed to the idea of an act, without any regard to its consequences, is a sufficient foundation for him to judge and act upon, let him ask himself whether his sentiment is to be a standard of right and wrong, with respect to every other man, or whether

every man's sentiment has the same privilege of being a standard to itself?

5. In the first case, let him ask himself whether his principle is not despotical, and hostile to all the rest of the human race?

6. In the second case, whether it is not anarchical, and whether at this rate there are not as many different standards of right and wrong, as there are men? and whether even to the same man, the same thing, which is right today, and may not (without the least change in its nature) be wrong tomorrow? and whether the same thing is not right and wrong in the same place at the same time? and in either case, whether all argument is not at an end? and whether, when two men have said, "I like this," and "I don't like it," they can (upon such a principle) have any thing more to say?

7. If he should have said to himself, No: for that the sentiment which he proposes as a standard must be grounded on reflection, let him say on what particulars the reflection is to turn? If on particulars having relation to the utility of the act, then let him say whether this is not deserting his own principle, and borrowing assistance from that very one in opposition to which he sets it up: or if not on those particulars, on what other particulars?

8. If he should be for compounding the matter, and adopting his own principle in part, and the principle of utility in part, let him say how far he will adopt it?

9. When he has settled with himself where he will stop, then let him ask himself how he justifies to himself the adopting it so far? and why he will not adopt it any farther?

10. Admitting any other principle than the principle of utility to be a right principle, a principle that it is right for a man to pursue; admitting (what is not true) that the word *right* can have a meaning without reference to utility, let him say whether there is any such thing as a motive that a man can have to pursue the dictates of it: if there is, let him say what that motive is, and how it is to be distinguished from those which enforce the dictates of utility: if not, then lastly let him say what it is this other principle can be good for?

CHAPTER II

I. If the principle of utility be a right principle to be governed by, and that in all cases, it follows from what has been just observed, that whatever principle differs from it in any case must necessarily be a wrong one. To prove any other principle, therefore, to be a wrong one, there needs no more than just to show it to be what it is, a principle of which the dictates are in some point or other different from those of the principle of utility: to state it is to confute it.

II. A principle may be different from that of utility in two ways: 1. By being constantly opposed to it; this is the case with a principle which may be termed the principle of asceticism. 2. By being sometimes opposed to it, and sometimes not, as it may happen: this is the case with another, which may be termed the principle of sympathy and antipathy.

III. By the principle of asceticism I mean that principle, which, like the principle of utility, approves or disapproves of any action, according to the tendency which it appears to have to augment or diminish the happiness of the party whose interest is in question; but in an inverse manner: approving of actions in as far as they tend to diminish happiness; disapproving of them in as far as they tend to augment it.

IV. It is evident that any one who reprobates any the least particle of pleasure, as such, from whatever source derived, is *pro tanto* a partizan of the principle of asceticism. It is only upon that principle, and not from the principle of utility, that the most abominable pleasure which the vilest of malefactors ever reaped from his crime would be to be reprobated, if it stood alone. The case is, that it never does stand alone; but is necessarily followed by such a quantity of pain (or, what comes to the same thing, such a chance for a certain quantity of pain) that the pleasure in comparison of it, is as nothing: and this is the true and sole, but perfectly sufficient, reason for making it a ground for punishment.

V. There are two classes of men of very different complexions, by whom the principle of asceticism appears to have been embraced; the one a set of moralists, the other a set of religionists. Different accordingly have been the motives which appear to have recommended it to the notice of these different parties. Hope, that is the prospect of pleasure, seems to have animated the former: hope, the aliment of philosophic pride: the hope of honour and reputation at the hands of men. Fear, that is, the prospect of pain, the latter: fear, the offspring of superstitious fancy: the fear of future punishment at the hands of a splenetic and revengeful Deity. I say in this case fear: for of the invisible future, fear is more powerful than hope. These circumstances characterize the two different parties among the partizans of the principle of asceticism; the parties and their motives different, the principle the same.

VI. The religious party, however, appear to have carried it farther than the philosophical: they have acted more consistently and less wisely. The philosophical party have scarcely gone farther than to reprobate pleasure: the religious party have frequently gone so far as to make it a matter of merit and of duty to court pain. The philosophical party have hardly gone farther than the making pain a matter of indifference. It is no evil, they have said: they have not said, it is a good. They have not so much as reprobated all pleasure in the lump. They have discarded only what they have called the gross; that is, such as are organical, or of which the origin is easily traced up to such as are organical: they have even cherished and magnified the refined. Yet this, however, not under the name of pleasure: to cleanse itself from the sordes of its impure original, it was necessary it should change its name: the honourable, the glorious, the reputable, the becoming, the *honestum,* the *decorum,* it was to be called: in short, any thing but pleasure.

VII. From these two sources have flowed the doctrines from which the sentiments of the bulk of mankind have all along received a tincture of this principle; some from the philosophical, some from the religious, some from both. Men of education more frequently from the philosophical, as more suited to the elevation of their sentiments: the vulgar more frequently from the superstitious, as more suited to the narrowness of their intellect, undilated by knowledge: and to the abjectness of their condition, continually open to the attacks of fear. The tinctures, however, derived from the two sources, would naturally intermingle, insomuch that a man would not always know by which of them he was most influenced: and they would often serve to corroborate and enliven one another. It was this conformity that made a kind of alliance between parties of a complexion otherwise so dissimilar: and disposed them to unite upon various occasions against the common enemy, the partizan of the principle of utility, whom they joined in branding with the odious name of Epicurean.

VIII. The principle of asceticism, however, with whatever warmth it may have been embraced by its partizans as a rule of private conduct, seems not to have been carried to any considerable length, when applied to the business of government. In a few instances it has been carried a little way by the philosophical party: witness the Spartan regimen. Though then, perhaps, it may be considered as having been a measure of security: and an application, though a precipitate and perverse application, of the principle of utility. Scarcely in any instances, to any considerable length, by the religious: for the various monastic orders, and the societies of the Quakers, Dumplers, Moravians, and other religionists, have been free societies, whose regimen no man has been astricted to without the intervention of his own consent. Whatever merit a man may have thought there would be in making himself miserable, no such notion seems ever to have occurred to any of them, that it may be a merit, much less a duty, to make others miserable: although it should seem, that if a certain quantity of misery were a thing so desirable, it would not matter much whether it were brought by each man upon himself, or by one man upon another. It is true, that from the same source from whence, among the religionists, the attachment to the principle of asceticism took its rise, flowed other doctrines and practices, from which misery in abundance was produced in one man by the instrumentality of another: witness the holy wars, and the persecutions for religion. But the passion for producing misery in these cases proceeded upon some special ground: the exercise of it was confined to persons of particular descriptions: they were tormented, not as men, but as heretics and infidels. To have inflicted the same miseries on their fellow-believers and fellow-sectaries, would have been as blameable in the eyes even of these religionists, as in those of a partizan of the principles of utility. For a man to give himself a certain number of stripes was indeed meritorius: but to give the same number of stripes to another man, not consenting, would have been a sin. We read of saints, who for the good of their souls, and the mortification of their bodies, have voluntarily yielded themselves a prey to vermin: but though many persons of this class have wielded the reins of empire, we read of none who have set themselves to work, and made laws on purpose, with a view of stocking the body politic with the breed of highwaymen, housebreakers, or incendiaries. If at any time they have suffered the nation to be preyed upon by swarms of idle pensioners, or useless placemen, it has rather been from negligence and imbecility, than from any settled plan for oppressing and plundering of the people. If at any time they have sapped the sources of national wealth, by cramping commerce, and driving the inhabitants into emigration, it has been with other views, and in pursuit of other ends. If they have declaimed against the pursuit of pleasure, and the use of wealth, they have commonly stopped at declamation: they have not, like Lycurgus, made express ordinances for the purpose of banishing the precious metals. If they have established idleness by a law, it has been not because idleness, the mother of vice and misery, is itself a virtue, but because idleness (say they) is the road to holiness. If under the notion of fasting, they have joined in the plan of confining their subjects to a diet, thought by some to be of the most nourishing and prolific nature, it has been not for the sake of making them tributaries to the nations by whom that diet was to be supplied, but for the sake of manifesting their own power, and exercising the obedience of the people. If they have established, or suffered to be established, punishments for the breach of celibacy, they have done no more than comply with the petitions of those deluded rigorists, who, dupes to the ambitious and deep-laid policy of their rulers, first laid themselves under that idle obligation by a vow.

IX. The principle of asceticism seems originally to have been the reverie of certain hasty speculators, who having perceived, or fancied, that certain pleasures, when reaped in certain circumstances, have, at the long run, been attended with pains more than equivalent to them, took occasion to quarrel with every thing that offered itself under the name of pleasure. Having then got thus far, and having forgot the point which they set out from, they pushed on, and went so much further as to think it meritorious to fall in love with pain. Even this, we see, is at bottom but the principle of utility misapplied.

X. The principle of utility is capable of being consistently pursued; and it is but tautology to say, that the more consistently it is pursued, the better it must ever be for human-kind. The principle of asceticism never was, nor ever can be consistently pursued by any living creature. Let but one tenth part of the inhabitants of this earth pursue it consistently, and in a day's time they will have turned it into a hell.

XI. Among principles adverse to that of utility, that which at this day seems to have most influence in matters of government, is what may be called the principle of sympathy and antipathy. By the principle of sympathy and antipathy, I mean that principle which approves or disapproves of certain actions, not on account of their tending to augment the happiness, nor yet on account of their tending to diminish the happiness of the party whose interest is in question, but merely because a man finds himself disposed to approve or disapprove of them: holding up that approbation or disapprobation as a sufficient reason for itself, and disclaiming the necessity of looking out for any extrinsic ground. Thus far in the general department of morals: and in the particular department of politics, measuring out the quantum (as well as determining the ground) of punishment, by the degree of the disapprobation.

XII. It is manifest, that this is rather a principle in name than in reality: it is not a positive principle of itself, so much as a term employed to signify the negation of all principle. What one expects to find in a principle is something that points out some external consideration, as a means of warranting and guiding the internal sentiments of approbation and disapprobation: this expectation is but ill fulfilled by a proposition, which does neither more nor less than hold up each of those sentiments as a ground and standard for itself.

XIII. In looking over the catalogue of human actions (says a partizan of this principle) in order to determine which of them are to be marked with the seal of disapprobation, you need but to take counsel of your own feelings: whatever you find in yourself a propensity to condemn, is wrong for that very reason. For the same reason it is also meet for punishment: in what proportion it is adverse to utility, or whether it be adverse to utility at all, is a matter that makes no difference. In that same proportion also is it meet for punishment: if you hate much, punish much: if you hate little, punish little: punish as you hate. If you hate not at all, punish not at all: the fine feelings of the soul are not to be overborne and tyrannized by the harsh and rugged dictates of political utility.

XIV. The various systems that have been formed concerning the standard of right and wrong, may all be reduced to the principle of sympathy and antipathy. One account may serve for all of them. They consist all of them in so many contrivances for avoiding the obligation of appealing to any external standard, and for prevailing upon the reader to accept of the author's sentiment or opinion as a reason for itself. The phrases different, but the principle the same.

The following passage occurs at this point as a footnote in Bentham's text:

It is curious enough to observe the variety of inventions men have hit upon, and the variety of phrases they have brought forward, in order to conceal from the world, and, if possible, from themselves, this very general and therefore very pardonable self-sufficiency.

1. One man says, he has a thing made on purpose to tell him what is right and what is wrong; and that it is called a moral sense: and then he goes to work at his ease, and says, such a thing is right, and such a thing is wrong—why? "because my moral sense tells me it is."

2. Another man comes and alters the phrase: leaving out moral, and putting in common, in the room of it. He then tells you, that his common sense teaches him what is right and wrong, as surely as the other's moral sense did: meaning by common sense, a sense of some kind or other, which, he says, is possessed by all mankind: the sense of those, whose sense is not the same as the author's, being struck out of the account as not worth taking. This contrivance does better than the other; for a moral sense, being a new thing, a man may feel about him a good while without being able to find it out: but common sense is as old as the creation; and there is no man but would be ashamed to be thought not to have as much of it as his neighbours. It has another great advantage: by appearing to share power, it lessens envy: for when a man gets up upon this ground, in order to anathematize those who differ from him, it is not by a *sic volo sic jubeo*, but by a *velitis jubeatis*.

3. Another man comes, and says, that as to a moral sense indeed, he cannot find that he has any such thing: that however he has an understanding, which will do quite as well. This understanding, he says, is the standard of right and wrong: it tells him so and so. All good and wise men understand as he does: if other men's understandings differ in any point from his, so much the worse for them: it is a sure sign they are either defective or corrupt.

4. Another man says, that there is an eternal and immutable Rule of Right: that that rule of right dictates so and so: and then he begins giving you his sentiments upon any thing that comes uppermost: and these sentiments (you are to take for granted) are so many branches of the eternal rule of right.

5. Another man, or perhaps the same man (it's no matter) says, that there are certain practices conformable, and others repugnant, to the Fitness of Things; and then he tells you, at his leisure, what practices are conformable and what repugnant: just as he happens to like a practice or dislike it.

6. A great multitude of people are continually talking of the Law of Nature; and then they go on giving you their sentiments about what is

right and what is wrong: and these sentiments, you are to understand, are so many chapters and sections of the Law of Nature.

7. Instead of the phrase, Law of Nature, you have sometimes, Law of Reason, Right Reason, Natural Justice, Natural Equity, Good Order. Any of them will do equally well. This latter is most used in politics. The three last are much more tolerable than the others, because they do not very explicitly claim to be any thing more than phrases: they insist but feebly upon the being looked upon as so many positive standards of themselves, and seem content to be taken, upon occasion, for phrases expressive of the conformity of the thing in question to the proper standard, whatever that may be. On most occasions, however, it will be better to say *utility*: *utility* is clearer, as referring more explicitly to pain and pleasure.

8. We have one philosopher, who says, there is no harm in any thing in the world but in telling a lie: and that if, for example, you were to murder your own father, this would only be a particular way of saying, he was not your father. Of course, when this philosopher sees any thing that he does not like, he says, it is a particular way of telling a lie. It is saying, that the act ought to be done, or may be done, when, in truth, it ought not to be done.

9. The fairest and openest of them all is that sort of man who speaks out, and says, I am of the number of the Elect: now God himself takes care to inform the Elect what is right: and that with so good effect, and let them strive ever so, they cannot help not only knowing it but practising it. If therefore a man wants to know what is right and what is wrong, he has nothing to do but to come to me.

It is upon the principle of antipathy that such and such acts are often reprobated on the score of their being unnatural: the practice of exposing children, established among the Greeks and Romans, was an unnatural practice. Unnatural, when it means any thing, means unfrequent: and there it means something; although nothing to the present purpose. But here it means no such thing: for the frequency of such acts is perhaps the great complaint. It therefore means nothing; nothing, I mean, which there is in the act itself. All it can serve to express is, the disposition of the person who is talking of it: the disposition he is in to be angry at the thoughts of it. Does it merit his anger? Very likely it may: but whether it does or no is a question, which, to be answered rightly, can only be answered upon the principle of utility.

Unnatural, is as good a word as moral sense, or common sense; and would be as good a foundation for a system. Such an act is unnatural; that is, repugnant to nature: for I do not like to practise it: and, consequently, do not practise it. It is therefore repugnant to what ought to be the nature of every body else.

The mischief common to all these ways of thinking and arguing (which, in truth, as we have seen, are but one and the same method, couched in different forms of words) is their serving as a cloke, and pretence, and aliment, to despotism: if not a despotism in practice, a despotism however in disposition: which is but too apt, when pretence and power offer, to show itself in practice. The consequence is, that with intentions very commonly of the purest kind, a man becomes a torment either to himself or his fellow-creatures. If he be of the melancholy cast, he sits in silent grief, bewailing their blindness and depravity: if of the irascible, he declaims with fury and virulence against all who differ from him; blowing up the coals of fanaticism, and branding with the charge of corruption and insincerity, every man who does not think, or profess to think as he does.

If such a man happens to possess the advantages of style, his book may do a considerable deal of mischief before the nothingness of it is understood.

These principles, if such they can be called, it is more frequent to see applied to morals than to politics: but their influence extends itself to both. In politics, as well as morals, a man will be at least equally glad of a pretence for deciding any question in the manner that best pleases him, without the trouble of inquiry. If a man is an infallible judge of what is right and wrong in the actions of private individuals, why not in the measures to be observed by public men in the direction of those actions? accordingly (not to mention other chimeras) I have more than once known the pretended law of nature set up in legislative debates, in opposition to arguments derived from the principle of utility.

"But is it never, then, from any other considerations than those of utility, that we derive our notions of right and wrong?" I do not know: I do not care. Whether a moral sentiment can be originally conceived from any other source than a view of utility, is one question: whether upon examination and reflection it can, in point of fact, be actually persisted in and justified on any other ground, by a person reflecting within himself, is another: whether in point of right it can properly be justified on any other ground, by a person addressing himself to the community, is a third. The two first are questions of speculation: it matters not, comparatively speaking, how they are decided. The last is a question of practice: the decision of it is of as much importance as that of any can be.

"I feel in myself," (say you) "a disposition to approve of such or such an action in a moral view: but this is not owing to any notions I have of its being a useful one to the community. I do not pretend to know whether it be an useful one or not: it may be, for aught I know, a mischievous one. "But is it then," (say I) "a mischievous one? examine; and if you can make yourself sensible that it is so, then, if duty means anything, that is, moral duty, it is your duty at least to abstain from it: and more than that, if it is what lies in your power, and can be done without too great a sacrifice, to endeavour to prevent it. It is not your cherishing the notion of it in your bosom, and giving it the name of virtue, that will excuse you."

"I feel in myself," (say you again) " a disposition to detest such or such an action in a moral view; but this is not owing to any notions I have of its being a mischievous one to the community. I do not pretend to know whether it be a mischievous one or not: it may be not a mischievous one; it may be, for aught I know, an useful one."—"May it indeed," (say I) "an useful one? but let me tell you then, that unless duty, and right and wrong, be just what you please to make them, if it really be not a mischievous one, and any body has a mind to do it, it is no duty of yours, but, on the contrary, it would be very wrong in you, to take upon you to prevent him: detest it within yourself as much as you please; that may be a very good reason (unless it be also a useful one) for your not doing it yourself: but if you go about, by word or deed, to do any thing to hinder him, or make him suffer for it, it is you, and not he, that have done wrong: it is not your setting yourself to blame his conduct, or branding it with the name of vice, that will make him culpable, or you blameless. Therefore, if you can make yourself content that he shall be of one mind, and you of another, about that matter, and so continue, it is well: but if nothing will serve you, but that you and he must needs be of the same mind, I'll tell you what you have to do: it is for you to get the better of your antipathy, not for him to truckle to it."

XV. It is manifest, that the dictates of this principle will frequently coincide with those of utility, though perhaps without intending any such thing. Probably more frequently than not: and hence it is that the business of penal justice is carried on upon that tolerable sort of footing upon which we see it carried on in common at this day. For what more natural or more general ground of hatred to a practice can there be, than the mischievousness of such practice? What all men are exposed to suffer by, all men will be disposed to hate. It is far yet, however, from being a constant ground: for when a man suffers, it is not always that he knows what it is he suffers by. A man may suffer grievously, for instance, by a new tax, without being able to trace up the cause of his sufferings to the injustice of some neighbour, who has eluded the payment of an old one.

XVI. The principle of sympathy and antipathy is most apt to err on the side of severity. It is for applying punishment in many cases which deserve none: in many cases which deserve some, it is for applying more than they deserve. There is no incident, imaginable, be it ever so trivial, and so remote from mischief, from which this principle may not extract a ground of punishment. Any difference in taste: any difference in opinion: upon one subject as well as upon another. No disagreement so trifling which perseverance and altercation will not render serious. Each becomes in the other's eyes an enemy, and, if laws permit, a criminal. This is one of the circumstances by which the human race is distinguished (not much indeed to its advantage) from the brute creation.

XVII. It is not, however, by any means unexampled for this principle to err on the side of lenity. A near and perceptible mischief moves antipathy. A remote and imperceptible mischief, though not less real, has no effect. Instances in proof of this will occur in numbers in the course of the work. It would be breaking in upon the order of it to give them here.

XVIII. It may be wondered, perhaps, that in all this while no mention has been made of the theological principle; meaning that principle which professes to recur for the standard of right and wrong to the will of God. But the case is, this is not in fact a distinct principle. It is never any thing more or less than one or other of the three before-mentioned principles presenting itself under another shape. The will of God here meant cannot be his revealed will, as contained in the sacred writings: for that is a system which nobody ever thinks of recurring to at this time of day, for the details of political administration: and even before it can be applied to the details of private conduct, it is universally allowed, by the most eminent divines of all persuasions, to stand in need of pretty ample interpretations; else to what use are the works of those divines? And for the guidance of these interpretations, it is also allowed, that some other standard must be assumed. The will then which is meant on this occasion, is that which may be called the presumptive will: that is to say, that which is presumed to be his will on account of the conformity of its dictates to those of some other principle. What then may be this other principle? it must be one or other of the three mentioned above: for there cannot, as we have seen, be any more. It is plain, therefore, that, setting revelation out of the question, no light can ever be thrown upon the standard of right and wrong, by any thing that can be said upon the question, what is God's will. We may be perfectly sure, indeed, that whatever is right is conformable to the will of God: but so far is that from answering the purpose of showing us what is right, that it is necessary to know first whether a thing is right in order to know from thence whether it be conformable to the will of God.

Bentham's footnote at this point:

The principle of theology refers everything to God's pleasure. But what is God's pleasure? God does not, he confessedly does not now, either speak or write to us. How then are we to know what is his pleasure? By observing what is our own pleasure, and pronouncing it to be his. Accordingly, what is called the pleasure of God, is and must necessarily be (revelation apart) neither more nor less than the good pleasure of the person, whoever he be, who is pronouncing what he believes, or pretends, to be God's pleasure. How know you it to be God's pleasure that such or such an act should be abstained from? whence come you even to suppose as much? "Because the engaging in it would, I imagine, be prejudicial upon the whole to the happiness of mankind"; says the partizan of the principle of utility: "Because the commission of it is attended with a gross and sensual, or at least with a trifling and transient satisfaction"; says the partizan of the principle of asceticism: "Because I detest the thoughts of it; and I cannot, neither ought I to be called upon to tell why"; says he who proceeds upon the principle of antipathy. In the words of one or other of these must that person necessarily answer (revelation apart) who professes to take for his standard the will of God.

XIX. There are two things which are very apt to be confounded, but which it imports us carefully to distinguish:—the motive or cause, which, by operating on the mind of an individual, is productive of any act: and the ground or reason which warrants a legislator, or other by-stander, in regarding that act with an eye of approbation. When the act happens, in the particular instance in question, to be productive of effects which we approve of, much more if we happen to observe that the same motive may frequently be productive, in other instances, of the like effects, we are apt to transfer our approbation to the motive itself, and to assume, as the just ground for the approbation we bestow on the act, the circumstance of its originating from that motive. It is in this way that the sentiment of antipathy has often been considered as a just ground of action. Antipathy, for instance, in such or such a case, is the cause of an action which is attended with good effects: but this does not make it a right ground of action in that case, any more than in any other. Still farther. Not only the effects are good, but the agent sees before-hand that they will be so. This may make the action indeed a perfectly right action: but it does not make antipathy a right ground of action. For the same sentiment of antipathy, if implicitly deferred to, may be, and very frequently is, productive of the very worst effects. Antipathy, therefore, can never be a right ground of action. No more, therefore, can resentment, which, as will be seen more particularly hereafter, is but a modification of antipathy. The only right ground of action, that can possibly subsist, is after all, the consideration of utility, which, if it is a right principle of action, and of approbation, in any one case, is so in every other. Other principles in abundance, that is, other motives, may be the reasons or causes of its being done: but it is this alone that can be the reason why it might or ought to have been done. Antipathy or resentment requires always to be regulated, to prevent its doing mischief: to be regulated by what? always by the principle of utility. The principle of utility neither requires nor admits of any other regulator than itself.

Influence. Utilitarianism is a secular ethics. It neither requires nor permits the introduction of the notion of the will of God into its formulation as a first principle. It says: There is such a thing as happiness. It is the only thing that is good in and for itself. It can be increased or decreased. To increase it is everywhere and always right; to decrease it is everywhere and always wrong. There is a seductive simplicity and clarity about this doctrine. It promises to act as a powerful dissolvent of obscurantism, narrowness, and authoritarianism. It, so to speak, puts the issue out there where everyone can see it and catch hold of it. It gives an engagingly "scientific" form to the attempt to estimate the rightness of an act: to set yourself to show, for example, that stealing decreases the greatest happiness of the greatest number, and is therefore wrong, is no less scientific in its intention than to set yourself to show that if you heat water beyond a certain point it will boil away in steam. It is empirical, as philosophers say, meaning that it refers you to experience for your answers: the only way to find out what effect an act has on human happiness is to consult experience. It is experimental: it says, try this and try that, proceed by the method of trial and error. It is objective: it refers you to something whose existence is independent of your thinking about it, and independent of what you think about it; an act either does or does not affect the happiness of men, and it does this whether you think so or not. It is humane: there is something genial and neighborly in the idea that the whole duty of man is to strive to create, maintain, and increase the happiness of his fellow-man. These are virtues in a philosophical doctrine. They do not guarantee the truth of the doctrine, but they commend it to those who profess it and act upon it.

At least they have done so, historically. It is probably no exaggeration to say that Utilitarianism has had more professed believers than any other secular moral philosophy in the modern world. Bentham's book became a rallying cry for a crowded century of legislative social reform. The history of the western world during the nineteenth century is dotted with men and movements which pointed to Utilitarianism as the principle upon which they would justify themselves. The book arrived at about the same time as the political revolutions in America and France, and the industrial revolution in England. These gave it a busy and colorful world in which to ferment and germinate. In A. V. Dicey's *Law and Public Opinion in England during the Nineteenth Century,* you will find the story of this ism in the life of one great people. There are comparable volumes for other peoples. Liberalism is the broader thing which Utilitarianism became. A people who chose "Life, Liberty, and the Pursuit of Happiness' as its major words have had much to say in the name of this doctrine. American Pragmatism is essentially a sophisticated reformulation of English Utilitarianism. You have, in Utilitarianism, a doctrine possessing demonstrated power to supply men with the principle upon which they seek to criticize and revise their attempts to do what is right and avoid doing what is wrong.

John Stuart Mill. Utilitarianism has been an important factor in the reflective as well as the active life of modern man. One question to ask of a doctrine is, "Will men act on it?" Another question is, "Will they *think* about it, and trouble to embody their thoughts in significant writing?" Judged by this criterion, Utilitarianism has done well for itself. Many men and many books could be cited in evidence. The most outstanding, I suppose, would be John Stuart Mill and such books of his as *On Liberty* (1859), *On Representative Government* (1861), *Utilitarianism* (1863), and *The Subjection of Women* (1869). That this doctrine inspired Mill to write these and similar books is no small tribute to its power.

One of Bentham's early friends and propagandists was James Mill, the father of John Stuart Mill. John Stuart was born in 1806 and was educated privately under the watchful eyes of his father and his father's friend, Bentham. He was carefully groomed for the job of second-generation expounder and defender of the utilitarian position. His elders were rewarded for their efforts: John Stuart became, for the period 1830 to 1870, one of the molders of opinion in Victorian England, and a saint of liberalism in the modern world.

Mill's 1859 tract, *On Liberty*, is a classic, a finished job. If you are a Utilitarian and a liberal, there are few other books so well calculated to clarify your position to yourself. It contains an elaborately reasoned and passionately asserted defence of the right of the individual to think and act for himself. To work through its pages is, for many readers, an unforgettable experience. The author's claim is that the case for liberty is its utility, its power to create, to maintain, to augment, the greatest happiness of the greatest number. If the case for liberty is its utility, then Mill has argued that case clearly and forcibly.

Two years later (1861) he published *Considerations on Representative Government,* giving the nineteenth century a second demonstration of the persuasive power of Bentham's Utilitarianism. The book is addressed to the central problem of community self-government: how shall men devise and revise the laws under which they are to live? The answer of the great political revolutions had been: those who are to live under laws shall choose those who are to make and administer the laws. This was the principle of representative government. Mill set himself to capture this idea for Utilitarianism; to show that government by elected representatives is best calculated to ensure the greatest happiness of the greatest number. It aimed to show democratically-minded men what they wanted to do, and to convince them of the reason for doing it. It was an able sequal to the *Liberty* and an added jewel to Utilitarianism's crown.

Two years later (1863) Mill published his small volume, *Utilitarianism*. In this book he reviewed the fortunes of the doctrine during the seventy-four years since Bentham had published his *Introduction*. Mill's intention was to answer the critics whom Bentham had stirred up. The volume is therefore essentially polemical. It says in effect: "Here is what men have said against Utilitarianism for three-quarters of a century. Here is Utilitarianism's answers to what they have said." If you are, or aim to be, a "greatest happiness" moralist, you cannot afford to ignore this wiry little book. I know of no better attempt to scrape off the stock misunderstandings and objections which Utilitarianism had gathered to itself, like barnacles, as it ploughed through the nineteenth century. It has another virtue: the author's integrity and persistence led him to make concessions. These would, in all probability, have scandalized the more doctrinaire Bentham, but they operated to assure readers that the doctrine, even if it did not contain the whole truth about right and wrong, was in good hands. A certain unbending fanaticism is sometimes needed to secure an initial hearing for a doctrine. This Bentham had provided. But moralists are fallible, and unbending fanaticism is therefore not enough to keep a doctrine alive for later and more seasoned customers.

Six years later (1869) Mill published *The Subjection of Women*. The title might better have been *The Emancipation of Women*. The book extends the argument of his *Liberty* to the position of women in the modern world. It contains a protest against their political, economic, professional, and social subjection, and an impassioned plea for their emancipation. Like its predecessors, the tract captured the field. It is the best of its kind. No other book has presented the case for the emancipation of women as generously and convincingly. The relevance of the book to the story of Utilitarianism is this: Mill rests his case against the subjection of women, and for their emancipation, on the principle of utility. In the long run, and from an over-all point of view, their subjection works against the greatest happiness of the greatest number; and their emancipation works for it.

Mill died in 1873. Among his posthumous publications was a volume called *Three Essays on Religion*. The first of these three essays was entitled "Nature." Mill had written this essay some twenty years earlier but had let it remain unpublished during his own lifetime. In the development of his own thought, therefore, it came before the 1859 *Liberty*. It is one of the author's best pieces of philosophical criticism and forms an introduction to the volumes which began with the *Liberty* and ended with *The Subjection of Women*. It would seem that the author intended it to clear the ground for the principle of utility and for the books in which he expounded, defended, or applied that principle. This essay, "Nature," [1] contains a searching and incisive criticism of the doctrine that an act is right if it is according to nature, or wrong if it is contrary to nature. Mill's criticism of "the appeal to nature," of the injunction to "follow nature" in matters of right and wrong, leaves little to be desired.

Utilitarianism has had a deep and lively influence on the active and reflective life of the modern world. This fact is one of its credentials, evidence of its power to attract men of integrity and good will. When you have said that, you have sung its praises high. It can be said of moral philosophies, as of fig trees, "by their fruits ye shall know them." The fruits of Utilitarianism are abundant and of good report. They would be a credit to any philosophical tree. Only an arrogant bigot could fail to be impressed by this fact. It has operated to clarify those ends which many good men propose for action, and to clarify, too, their ef-

---

[1] Mill's "Nature" has been published separately, in pamphlet form, by the University of Oregon Co-operative Store, Eugene, Oregon.

forts to think about these matters in principle. If a man cannot see these as strong points, he must be either fanatic or stupid.

Comment. Our two moralists thus far, Paley and Bentham, cover a lot of territory. Many people would agree with one or the other of them. Indeed, the question is, who wouldn't? And, why wouldn't he? And, what alternative would he propose? If a person says, "I do not think that rightness can be defined with reference to either the will of God or the happiness of men," we would ask him, why not? And, with reference to what, then?

Some reasons were suggested, in the section on Paley, which might incline a person to say, "Not Paley." But how about Bentham? A person who disagreed with Bentham would be claiming that the essence of the matter, the rightness of a right act, is not to be found in its power to create, to preserve, to augment, the happiness of men. Such a person would want to be free to argue that an act might do this, and still not be right; or might not do this, and still be right. He would be claiming to have a more penetrating insight into what it is about a right act which makes it right. Our next moralist (Kant) made such a claim. Let us examine some possible reasons for such a claim.

(1) To begin with, Utilitarianism proposes to judge the rightness of an act by reference to its consequences. An act, it says, is right if, and only if, it contributes more to the greatest happiness of the greatest number than any other act possible under the circumstances. Does Utilitarianism mean actual consequences or intended consequences? If actual consequences, then it is letting the notion of the accidental, the unintended, become ingredient in the notion of rightness. This is to part company with much legal and common sense thinking, a somewhat paradoxical business for a moral philosophy which, historically at least, was generated by a concern for just such considerations. Common sense and the law distinguish between what a man intends and what, in point of fact, sometimes happens. We may regret unintended consequences as unfortunate, but we do not condemn them as wrong. If someone asks you the shortest way to a certain place, and that way lies over a bridge,

it is not wrong to tell him so, if at the time you don't know that the bridge is about to collapse. Your intentions are right, even though the consequences are exceedingly unfortunate. If you know that the bridge is about to collapse, the matter is different: the man's death forms part of what you intend and becomes, under assignable circumstances, grounds for calling your act wrong.

(2) If actual consequences are to be retained as alone decisive, we are threatened with skepticism. We do not know all, perhaps not even most, of the actual consequences of any act. The consequences of an act ramify in ever widening circles. If we guess, we may guess wrong. If we try to find out, we set ourselves a seemingly endless task. If we do neither, we admit that we cannot say whether the act was right or wrong, and this is to admit ethical skepticism. There is an added difficulty. Utilitarianism bids us judge a particular deed, not only with reference to its actual consequences, but with reference to other deeds which were also possible at the time. We must be able to say that our act produced more happiness than any other act we might have done. Now, if the actual consequences of an actual deed are difficult to discover, what shall be said of the hypothetical consequences of a hypothetical deed? The price tag on a right-wrong judgment becomes, at this point, very steep indeed.

(3) Suppose Utilitarianism shifts from actual consequences to intended consequences, and says that an act is right if, and only if, it intends the greatest happiness of the greatest number. A man would then say, "I acted rightly because I intended, by my action, to bring about the greatest happiness of the greatest number. You must judge the morality of my action by its intended outcome, not its actual outcome. If the consequences did not actualize my intention, you can say that I failed. But can you say that I did wrong?" The answer is not immediately apparent. It would be no final rejoinder to such a person to murmur that the road to hell is paved with good intentions. He could admit that sad fact, but insist that it constituted a criti-

cism not of him but of the nature of things, for refusing to cooperate with his good intentions. It could be pointed out, of course, that this modification of theory, from actual consequences to intended consequences, is a real abandonment of the Utilitarianism of Bentham and Mill: they insisted upon actual consequences. It would seem as though the matter would have to be left at that.

(4) One criticism which has been persistently directed at Utilitarianism is to the following effect. Utilitarianism divides all good things into two classes: those which are good in themselves, good intrinsically; and those which are good instrumentally, good as a means to things which are themselves good intrinsically. Let us refer to these two kinds of goods as first-order goods (good in themselves) and second-order goods (good as means to first-order goods). So far, no objection is interposed. But at this point Utilitarianism enters its basic claim: there is only *one* first-order good, namely happiness. Happiness is the only intrinsically good thing. All other good things are good because, and only because, they are means to or conditions for happiness. Everything except happiness is a second-order good. Now this claim is cordially rejected by many critics. They do not deny that happiness is a first-order good; they deny that it is the *only* first-order good. What, for example, shall we say of such things as the disinterested pursuit of knowledge, shared affection, the appreciation of beauty? Are not these good things? And are they not first-order goods? Are they not intrinsically good, as clearly as happiness is? If you say "Yes" to that question, you break with orthodox Utilitarianism. You still find yourself in good company, but the company is no longer Bentham and Mill.

(5) Utilitarianism, as formulated by Bentham and Mill, invites a criticism which may not be relevant to all formulations. Bentham and Mill would have difficulties with the following: "An act is right if, and only if, it produces a greater balance of happiness than any other act possible under the circumstances."

The difficulty would arise over the phrase "other act possible under the circumstances." So formulated, Utilitarianism would presuppose that other acts are possible, that alternatives confront the person who acts. This is free will, and both Bentham and Mill took a dim view of free will. It cannot be said that the principle of utility committed them to a denial of free will. Why should it? Nevertheless they looked askance at the notion of free will. They felt that their theory of right and wrong implied a certain theory of human nature, namely that it is not the locus of free will. If they were mistaken in suspecting this implication, the present criticism cannot be urged. But if they were not mistaken, then Utilitarianism implies a denial of free will. This would be grounds for criticism. If free will is denied, then the theory cannot presuppose that alternative possibilities confront the person who acts. If it cannot presuppose that, then it is not clear how it can propose to criticize a person whose act violates the principle of utility.

It is important to distinguish between criticism and repudiation. Utilitarianism has often been repudiated, very colorfully so by Mill's contemporary, Thomas Carlyle, who called it a pig-philosophy and would have none of it. When you criticize a man's position you show him that some point in that position is inconsistent with some other point. You say to him: "Your position includes elements X and Y, and these are inconsistent. You must modify your position in respect to either X or Y." It is otherwise with repudiation. Both Paley and Bentham provide examples of what I mean. If you should ask Paley whether, under assignable circumstances, it is wrong to steal, he would answer, "Yes." If you should then ask him why, he would answer, "Because it is contrary to the will of God." If you persisted, and asked, "Why does being contrary to the will of God make an act wrong? Why is it wrong to act contrary to the will of God?" he would, I think, realize that you were asking him a question which defined his position, which, therefore, fell outside of his position. He would not undertake to answer that question. To say to Paley, "It is not wrong to act contrary to God's will," would not be to criticize his position; it would be to repudiate his position. Now, a comment sometimes directed against Utilitarianism seems to me to illustrate this distinction between criticism and repudiation. If you deny that happiness is an intrinsically good thing or that minimizing happiness is wrong, you are not criticizing Utilitarianism. You are repudiating it. This, it seems, many of its "critics" have done. They have, in effect, put to Utilitarianism the one question which it does not have to answer, namely, "Why is an act right because it maximizes the greatest happiness of the greatest number?" That is on a par with asking Paley, "Why is an act right because it agrees with the will of God?" To intend these questions in all seriousness is not to propose criticisms of these positions. It is to repudiate them.

QUESTIONS

1. Bentham's first paragraph has become famous. Why, do you suppose? Is there a contradiction running through it?

2. Distinguish (a) the principle of utility, (b) the principle of asceticism, (c) the principle of sympathy-antipathy.

3. Answer the following questions about those principles: (a) Why can the principle of utility not be proved? (b) Why can the principle of asceticism not be consistently pursued? Would that be an incisive criticism of it? (c) Why is the principle of sympathy-antipathy the negation of all principle? (d) Why does Bentham not consider the theological principle as a fourth, along with the other three?

4. What is Bentham's purpose in the set of ten questions in Chapter I, Section XIV? Which of these questions is the most effective? Why? Could question 8 be directed at Paley?

5. Why is Utilitarianism called a "secular" ethics? Is that a count against it?

6. As theories go, Utilitarianism has had many followers and has exerted considerable influence. It has also had many critics. How would you account for these facts about it?

7. Use the titles of J. S. Mill's writings to indicate their relation to Utilitarianism.

8. The principle is this: An act is right if, and only if, it produces more happiness than any other act possible under the circumstances. What presuppositions can you point out? Can the principle be critized through any of its presuppositions?

3. KANT

Suppose a man is doing something. We take note of what he is doing and reflect that, under the circumstances, it is wrong. We thereupon ask him why he is doing it. Suppose he were to answer, "I am doing it *because* I believe it to be wrong." We would, I think, be somewhat puzzled; more puzzled than if he had said, "I am doing it *although* I believe it to be wrong." There is a difference here between "because" and "although": to say "although" conveys the notion of weakness or selfishness, whereas to say "because" conveys the notion of perversity. You have something here upon which moralists might agree, even though they differed as to what makes an act wrong. Paley and Bentham differ as to what makes an act wrong, but both would look askance at the person who said, "I am doing this *because* I believe it to be wrong." Both would approve of the man who said, "I am doing this because I believe it to be right," although each might feel that the man had a mistaken notion of what makes an act right. Both would disapprove of the man who said, "I am doing this although I believe it to be wrong," despite the fact that each might feel that the man had a mistaken notion of what makes an act wrong. But both would be scandalized by the man who gave as his reason for doing something, the fact that he believed it to be wrong; although, again, each might feel that the man had a mistaken notion of what makes an act wrong. Both would respect the *conscientious* man, the man who did what he believed to be right, although each might feel that the man had a misguided conscience. Both would agree that rightness makes a *demand* upon us, and that wrongness does not, although each would differ from the other as to the nature of rightness and wrongness. Paley would say that the rightness of an act is to be found in the fact that God demands it: whatever God demands, it is right to do. Bentham would say that it is to be found in the fact that the greatest happiness of the greatest number demands it: whatever the greatest happiness of the greatest number demands, it is right to do.

No moralist would deny this demand character of rightness. Its presence is acknowledged by the use of such a word as "ought" in connection with the idea of rightness, as, for example, in the statement, "You ought to do what is right," or, "If it is right, then you ought to do it." Rightness puts us under an obligation to enact it; wrongness does not. Some moralists, however, are more impressed by this demand character than others, in the sense that they give it a more prominent place in their account of the nature of rightness. Among modern moralists, none have been more insistent upon it than Immanuel Kant. He introduced the word "categorical" to convey the unqualified character of the demand which rightness makes. This was to put the matter in the strongest possible language. To say that rightness makes a categorical demand is not, however, except in point of language, peculiar to Kant. Paley would say that what God demands is demanded categorically. Bentham would say that what the greatest happiness of the greatest number demands is demanded categorically, without any qualification. Nevertheless, it is Immanuel Kant who makes the clear, sharp emphasis upon the demand character of rightness, and the categorical character of that demand. The jolt which is administered by the statement, "I am doing this because I believe it to be wrong," testifies to the correctness of Kant's insight here.

In the year 1785 Immanuel Kant published a small book with a large and somewhat forbidding title, *The Groundwork of the Metaphysics of Morals*. It has become one of the most significant volumes in the history of moral philosophy in the modern world. The book was written with a clear knowledge of the positions illustrated by Paley and Bentham, and it proposed an alternative to both. It addressed itself to two matters, the principle of morality and the freedom of the will. When is an act right? And, Is choice a fact? It is an important book. For the student of moral philosophy in the modern world there is no way around it: it is necessary to go through it.

Kant's book was published in the same year as Paley's *Principles of Moral and Political Philosophy*, and four years before Bentham's *Introduction to the Principles of Morals and Legislation;* all three in the 1780's. Kant was sixty-one years old at the time. *The Groundwork of the Metaphysics of Morals* is therefore not a young man's book. The author had had ample time to think over what he wanted to say. He had already, in 1781, published one of the half-dozen greatest books in philosophy, namely, *The Critique of Pure Reason*. His concern there had been with knowledge, not action. He had there argued that knowledge is a joint product, arising in experience, of the mind and the external world; and he had set himself to isolate and describe the mind's contribution. If you had asked him, "what does the mind contribute to knowledge?" he would have pointed to his *Critique* and said, "My answer is there." Having dealt with knowledge, he turned to morality and repeated his question: What does the mind contribute to morality? If the mind contributes something to knowledge, then it may be that it also contributes something to morality. You have here a somewhat novel approach. If the mind *does* contribute something to morality, what is it?

Kant on History. The year before Kant published his *Groundwork,* he had published an interesting and important paper on the philosophy of history, *The Idea of a Universal History*. Since the *Groundwork* is longer than the essay and was published only a year later, it is reasonable to suppose that Kant worked on both at the same time. The 1784 essay also has something to say about morality, so examining it may help us to follow the argument of the 1785 book. The essay gives us Kant's view of human nature and society, two matters that lie very close to the notion of morality, and of history as the development of those capacities in man by which he can raise his actions from the instinctive and the customary to the moral.

The argument of Kant's essay on history is as follows. The human race has no over-all purpose of its own which it is working out for itself in history. But nature has a purpose, which she is engaged in working out through humanity in history. Nature's purpose in human history is this: she produced in man a combination of the mechanical and the rational, e.g., his body is mechanical, his mind rational. As man came originally from the hand of nature, his rational powers were undeveloped. They existed as potentialities, not as actualities, of human nature. Nature's problem was, then, how to develop man's rational powers. She recognized that these powers must be developed in the race, not in the individual: the life of a single generation would not be long enough. She recognized also that man must do it for himself. She could provide him with a body; he must develop his mind. To realize her purpose, she instituted two arrangements. First, she fixed it that man could find lasting satisfaction, and increasing perfection, only in what he produces through the use of his rational powers. Second, she fixed it that those tendencies in human nature which, if given free play, would result in the growth of his rational powers—that those tendencies would force man to live in society and would also generate tension and conflict in society. By this second arrangement she set man a problem: to organize society so that the necessity and fruitfulness of tension and conflict will be provided for. Tension and conflict, to be both necessary and fruitful, require an order which permits their resolution and also the consolidation of the gains which they generate. Social arrangement founded in law, and social process regulated by law, provided the solution to this problem. But this requires eventually a universal civil society founded on political justice. Nature has here set humanity its most difficult problem, but upon the solution to it depends the continued growth of the rational powers of man.

Nature's purpose in human history, then, is to develop the rational powers of man. This purpose requires that man create for himself a universal civil society founded on political justice.

He will use his rational powers in doing this; and, to the extent that he succeeds in doing it, he will create an area, a milieu, within which those rational powers can themselves continue to develop. This is man's "natural" destiny as a rational and historical animal.

These rational powers of man, which it is nature's purpose to develop through man in history, manifest themselves in many ways. They manifest themselves, for example, in the growth of science, mathematics, literature and art, religion, philosophy, society, and, within this latter, morality. These are areas and achievements in the life of reason, achievements which nature can produce only through the agency of man.

Kant on Morals. Kant's little book on ethics, published a year later than the essay on history, is an inquiry into the nature of a rational morality, an inquiry into the nature of right and wrong, guided by the assumption that this distinction, like, for example, the distinction between true and false or between appearance and reality, is an expression of man's reason. This is to claim two things: first, that reason demands this distinction between right and wrong, that it is a rational distinction; and second, that reason demands that this distinction be drawn in one way—reason's way—and not in some other way.

If you strip off Kant's mythologizing about "nature," what remains? What have you said about the distinction between right and wrong as applied to acts, when you say that it is a rational distinction and compare it, in that respect, to, say, the distinction between true and false as applied to beliefs? You have said, if I follow Kant correctly, that it is a *necessary* distinction, one which you cannot repudiate. It would be as impossible for a rational animal to deny the distinction between right and wrong as to deny the distinction between true and false. A rational distinction is a necessary distinction. To verify the necessity, try getting along without drawing the distinction. The distinctions between right and wrong and true and false are not, of course, the only rational distinctions. There are others which are equally mandatory, equally necessary. It would be a good exercise in self-knowledge for the reader to enumerate as many more as he can. Among necessary distinctions some apply to belief and action and some apply to objects and processes in nature. Thus the distinctions between right and wrong and true and false belong in the first group. If an act is right, it makes a demand upon us that we do it. If a belief is true, it makes a demand upon us that we accept it. If we do not meet this demand, we open ourselves to criticism. This is a double-barrelled demand. We can be mistaken in our belief that an act is right, and be open to criticism on that score. We can choose to do the wrong act, and be open to criticism on that score. The point is that the distinction between right and wrong is one which creates for us the possibility of wrong choice, and hence opens us to criticism and the need for revision. I said above that some necessary distinctions apply to objects and processes in nature. Examples of the latter sort would be here–there, now–then, cause–effect, before–after. You cannot repudiate these distinctions. If you deny them, or refuse to admit them, you find yourself instantly cut off from wide areas of experience. Their necessity is obvious. If necessity be diagnostic of rational, they are rational distinctions. Of things in nature you have to say that they are here or there, now or then, cause or effect.

These rational distinctions, of either kind, are necessary, mandatory, binding, upon all rational beings. If Smith and Jones are both rational animals, then both will admit such distinctions as right–wrong, true–false, before–after, here–there, and the like. This in itself is not to say that they will draw this distinction in the same way, nor apply it to the same cases. It is merely to say that they will not refuse to make the distinction nor refuse to apply it.

This detour into the character of the distinction between right and wrong is intended to enable the reader to see the problem as Kant saw it. His approach was this: Since the distinction between right and wrong is a rational distinction (necessary, and necessary for all rational beings) how shall it be drawn? On what principle? As he says, "The present treatise is . . . (an) investigation . . . of the supreme principle of morality." It is as though, of a book on trueness in belief (in contrast to rightness in action), he were to say, "The present treatise is an investigation of the supreme principle of knowledge."

You have then the notion of "morality" as what reason demands in the matter of right and wrong. How shall this demand be characterized or defined in principle? If "right" is "what reason demands," we are led to ask, "Well, what does reason demand?" How are we to judge of an act, whether it is, or is not, what reason demands? How must we act if we want to act rightly, and if "acting rightly" means doing as reason demands? It is important in reading Kant to bear in mind the distinction between what you take for granted and what you want to show. Thus he takes for granted that "right" confronts us as a "demand," that the demand is categorical (without qualification), and that it is universal (holding *for* all men) and necessary (binding *on* all men). That being granted, Kant is in a position to put the question as he sees it, namely, "If you claim that an act is wrong what must you be prepared to show about it in principle?" Suppose you say that it is wrong to steal, or cheat, or lie. It is not Kant's purpose to supply you with that conviction. His aim is to tell you what you must be prepared to show if you want to make good your claim that these actions are wrong and ought not to be done.

His claim here is simple. He directs your attention to what he calls the "maxim" of your act. A maxim of an action might be compared to the major premise of a syllogism. The act would be the minor premise. Thus—Maxim: "When in a tight spot, lie your way out of it." Minor premise: "I am now in a tight spot." Conclusion: "Lie my way out of it." Again—Maxim: "When unable to handle an examination, get the answers by cheating." Minor: "I am unable to handle this examination." Conclusion: "Get the answers by cheating." Again—Maxim: "When in need of something you do not possess and cannot honestly obtain, steal it." Minor: "I am in need of X, and cannot obtain it honestly." Conclusion: "Steal it." These illustrate what Kant means by the maxim of your action. He would ask a question of the maxim which, if answered, would enable him to diagnose whether the act was right or wrong. This diagnostic question is: Could you will that the maxim of your action should become a universal law, binding upon all men? If your answer to that question is "No," then the act is wrong. If the maxim upon which you perform an act could not be universalized, then you have the grounds for claiming that it is wrong, that is, not what reason would demand. If a person who admits that it is wrong to cheat were to formulate the principle upon which he acts, and then were to ask himself whether he could will to have the principle become a universal law, binding upon all who, for example, play cards or take exams, he would, Kant argues, say "No." If there is to be any point to cheating, it must occur as the exception, not as the rule. You can say that sort of thing, Kant claims, about every wrong act. In committing a wrong act you are making an exception in favor of yourself in respect to a rule which others must observe if there is to be any point to what you are doing. If you think that it is wrong to lie or steal, you must be able to show, says Kant, that stealing or lying would lose their point if everyone were to steal or lie. Right action creates an area within which wrong can occur and have point. To say that a way of acting is right is to say that no matter how many were to act that way their doing so would not prevent others from doing likewise.

Paraphrase from Kant. The following is offered as a paraphrase of Kant's argument. His own words are used whenever convenient.

1. Good Will

A good will is the only thing that is unconditionally good.

Such things as intelligence, judgment, courage, resolution, and perseverance are good, but not unconditionally so. They are good if, and only if, the will which makes use of them is good. Such things as power, riches, honor, health, happiness are good, but not unconditionally so. They can, for example, inspire pride and presumption. Such things as moderation in the passions, self-control, and calm deliberation are good, but not unconditionally so. They may characterize the behavior of a bad man.

The "unconditional goodness" of a good will may be expressed by other words and phrases, e.g., absolutely good, intrinsically good, supremely good, good without qualification or limitation, good in itself, etc.

A good will is not good because of what it actually accomplishes in the way of external results. Even if it lacked the power to accomplish its purpose, it would still be good. Its usefulness and its fruitfulness neither add to nor detract from its goodness.

2. REASON NECESSARY TO A GOOD WILL

This idea of the unconditional goodness of a good will, in which no account is taken of its utility, may seem strange, not to say fantastic; so much so, indeed as to cause us to suspect that we have misunderstood the purpose of nature in assigning reason to be the governor of our will. Did nature make men rational in order to ensure their goodness, or their happiness?

Let us see. We must assume, to begin with, that nature provides those organs and capacities which are best adapted to carry out her purposes. Now, if nature's purpose was to make men happy, and keep them so, then, in selecting reason, she hit upon a very poor arrangement: Instinct would have been better. We infer, then, that in making men rational, nature's primary intention was not to ensure man's happiness.

Since nature always adapts means to ends, we infer that she had some other end when she gave men a reason which could influence their will. The function of reason is to produce a good will. To this end instinct would not have sufficed: reason was necessary. Reason indeed recognizes the establishment of a good will as her highest practical destination.

3. GOOD WILL AND THE IDEA OF DUTY

We have, then, to develop the notion of a good will. This notion exists already in the sound natural understanding. It requires rather to be cleared up, than taught. The common moral consciousness contains the notion of a good will, and perceives its unconditional goodness: the task of philosophy is to clarify the idea, not to contribute it.

In order to do this, we shall consider the notion of duty. It includes the notion of good will, although the two are not exactly equivalent. What can we say about duty that will throw light upon good will?

To get at the notion of duty we must first distinguish between acting *as* duty requires and *because* duty requires. If duty requires you to do *X*, and you do *X*, that in itself does not make the doing of *X* a dutiful act. An act is dutiful if, and only if, it is done *because* duty requires it. Duty requires a store-keeper to refrain from cheating his customers. If he so refrains *because* duty requires it, his act is dutiful. If he so refrains for any other reason, his act is not dutiful in the full and proper sense of the word. Under assignable circumstances, it is a duty to maintain one's life; to be beneficent; to secure one's own happiness; to love our neighbors. If we do these things *because* duty requires them, our actions are dutiful. If we do them for any other reason, then it would be incorrect to speak of our actions as dutiful. They would not illustrate what duty means.

We may sharpen our analysis of the notion of duty even further. The thing which makes an act dutiful is not its actual results, nor even its intended results. It is the maxim or principle upon which the act is done. This is under our control, and can, therefore, be required of us by duty. To say that something is a *duty* implies that in the full sense of the word we *can* do it. We cannot guarantee the *outcome* of an action, but we *can* guarantee the maxim or principle upon which we perform the action. This, duty can require of us.

We can add a third point. An act is dutiful, in the full and proper sense, when it is done out of *respect* for the maxim or principle. Respect is not inclination and not necessity: it is a notion we need if we are to distinguish between "I want to," "I have to," and "I ought to." If we can state the kind of maxim or principle which would make an act dutiful, we can say the act must be performed out of respect for that.

4. Principle of a Good Will

Now, what is it that must serve the will as a principle, if its action is to be dutiful, if the will is to be a good will? It cannot be any particular principle prescribing a particular class of acts because goodness is not limited to any one class of acts. For example, it could not be the principle "Pay your debts" or "Tell the truth" or "Do not steal," because each of these delineates a particular class of actions and would, if taken as *the* principle, exclude the others. The principle, whatever it is, must be wholly general, must cover all particular principles.

We can add also that it must be of such a character as to require reason in man. The principle must reflect the fact that nature gave man reason to be the guide of his will, that reason and not some other capacity is necessary to the production of a good will.

Reason, in its broadest sense, is the capacity for rules or laws. It is either theoretical, concerned with knowing; or practical, concerned with doing. Reason, as theoretical, is the capacity to formulate or detect the rules or laws which describe or govern man's attempts to discover the order of nature. Reason, as practical, is the capacity to formulate or detect the rules or laws which describe or govern man's attempts to produce morality, to do what is right.

If we combine paragraphs one ("it must be general") and three ("it must be a rule or law") we see that there remains nothing but conformity to law in general. This alone is to serve the will as its principle: I am never to act otherwise than so that I could also will that my maxim should become a universal law. This is awkwardly stated, and remains to be clarified and illustrated; but we have here the notion of conformity to law in general, without assuming any particular law applicable to certain actions but not to others. The common reason of men in its practical judgments perfectly coincides with this, and always has in view the principle here suggested.

Suppose a customer who has received too much change from a store-keeper draws his attention to this fact and hands him back the extra change. What would we need to know of this act, if we wanted to say that it was right, dutiful, and an expression of good will? We would want to know first the maxim upon which the customer acted. Suppose it were a maxim defining a particular class of acts, e.g., be honest in money matters with store-keepers. This would not suffice us. Such a maxim does not, by itself, disclose the rightness of the act. We have, then, to know something more about the maxim before we can diagnose the rightness of the act. We have to know whether we could consistently will that this maxim should become a universal law, i.e., be binding upon all persons in similar circumstances. Could we consistently will that all persons be honest in dealing with store-keepers? If so, we have the data we need to pronounce the act right; if not, then we have the data we need to pronounce it wrong.

5. GOODNESS A CATEGORICAL IMPERATIVE

Our general principle ("So act," etc.) defines a good will. A good will is one which acts upon that principle. You can put the matter in other ways. You can say, for example, that it defines a right act, or morality, or moral obligation, or duty.

The relation of our will to this principle is expressed by the word *ought*. If we were wholly rational beings, the principle would characterize the way we *do* act. But we are not wholly rational beings. We are creatures also of impulse, feeling, emotion, incli-nation, passion, etc. When these get the upper hand they drive reason from its throne. On such occasions the principle of morality does *not* characterize our actions. You can still say, however, that it *ought* to, even though it doesn't. You can always say that we *ought* to do what is right even though we do not do so. Goodness does not force itself upon us. It places us under an "ought," a moral obligation.

This relation between goodness and our will can be further in-dicated by means of the distinction between a hypothetical and a categorical imperative. Something which you must do *if* you want the results it will bring, is hypothetically imperative. If you want A, and B is a condition for getting A, then B is hypothetically im-perative for you. This notion of a hypothetical imperative does not indicate the relation between goodness and our will. You cannot say that goodness is hypothetically imperative, that it is a condition for something else, something other than goodness, which we want. That would be to mistake its nature. It is categorically imperative; and, as we said in the beginning, it is the only thing which is cate-gorically imperative. If a person does not see that goodness con-fronts his will with an ought, an obligation, a categorical impera-tive, then he does not understand the nature of goodness, or he does not understand the nature of his own will.

We can say, then, that the principle, "So act, etc," is categorically imperative for any creature whose will is subject to his reason but capable also of being swayed by his passions, etc. It is an uncon-ditional objective principle which every rational creature, regardless of particular desires, *would* obey if his reason had complete control over his passions, and *ought* to obey even if tempted to do otherwise.

6. ALTERNATIVE STATEMENTS

The principle of morality, the only principle which is categorically imperative, may be worded in different ways. It can be worded thus: Act only on that maxim which you can will should become a universal law.

It can also be worded thus: Act as if the maxim of your action were through your will to become a universal law of nature.

It can also be worded thus: So act as to use humanity, both in your own person and in the person of every other, always at the same time as an end, never simply as a means.

It can also be worded thus: So act that your will can regard itself at the same time as making universal law through its maxim.

It can also be worded thus: So act as if you were, through your maxims, a law-making member of a kingdom of beings each of whom is an end in himself.

7. THE GOOD WILL AS AUTONOMOUS

The word *autonomous* means self-legislating. It is derived from two Greek words, *autos* and *nomos,* meaning *self* and *law.* If a person acts upon a law of his own making, he is autonomous; he exercises autonomy.

A good will, as we have defined it in principle, is one which could be autonomous, could exercise autonomy. It should so regard itself.

The reasoning here is this: A good will acts on the general principle that its particular maxims shall be such that they could each become a universal law, that is, a law for all. It proposes a law for itself which could be a law for all. This law can be conceived as originating with the will itself, hence *autos;* and as valid for all, hence *nomos.*

You can, therefore, speak of the autonomy or self-legislative character of the will as the supreme principle of morality, since only a good will could propose *its* law as a law for *all.*

Comment on Kant. Kant is a shrewd and common sense moralist. Sometimes his polysyllables and his heavy style tend to obscure this fact. He can be the despair of those who are coming at him for the first time. Any doubt on this point can be dispelled by sitting down with a copy of his *Groundwork* and reading it for an hour or so. Nevertheless, the man is a challenge. After sweating through his pages you begin to realize that it would be difficult to produce a really good idea which he has not already spotted and nailed down. We say, sometimes casually enough, that so-and-so is "a man of good will." We do not stop to consider the presuppositions of our remark. What is a man? What is a will? What is goodness? You can say of these questions what St. Augustine said of the question "What is time?"; namely, that everyone knows the answers until someone asks the questions. Aside from his eighteenth-century mythologizing about "nature," Kant had a sharp eye when it came to detecting the presuppositions of our everyday thinking on questions of right and wrong. Kant lived in and wrote for that period of European history which is known as the Age of Reason. His intention to be a spokesman for an "age of reason" is patent in much of his language. It is one of his virtues that he was not willing to use the language of his age without endeavoring to make clear what meanings that language conveys. To say that is not to write him off as "an expression of his times" and let it go at that. There *is* some connection between an act being "right" and being "reasonable." Kant's book underlines this fact; and the underlining continues to be visible even though we no longer refer to ourselves as living in the Age of Reason.

QUESTIONS

1. Use (*a*) health or wealth and (*b*) courage or perseverance to illustrate Kant's claim that only a good will is good without qualification.

2. Do you go along with Kant in his claim that nature made men rational because that was her only way of ensuring that they could become men of good will?

3. Kant seems to say that a good man is one who acknowledges his obligations. Do you agree with his further claim that obligation,

duty, is definable through principle rather than results? Would this raise an argument with Bentham?

4. Illustrate Kant's three-fold distinction: act, maxim, principle. Show how the maxim and the principle enter into the judgment of the act.

5. What fact about human nature, according to Kant, gives rise to the notion of *ought*?

6. Distinguish between a hypothetical and a categorical imperative. Why the term imperative? Since imperatives are neither true nor false, should it follow, for Kant, that moral judgments are neither true nor false?

7. Show that Paley and Bentham could (or could not) avail themselves of Kant's notion of an imperative being categorical.

8. The obligation to act rightly confronts us with which kind of imperative? How would Kant answer this question: "If you want to act rightly, on what principle must you act?"

9. Kant speaks of the autonomy of the good will. Meaning what? What, by contrast, would be meant by "heteronomy"? Would Kant's notion of the autonomy of the good will get him into an argument with either Paley or Bentham? Would you distinguish between the autonomy and the freedom of the will?

III. Alternatives to Ethical Theory

It may be well to review the steps by which we have arrived at this point. Chapter One indicates the data upon which an ethical theory is based, and some of the problems to which it is directed. It draws attention to the distinction between and the relation between moral judgment and ethical theory. Chapter Two presents three examples of traditional ethical theory, three attempts to formulate the principle of moral judgments. We come now to three alternatives to traditional ethical theory.

There is a reason for assigning separate chapters to these two groups of moralists. The first three moralists, although they differ importantly among themselves, acknowledge a common problem. Each tries to formulate the principle of morality; to define morality, to distinguish between right and wrong, with reference to a single principle; to state what principle is illustrated by all right acts and violated by all wrong acts. Each would acknowledge the propriety of our question, "What fact, common to all cases of wrongdoing, is the reason for calling them cases of wrongdoing?" The second three moralists—Nietzsche, Dewey, Ayer—not only differ among themselves, they differ as a group from Paley, Bentham, and Kant. You cannot diagnose this difference by saying that they propose different answers to the question dealt with by Paley, Bentham, and Kant. You have to put it that in one way or another they object to the question itself. There is a difference between questioning a man's answer, and questioning his question. The latter procedure is more radical. A man says he is trying to answer the question, "What do all right acts have in common?"

You say to him, "Your question presupposes that they *do* have something in common. I doubt that." You are questioning his question. Nietzsche, Dewey, and Ayer do not agree among themselves except in respect to calling into question the question which was common to Paley, Bentham, and Kant. Each does it in a different way, or for a different reason. Each would criticize and argue with the other but each would shy away from the question, "What fact, common to all cases of wrongdoing, is the reason for calling them cases of wrongdoing?" They would close ranks against all who accepted that question as central. Their common insistence is that the question carries presuppositions about morality which need not or cannot be granted. If that is so, the argument shifts radically. If those presuppositions are denied, then the problem, as traditionally conceived, cannot be put. Each repudiates traditional theory. Each does it for reasons peculiar to himself. And each proposes to substitute something for traditional ethical theory.

1. NIETZSCHE

We used one question to examine the views of three eighteenth-century moralists; namely: What fact common to all cases of wrongdoing is the reason for calling them cases of wrongdoing? These moralists gave three different answers to our question; one finding it in the will of God, another in the greatest happiness of the greatest number, another in the rationality of the maxim. The matter could be put this way: they presupposed a common morality; they philosophized within this common morality; but they differed in what they took the principle of this morality to be.

Our fourth moralist, Friedrich Nietzsche, differs from them on this point on which they agree among themselves. They ask, "What is the principle of morality?" suggesting that morality is one thing, that there is only one morality. He begins by insisting that there are many moralities; that they differ one from another; that moralists must begin by taking account of this fact; that such a question as "What is the principle of morality?" is misleadingly vague and general, unless you specify *which* morality you have in mind. The principle of one morality might differ from the principle of another morality; and this difference would not be detected if the moralities were not distinguished to begin with. Paley, Bentham, and Kant offered formulations of the principle of morality. But the question, "Which morality?" seems not to have occurred to them. They presupposed the morality of Christian Europe at the close of the eighteenth century. But there have been other moralities. Had they begun by emphasizing this they might have asked a different question. This shift from morality to moralities, from morals to mores, became increasingly important in the century between Kant and Nietzsche. It inclined Nietzsche to the opinion that he had little or nothing in common with traditional moralists; that their problems were not his; and that his problems were not theirs. It is usually worthwhile to look through the eyes of a man who believes that he is breaking with a long tradition. It sometimes enables one to see more clearly what the tradition is. For this reason Nietzsche is one of the most important and stimulating moralists in the century following Paley, Bentham and Kant.

The essential difference between a "traditional" moralist and Nietzsche can be set forth by means of two diagrams:

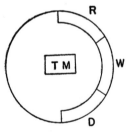

Here *T M* stands for "traditional moralists," for example, Paley, Bentham, or Kant; and *R*, *W*, and *D* stand respectively for "right," "wrong," and "doubtful." The *R* and *W* refer to acts which the moralist is prepared to judge right or wrong; the *D*, to acts about which he is in doubt. His question is this:

What fact, common to all the cases of right or wrong or doubtful is the reason for calling them right or wrong or doubtful? This diagram does not enable you to do justice to Nietzsche or any other writer proposing to break with traditional ethical theory. To get at Nietzsche you need some such diagram as the following:

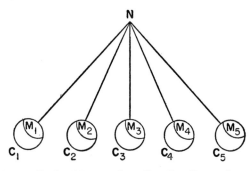

Here the N stands for Nietzsche; the C_1, C_2, and so forth stand for different cultures; and the M_1, M_2, and so forth stand for the moralities belonging to those cultures. You require that information before you can pose Nietzsche's question: What is the natural history, the genealogy, for each morality? Do their natural histories show any common traits?

Paley, Bentham, and Kant wrote in the 1780's, Nietzsche in the 1880's. You have, therefore, a flat century between them and him. In the 1780's you would have proposed a "philosophy of morals"; in the 1880's Nietzsche proposes "a natural history of morals." This shift in terminology is diagnostic of an altered point of view, a new climate of opinion. What is the difference between a "philosophy" of morals and a "natural history" of morals? The difference would not seem to be peculiar to morals. You could contrast, for example, a philosophy of art and a natural history of art; a philosophy of religion and a natural history of religion; a philosophy of the state and a natural history of the state; a philosophy of science and a natural history of science. The point is not that Paley, Bentham, and Kant would not have understood this contrast, nor even denied it.

The point is that they were not concerned to make it; whereas, for Nietzsche, the distinction is initial and primary. His essay, "The Natural History of Morals," occures in a volume entitled *Beyond Good and Evil*, as if to say, "The natural history of morals presupposes a point of view that lies outside of morals, beyound good and evil." You have here a radical suggestion. The historical question it raises is this: What events, between 1780 and 1880, provided a man with reasons for insisting upon the distinction between a "philosophy of" and a "natural history of" morality?

From Kant to Nietzsche. The events in question are aspects of one large event, namely, the extension to the "life sciences" of the point of view of the "natural sciences." This was a many-sided business, and Nietzsche considered himself its full-fledged beneficiary. Between the 1780's and the 1880's, you have August Comte proposing a scientific sociology; the English economists and Karl Marx proposing scientific economics; H. T. Buckle proposing scientific history; Charles Darwin proposing scientific biology; Bain, Spencer, and others proposing scientific psychology; and E. B. Tylor proposing scientific anthropology. The point is not that Nietzsche borrowed from these others. It is that he shared with them the conviction that nature is amenable to the scientific point of view and that man is part of nature. A physicist, a chemist, and an astronomer are recognized instances of the scientist in action. They have a characteristic way of regarding their subject and a characteristic way of going about their business. Let the biologist, the sociologist, the economist, the historian, the anthropologist, and the psychologist have an eye to these ways of the natural or physical sciences, and extend them to the life sciences. An astronomer can propose a "natural history of the solar system." By parity of reasoning, an economist can propose a "natural history of trade cycles." So, by parity of reasoning again, why cannot a moralist propose a "natural history of morals"?

This crescent "naturalism" is a first point to be kept in mind when you pass from Kant to Nietzsche. There is a second, however, and here Nietzsche is in opposition. In the century following Paley, Bentham, and Kant, much writing and much social action was broadly "humanitarian." This too was a many-sided business, and Nietzsche considered himself its full-fledged critic and opponent. Between the 1780's and the 1880's you have the French Revolution proposing liberty, equality, and fraternity. You have English Utilitarianism proposing a landslide of legislative social reform intended to preserve and increase the greatest happiness of the greatest number. You have political liberalism insisting upon the right of all men to a voice in the selection and control of those who are to make and administer the laws. You have labor movements protesting against the inequalities and iniquities of competitive capitalism; and socialism proposing that such arrangements be replaced by collective ownership and control of the economic order. You have feminism proposing the emancipation of women, pacifism proposing the abolition of war, and anarchism proposing to abolish force in the administering of law. You have literature, particularly in the novel, reflecting and dramatizing these humanitarian aspirations, a popular press demanding them, and popular education claiming to prepare everyone to share responsibly in them. You have religion proclaiming Christian socialism, the social gospel, the brotherhood of man, and this sometimes with an emphasis inversely proportioned to their "fundamentalism" and orthodoxy. You have in all of this the emergence of what has been called the "century of the common man." This became a kind of spectre in Nietzsche's imagination. Insistence upon naturalism and repudiation of humanitarianism became two powerful drives in his meditations upon morals in the modern world.

These shifts in point of view place Nietzsche in sharp contrast to Kant. The contrast is almost systematic. Kant's 1785 *Groundwork of the Metaphysics of Morals* dealt with what the author considered the two fundamental problems in any philosophy of morals, namely, the principle of morality and the freedom of the will. Nietzsche's 1885 *Beyond Good and Evil* repudiates both of these ideas and proposes a natural history of morals. Kant located the object of the moral judgment in the maxim upon which a person acts; Nietzsche rules this out as irrelevant. Kant finds that act right whose maxim could be made universal, for all men, regardless of time or place. Nietzsche insists that since men are in no sense "equal," the universality of a maxim would fly in the teeth of nature. Kant sees in Christianity a religion that presents men with high moral teachings and a clear exemplar of these teachings, and does this, whether you accept its supernatural theology or not. Nietzsche repudiates Christianity, holding that its humanitarianism has made European morality decadent, and its supernaturalism has made it superstitious. Kant insists that genuine morality is unconditionally valuable, the crowning manifestation of rationality in man, and categorically binding upon all rational beings, regardless of time and place. Nietzsche argues that morality is indeed not unconditionally valuable; that its value is a matter for investigation and assessment; that such investigation and assessment presuppose a position "beyond good and evil"; and that it is cultural provincialism for any morality to look upon itself as categorically binding upon anyone, let alone everyone. Kant emphasizes that a philosophy of morals secures its initial data by examining the common moral consciousness; and that its task is to clarify these, not to criticize them. Nietzsche regards such a procedure as foolish truckling to the conscience of the average man, a reservoir of ignorance, prejudice, and confusion. Kant would make morality the basis for a criticism of custom; Nietzsche insists that custom generates morality, that the mores make anything right. Kant among moderns, like Socrates among the ancients, comes close to being "the moralist," symbolizing the spirit, if not the teachings, of much modern moral philosophy. Nietzsche, having a sense for these matters, labelled himself "the immoralist," as if to say, "A man who begins by accepting 'morality' is a moralist. I begin by rejecting it. I am, therefore, an immoralist."

Biographical Note. Friedrich Nietzsche, the stormy petrel among modern moralists, was born in 1844 and died in 1900. During the ten years, 1878 to 1888, he published eight books on the morality of the modern world. These are a unique collection: it is difficult to see how anyone could be expected to agree with all, or even most, of their important claims; but it is equally difficult to see how anyone can afford to ignore them. They place modern civilization on trial in a manner that jars and alienates; but they do this with a vigor and singleness of purpose which in the end compels reflection. Nietzsche spoke of himself as philosophizing "with a hammer," that is, smashing things. On a first reading that is the impression conveyed by these commentaries on the modern scene. Socrates, addressing himself to the shortcomings of Athenian civilization, spoke of himself as a "gadfly." It would not, I think, occur to Nietzsche or a reader of Nietzsche to use any such metaphor. The man is not engaged in "needling" his age: he is hammering it. Nietzsche lived in an age of great critics: Matthew Arnold and Samuel Butler in England, Anatole France and Zola across the channel, Tolstoy in Russia, Marx in Germany, Ibsen among the Scandinavians, were not exactly buttering up their age. But Nietzsche's vehemence sounds above all their voices, and there is an across-the-boards sweep to his criticisms which theirs do not possess.

This sequence of jeremiads began with *Human, All Too Human: A Book for Free Spirits,* in 1878, just one century, as Nietzsche notes, after the death of Voltaire. The title means, "Where you see ideal things, I see human, alas all-too-human things." The book contains some fourteen hundred aphorisms, grapeshot by means of which the author conducts guerilla warfare on smug or highflying or wobbly idealism. By means of this book, he says, "I put an abrupt end to all the 'Superior Bunkum' that had percolated into my being." Three years later, 1881, came the *Dawn of Day: Thoughts About Morality as a Prejudice.* The title indicates that the author is narrowing his scope a little. Having, so to speak, "cleaned house," he will begin to put things to rights. The book contains some six hundred aphorisms. By means of them Nietzsche bears down on the fact that all too frequently "goodness" is little more than a feeble and fumbling cover-up for "softness." The thing which has "dawned" on him is that goodness must contain an element of pugnacity. "With this book," he says, "I opened my campaign against morality . . . I first engaged in a struggle against the morality of self-reunuciation." If goodness must be affirmative, if renunciation and resignation are not its essential moods, if criticism presupposes *some* ideal which authorizes the criticism, you have, following the dawn of day, the task of hoisting the sun into the sky. This gets under way in Nietzsche's next book, *Joyful Wisdom,* published in 1882. It aims, he says, to be a "yea-saying book." The title acknowledges, by implication, that wisdom can upon occasion be sad, but insists that it need not always be so, that in its affirmative insight it will not be so. It contains some four hundred aphorisms. *Joyful Wisdom* bids all "preachers of death," all cynics, pessimists, nay-sayers and re-nunciation-mongers, to look again at the facts of life. The argu-ment of these three books *(Human, All Too Human; Dawn of Day;* and *Joyful Wisdom)* culminates in *Thus Spake Zarathus-tra: A Book for All and None,* published in 1883. This was Nietzsche's "New Testament." The subtitle, "for all and none," indicates the author's own opinion of what he was attempting, namely, that it ought to concern everyone but will concern no one. In this he was substantially correct. The book urges upon mankind the necessity of willing into existence a race which will surpass mankind in all important respects. Whether you say "Be ye perfect, even as God is perfect" or "Man is a creature to be surpassed" makes little difference: your injunction is not destined to receive any very effective consideration. It may be that criticism *of* man presupposes a point of view that lies *be-yond* man, but in saying this you open yourself to the question, "What is that to us?" It is not clear what rejoinder you can make to *that.* The book was, to use Nietzsche's words, an "arrow of longing." He did not cease to feel this longing, but he did not launch such an arrow again. The book puzzled those whom it did not alienate and offend. Thereafter Nietzsche addressed himself only to those who were puzzled. In 1885–86 he published *Beyond Good and Evil: Prelude to a Philosophy of the Future.* The title tells the story: a significant criticism of human morality presupposes a position *beyond* human morality; since no moralist thus far has seen this point, its formulation is of necessity addressed to the future. The book contains nine essays, of which the fifth, "The Natural History of Morals," and the ninth, "What Is Noble?" are the most important. The fifth rejects what has traditionally been meant by a "philosophy of morals," and demands in its place a "science or natural history of morals." Only if you thus completely objectify human morals can you see that unless man surpasses himself, his goodness will always remain at best a shoddy business. The ninth contrasts "good"—mankind at its ordinary best—with "noble"—the virtue of beings through whom and in whom the genus man would be itself surpassed. *Beyond Good and Evil* was followed in 1887 by *The Genealogy of Morals.* This book contains three essays on what the author has called the "natural history" of morals. They are examples of the *sort* of thing that he felt needed doing. The title is apt: morals have a genealogy, a structured coming-to-be and passing-away. It is the first concern of a moralist to make himself familiar with the natural history, or genealogy, of morals. Then he can offer himself as a critic of existing morals. Finally he can offer himself as a creator of new values.

All this by 1887. Nietzsche had two years left before he went insane. During these two years he wrote three short books and began work on one long one. The long one, which remained unfinished, was *The Will to Power: An Attempted Transvaluation of All Values.* It was to have been the great treatise. The title indicates that a will is, above all, a *will,* a striving, a source of power, never a renunciation. The subtitle indicates that human values are so wretched that they must be inverted, turned around, transvalued. As for the three small volumes, the first was *Twilight of the Idols: or How to Philosophize with the*

Hammer, a kind of manual summarizing the conclusions arrived at in the six major works already noted. An "idol" here is a false or invalid ideal. The title indicates the author's conviction that human ideals, most of them false, have had their day. Their "twilight" is setting in. It is a return to the spirit of his earlier phrase, "human, all too human." The second, *Anti-Christ: An Attempted Criticism of Christianity,* is a savage rejection of the tradition which, in Nietzsche's opinion, the churches had built up in the name of Christianity. Less than ten years before, Dostoievsky had included "The Grand Inquisitor" section in his novel, *The Brothers Karamazov.* Nietzsche's "Antichrist" and Dostoievsky's "Grand Inquisitor" differ in almost every respect but this: they are passionate protests against what their authors conceive historical Christianity to have done to mankind. The third short volume, *Ecce Homo: How One Becomes What One Is,* is Nietzsche's autobiography. The title means "Behold the Man," a phrase usually applied to Christ. The book is painful and exasperating. It was written late in 1888. By 1889, Nietzsche had lost the use of his mind, and, for eleven years until his death, remained tragically insane.

Themes from Nietzsche. The quotations which follow set forth some recurring themes. They do not exhaust what Nietzsche has to say about morals, but they enable a reader to get some notion of what was stirring in the man's mind. It is not possible to say that they occur in only one of Nietzsche's books. There is, no doubt, a steady progression from *Human, All Too Human* to *Twilight of the Idols,* but it is nevertheless true that he tended to back-track and tell over his whole story each time he wrote a book. The sets of quotations might be given some such titles as these: (1) As to Conscience; (2) As to the Philosophers; (3) Wanted: A "Science of Morals"; (4) Morality as Custom; (5) Morality as Expression of Emotion; (6) Not Wholly Negative.

Keynote. The entire group might carry the following paragraph as a kind of keynote. In it Nietzsche protests that when it come to morality our attitude, traditionally, is one of obedience rather than inquiry. We are more inclined to do what morality tells us than to challenge its right to tell us. In short, we haven't *thought* much about morality. It is high time we did.

So far it is on Good and Evil that we have meditated least profoundly: this was always too dangerous a subject. Conscience, a good reputation, hell, even the police, do not allow of impartiality. In the presence of morality we must not even think, we must obey. To criticize morals, to look upon morality as problematic, is not that itself immoral? Morality has at its disposal every means of intimidation to keep itself free from critical hands. It possesses also a certain art of enchantment, it knows how to "enrapture." It can often paralyze the critical will with a single look, even turn that will against itself. Morality has been an expert in all kinds of deviltry in the art of convincing. She has shown herself the greatest mistress of seduction ever since men began to discourse and persuade on earth.[1]

1. As to Conscience. Most people, if they ever get around to thinking about morality, come up with the notion of conscience, and offer that as the essence of the matter: an act is moral if done because believed to be right; and it is right if it is according to conscience. Nietzsche will have none of that. The notion of conscience, at worst a nest of superstitions, is at best a set of unquestioned assumptions. Where does conscience get its authority? Where did you get your conscience? What is conscience but the voice of tradition speaking in and to the individual?

Everyone seems inclined to say that when a man decides "this is right" and "it must therefore be done," and thereupon does what he has thus recognized as right, then the nature of his action is moral.

---

[1] The quotations in the numbered paragraphs which follow are from Oscar Levy, ed., *Nietzsche*, and are reprinted by permission of George Allen & Unwin Ltd.

Why do you regard this act, and just this act, as right? "Because my conscience tells me so. Conscience never speaks immorally. Indeed it determines what shall be moral." But why do you listen to your conscience? Are you justified in regarding such a judgment as true? This belief (in conscience)—is there no further conscience, no intellectual conscience, for it? Your decision, "this is right," has a previous history in your impulses, your likes and dislikes, your experiences and non-experiences. How has it originated? you must ask; and then further, what impels me to give ear to it? You can listen to its commands like a brave soldier who hears the command of his officer; or like a woman who loves him who commands; or like a flatterer and coward who is afraid of the commander; or like a blockhead who follows because he has nothing to say to the contrary. You can give ear to your conscience in a hundred different ways. But *that* you hear this or that judgment as the voice of conscience, *that* consequently you feel a thing to be right,—may have its cause in the fact that you have never reflected about yourself, have blindly accepted from childhood what has been designated to you as right. . . . If you had thought more acutely, observed more accurately, and learned more, you would no longer under all circumstances call this and that your "duty" and your "conscience." The knowledge of how moral judgments have in general originated would make you tired of those pathetic words, as you have already grown tired of other pathetic words. . . .

The sum-total of our conscience is all that has been regularly demanded of us, without reason, in the days of our childhood, by people whom we respected or feared. From conscience comes that feeling of obligation which does not ask, Why must I? . . . The belief in authority is the source of conscience.

2. As to the Philosophers. There is no point in turning from your own conscience to traditional moral philosophy. Nietzsche will pull you out of that bolthole. Traditional moral philosophy is naive: it never questions its own data and its own assumptions. It begins by accepting morality as a datum, and then proceeds to give morality a basis, to formulate the "principle" of morality. This won't do. It should begin by questioning morality, challenging its right to demand our obedience. What is morality but the voice of tradition speaking in and to the individual?

Morality is the veritable Circe of philosophers. Why else, from Plato onwards, have European philosophers built in vain? The answer is that all philosophers, even Kant, have built under the seductive influence of morality. They have aimed at certainty and truth only in appearance; in reality their attention was directed to what Kant calls "majestic moral edifices."

Hitherto philosophers, with a pedantic and ridiculous seriousness, have wanted to give a "basis" to morality; they believed that they had given it *a* "basis." But they regarded morality itself as something "given". . . . They knew the moral facts imperfectly, in an arbitrary epitome or an accidental abridgment, perhaps as the morality of their environment, their church, their zeitgeist, their climate, their zone. They were badly instructed with regard to nations, eras, past ages, and were by no means eager to know about these matters. Hence they did not come within sight of the real problems of morals, problems which are disclosed only by a comparison of many moralities.

What philosophers have called "giving a basis to morality" has been merely a learned form of good faith in prevailing morality, a new expression of *it*, a matter of fact within the sphere of a definite morality, a sort of denial that it is lawful for this morality to be called in question; the reverse of testing, analysing, doubting and vivisecting this very faith.

Philosophers seek to fix and systematize some existing body of valuations, i.e., creations of value which have become prevalant and are for the time called "the truth." It is for these thinkers to make conspicuous, conceivable, intelligible, what has happened and been esteemed hitherto.

Do not talk to me about the categorical imperative. That word tickles my ears, and I must laugh in spite of your seriousness. He who thinks that "each would have to act in this manner in this case" has not advanced half-a-dozen paces in self-knowledge. . . .

3. Wanted: A Science of Morals. What is wanted, in place of conscience and traditional moral philosophy, is a natural history of morals; that is, an objective inquiry into the nature, the origin, the social function of morality—a science of morals. Such a thing hardly exists at present. Almost everything remains to be done. There is little to be learned from historians of morality. They are either naive or skeptical, in either case, childish.

The "science of morals" is recent, awkward, and coarse-fingered. Indeed, the expression "science of morals" is, for the present, far too presumptuous. . . . What is still necessary here for a long time is the collection of material, the comprehensive survey and classification of an immense domain of sentiments of "worth," distinctions of "worth," which live, grow, propagate and perish; perhaps an attempt to give an idea of the more common and recurring forms of these living crystallizations, as preparation for a theory of types of morality.

There are systems of morals which are meant to justify their author in the eyes of other people; others that are meant to tranquillize him and make him self-satisfied; with others he wants to crucify and humble himself, or to take revenge, or to conceal himself, or to glorify himself, or to forget himself, or to exercise power and creative arbitrariness over mankind. In short, systems of morals are only a sign language of the emotions.

To get a glimpse of our European morality from a distance, in order to compare it with other moralities, one must do as the traveller who wants to know the height of the towers of a city: he leaves the city. Thoughts concerning moral prejudices, if they are not to be prejudices concerning prejudices, presuppose a position outside of morality, some sort of world beyond good and evil; in our case, a position beyond *our* good and evil. . . . The question is whether one can really get there. . . . The man of such a "Beyond" must first of all surmount his own age. It is the test of his power.

I have not met with anyone, not even in books, who knew morality as a problem. Up to the present, morality has not been a problem at all. It has, rather, been the very ground on which people have met, the hallowed place where thinkers could obtain rest even from themselves. No one has ventured to criticize the estimates of moral worth. I miss even the fastidious groping imagination of psychologists and historians which easily anticipates a problem and catches it on the wing without knowing rightly what it catches.

There is little to be learned from historians of morality. They are usually under the influence of a definite morality. Their usual error is to insist on a certain consensus among human beings, at least civilized human beings, with regard to certain propositions of morality, and then conclude that these propositions are absolutely binding upon you and me. Or, reversely, they conclude that no morality at all is binding after the truth has dawned on them that different peoples' moral valuations are necessarily different: both of which conclusions are equally childish follies.

The more subtle among them fall into a still different error. They set themselves to discover and criticize the probably foolish opinions of a people *about* its own morality. Thereupon they treat of its orgin, its religious sanctions, the superstition of free will, and such matters. They think that in doing this they have criticized the morality itself. But this is an error. The worth of a precept, a Thou Shalt, is different from and independent of such opinions about it. A morality could have grown out of an error; but knowing that does not even touch the problem of its worth. No one hitherto has tested the value of morality: for which purpose it is first of all necessary to call it in question. Well, that is just our work.

4. Morality as Custom. Nietzsche worked at this notion of a natural history, or science, of morals. It is never wholly absent from anything he wrote on morality. The titles of many of his books testify to this preoccupation, for example, *Human, All Too Human, Beyond Good and Evil, The Genealogy of Morals,* and so on. One thought that constantly recurs is that morality, whatever else you can say about it, is custom: morals are mores, folkways, traditions. Another is that a given morality normally has a certain survival value for the group whose needs and interests it expresses: its value is relative to those needs and interests. Another is that a morality confronts an individual as a set of do's and don'ts, a set of restrictions proposed for his private will: it does not express his will, it restrains it. "What is essential and valuable in every system of morals is that it is a long constraint." Another is that a given morality has a history: it originates, flourishes and decays: as individuals become sophisticated, its hold over their lives decreases. Those who defy it are often regarded as evil; but their defiance is often a salutory challenge directed at a moribund, outworn custom.

Morality is nothing else, and above all nothing more, than obedience to customs, of whatsoever nature they be. Where there is no tradition there is no morality; and the less life is governed by tradition, the narrower the circle of morality. But customs are simply the traditional way of acting and valuing. The freeman is "immoral" because it is his will to depend upon himself and not upon tradition.

What is tradition? A higher authority, which is obeyed, not because it commands what is useful to us, but merely because it commands. . . . This feeling for tradition is the fear of a higher intelligence which commands, the fear of an incomprehensible power, of something more than personal: there is superstition in this fear.

By morality the individual is taught to become a function of the herd, and to ascribe value to himself only as a function. As the needs of one community have been very different from those of another community, there have been very different moralities; and there will be very divergent moralities in the future. Morality is the herd instinct in the individual.

Morality is primarily a means of preserving the community. Next it is a means of maintaining the community on a certain plane. Its motives are fear and hope. The most terrible means of intimidation must be brought into play so long as milder forms have no effect. The strongest intimidation is the invention of a hereafter with an everlasting hell. Further grades are the commandments of a God. Still further are the commandments of an absolute sense of duty. . . .

In primitive times the domain of morality included education, hygenics, marriage, medicine, agriculture, war, speech and silence, the relation between man and man and between man and the gods. Morality required that a man should observe her prescriptions without thinking of himself as an individual. Everything was originally custom, and whoever wished to raise himself above it had first to *create* customs, a dangerous thing to do.

Those precepts which are called moral are in reality directed against individuals, and do not by any means make for the happiness of such individuals. The relationship of these precepts to the "happiness and well-being of mankind" is equally slight, for it is quite impossible to assign a definite conception to these words, and still less can they be employed as guiding stars on the dark sea of moral aspirations.

Who is the most moral man? On the one hand, he who most frequently obeys the law (custom), he who carries a consciousness of the law about with him, continually exercising his mind in finding opportunities for obeying the law. On the other hand, he who obeys the law in the most difficult cases, he who makes the greatest sacrifices to morality. . . . This distinction between the morality of the most frequent obedience and the morality of the most difficult obedience is of the greatest importance.

What is essential and valuable in every system of morals is that it is a long constraint. . . . "Thou must obey someone, and for a long time"—this seems to me to be the moral imperative of nature; and it is neither "categorical" (as old Kant wished) nor addressed to the individual but to nations, ages, races, to mankind generally.

Let us not be deceived as to this obedience to custom. It is not required because of its useful consequences for the individual, but so that custom and tradition may appear to be dominant. The individual shall sacrifice himself—so demands the morality of custom. Under the influence of the morality of custom, originality acquired a bad conscience. Even now the sky of the best minds seems to be more overcast by this thought than needs be.

Wherever we meet with a morality we find a valuation and order of rank of the human impulses and activity. The valuations and orders of rank are always the expression of the needs of a community or herd: that which is to its advantage is also the authoritative standard for the worth of every individual.

As the sense of causality increases, the domain of the morality of custom decreases. Every time one has been able to grasp effects as necessary, and conceive them as distinct from incidental and chance possibilities, one has destroyed "imaginary causalities" which had been believed in as the basis of morals. One casts away also a certain amount of one's anxiety and coercion, some of one's reverence for the authority of custom is lost. Morality thus undergoes a diminution. On the other hand, he who wishes to increase the domain of the morality of custom must prevent results from becoming controllable through a knowledge of their causes.

The strongest and most "evil" spirits have hitherto advanced mankind the most. They rekindle the sleeping passions: orderly society lulls the passions to sleep. They re-awaken the sense of comparison; of contradiction; of delight in the new, the adventurous, the untried. They compel men to set opinion against opinion, ideal plan against ideal plan, by appeal to *arms,* by upsetting boundary stones, most of all by violations of piety. . . . The same kind of "wickedness" is in every teacher and preacher of the new.

5. Morality as Expression of Emotion. It is one thing to defy a morality on the grounds that it is no longer valid for your time and place, that it has lost its "sanctions," that it is an outmoded custom. This was not Nietzsche's primary theoretical challenge. He had a bigger fish to fry, namely, the claim of a moral judgment to be at any time either true or false. This is to say that it is not a judgment at all: it is the expression of an emotion. He says there are no such things as moral facts—there are only moral feelings; and feelings, while they can be expressed, are never either true or false. Their expression is not a judgment. This thesis *about* moral judgments cuts the connection between Nietzsche and traditional moralists, and looks forward to twentieth-century emotivism.

There are two classes of people who deny morality. It may mean, in the first place, to deny inducements which, men pretend, have urged to actions. It may mean, in the second place, denying that moral judgments are founded on truths. . . . This is my point of view. . . . I deny morality in the same sense as I deny alchemy, i.e., I deny its hypotheses; but I do not deny that there have been alchemists who believed in these hypotheses and based their actions upon them. I also deny immorality—not that many people feel immoral, but that there is any true reason why they should feel so.

There are no such things as moral facts. Moral judgment believes in realities which are not real. Moral judgment belongs to a stage in which the distinction between real and imaginary is still lacking. That is why the moral judgment must never be taken literally; as such, it is sheer nonsense. As a "sign" code, however, it is invaluable: it reveals the most valuable facts concerning cultures and inner conditions which did not know enough to understand themselves. Morality is a sign-language, a symptom.

Of such assertions as "there is a categorical imperative in us" one can always ask: What does such an assertion indicate about him who makes it? Systems of morals are only sign-languages of emotions.

All actions may be referred back to valuations. All valuations are either our own or adopted, the latter being by far more numerous. A valuation of our own which is the appreciation of a thing in accordance with the pleasure or displeasure it causes us and no one else, is very rare.

6. Not Wholly Negative. Nietzsche was not satisfied to settle finally for a natural history of morals and an emotive theory of moral judgments. Once he had broken with past moralities and moral philosophies, he wanted something to put in their place. As he says, if humanity had a universally recognized goal, we could propose ways of acting, morals, which would make for its realization. However, for the time being there is no such goal. As he states it, "There have been a thousand-and-one-goals. There is lacking the one goal. As yet humanity hath not a goal." So Nietzsche proposes a goal, namely the superman. Humanity itself is something to be surpassed. There are two stages here: first, the self-liquidation of humanity; second, the replacement of humanity by a higher order of life. The first stage calls for an *interims-ethik*. Nietzsche gave much thought to this, as witness the sermons preached by his "Zarathustra." But beyond that he does not try to go. The character of the superhuman race of beings which would supersede the human race does not get much more than a few hints, a sort of office-sketch awaiting the architect who will draw the plans.

To us also there speaketh a "thou shalt." We likewise obey a law set above us. This is the last cry of morals. Here, if anywhere, we are still men of conscience: we will not return to that which we look upon as decayed, outlived, superseded. We will not return to something "unworthy of belief," whether it be called God, virtue, justice, neighbor-love, or what not. We will not permit ourselves to open up a lying path to old ideals. We are opposed to all forms of present-day faith; in us is consummated the auto-suppression of morals.

I should not, of course, deny—unless I were a fool—that many actions which are called immoral should be avoided and resisted; and in the same way that many which are called moral should be performed from motives other than those which have prevailed up to the present time. We must learn anew in order that at last, perhaps very late in the day, we may be able to do something more: feel anew.

It is only if humanity had a universally recognized goal that we could propose to do this or that: for the time being there is no such goal. It follows that the pretensions of morality should not be brought into any relationship with mankind: this would be merely childish and irrational. It is quite another thing to recommend a goal to mankind: this goal would then be something that would depend upon our own will and pleasure. Provided that mankind in general agreed to adopt such a goal, it could then impose a moral law upon itself, a law which would, at all events, be imposed by their own free will. Up to now, however, the moral law has had to be placed above our own free will: strictly speaking, men did not wish to impose this law upon themselves; they wished to take it from somewhere, to discover it, or to let themselves be commanded by it from somewhere.

Rèsumè. It would be possible to add many more quotations, and, by means of them, to work out more themes from Nietzsche. The possibility is tempting: few moralists write with such vigor and color and engaging destructiveness. No other modern moralist is so typical an example of the *enfant terrible*. Samuel Butler, Bernard Shaw, Anatole France, H. L. Mencken, are thin beer after a draught of Nietzsche when the "hammer" mood is on him. He is toxic, if you take him too seriously; but quite tonic if you do not.

There are two phases in Nietzsche's handling of morality, and within each phase he is both destructive and constructive. The first phase is addressed to mankind in general: "for all and none," as he puts it. Here he is a critic of traditional and modern moralities. These he will have none of. He wants them replaced by a new morality which will be a function of a new goal. In this phase of his work he is a "critic and creator of values." Neither Benthan nor Kant set himself to "create new values": they were concerned with clarifying and rendering explicit what they believed to be the nature of right and wrong. In this first phase Nietzsche is, as suggested, both constructive and destructive. In the constructive portion he sets a new goal before humanity: the idea that man is a "creature to be surpassed": the superman idea. This is stimulating though somewhat strident business. The difficulty, for our purposes, is that it throws no direct light on what right and wrong mean for man as he is. If you ask, "Human nature, man, humanity, being what it is, what kind of acts are right and what kind wrong?" it is disconcerting to be told: "The only right thing for man to do is to pass out of the picture, make way for the superman: man is a creature to be surpassed." That threatens the inquiry into the nature of rightness for man with abrupt dismissal. Nietzsche saw this and said so repeatedly. His whole protest against the idea of rightness was that even at its best it was only a function of human nature, "human, all too human"; that in itself was enough to condemn it. Human nature must be surpassed. There *is* no worthwhile ideal, except surpassing itself, that human nature *could* generate and enact. To *be* human, whether "good" or "bad," is *ipso facto* to be worthless. Until the superhuman has replaced the human, all talk about right and wrong is futile. Human nature's "best" is as irrelevant as its "worst." This one "constructive" suggestion carried with it many essays in destructive criticism. Their purpose was to clear the field for the new goal. Here Nietzsche directs a raking fire at human ideals and the institutions which embody them.

The second phase is directed at moral philosophers, thinkers who have addressed themselves to the task of working out a moral philosophy, in the manner, say, of Paley or Bentham or Kant. At all such persons Nietzsche directs two radical criticisms. The first is this, "You have misconceived the nature of morality and hence the nature of your task." It is in respect to this phase of his work that Nietzsche provides a transition from what you might call "first-order theories" to "second-order theories." You could imagine Paley, Benthan, and Kant agreeing to the statement, "An act is moral if done because believed to be right," and then settling down to clarify the nature of rightness. As we have seen, they would arrive at different conclusions, but they acknowledge a common ground ("morality") in respect to which their differences could be stated. They agree that some acts *are* right and some wrong. They attempt to set forth the character of this rightness and wrongness, to state what these are in principle, to define them. Their diagnostic question is always: "What is the principle of morality?"; meaning, "What fact, common to all right acts, is the reason for calling them right acts?" Wherever this or some variant is the diagnostic question, you have a "first-order theory." Now, you could indicate Nietzsche's relation and objection to tradional moralists, by supposing him to say: "They propose only first-order theories. They *can* propose only first-order theories. This limitation is radical: it discloses their misconception of the task and arises out of their misconception of the nature of morality. They propose a theory *of* morality. What is needed is a theory *about* morality. A theory of morality, obtained by first accepting morality and *then* asking for its principle, is a first-order theory. Now, all that is out. *Nous avons changé tout celà.* What is needed is a theory *about* morality, and, by implication, a theory about moral judgments. A theory about morality begins by objectifying morality. If you say that the distinction between right and wrong expresses a necessary aspect of human nature, it (a theory about morality) says, 'What of it? So much the worse, for human nature. Human nature is a thing to be surpassed.' A theory *of* morality begins by taking sides with morality. It cannot undo that initial mistake. It thereby sells its birthright. It should take an attitude of neutrality, of strictly impartial scientific curiosity. It should begin by asking what morality *is*, considered as an 'objective fact' in nature. Then it would be a theory *about* morality, that is, a science or natural history of morals. If you begin by endorsing morality, you cannot expect to get at the truth *about* morality."

The above imaginary remarks are intended to convey, by suggestion, this distinction between first- and second-order theories, and to indicate that recent and contemporary second-order theories could be derived from Nietzsche more easily than from such writers as Paley, Bentham, and Kant. I do not mean that recent and contemporary propounders of "second-order theories" are Nietzscheans. I mean that his writing frequently contains suggestions which point forward to such doctrines as relativism, subjectivism, emotivism; and that these are doctrines *about* morality, or *about* moral judgments. These latter-day theories have precipitated a great deal of confused and confusing argument. Without pronouncing against them, it seems to me that they have, in the hands of many persons, only managed to darken counsel. In the hope that some of this darkness may be dispelled, I am proposing to describe them as "second-order" theories, to contrast their propounders thus with Paley, Bentham, and Kant; and to suggest that their way of coming at things is reminiscent of Nietzsche's critique of traditional moral philosophy.

This notion of a second-order theory raises a question. You could come at it this way: If a man does not himself authorize any moral judgments, it is not clear that he could propound an ethical theory, a theory *of* morality, a first-order theory. To propound an ethical theory when you don't authorize moral judgments is to be at best hypothetical and at worst irresponsible. My suspicion is that the same restriction holds when you pass from ethical theories to theories about ethical theories, from first-order to second-order theories. If a man does not himself hold any ethical theory, it is not clear that he could propound a theory about ethical theories. To do so would seem to make his discourse either hypothetical or irresponsible. In these matters the rule seems to be that you put up or shut up. I am not sure that this is the case, but I think it is; if it is, you have a scale in which many second-order theories can be weighed and found wanting.

Free Will. Nietzsche broke with traditional ethical theory for two major reasons. One has been indicated: traditional ethical theory presupposes the unity and identity of morality, regardless of times and places, and proposes to formulate its principle. The second reason was this: traditional ethical theory usually presupposes free will in man, that a man guilty of wrongdoing could have done otherwise. This second ingredient Nietzsche flatly rejects. Thus the two items which Kant found diagnostic of the moral consciousness were Nietzsche's principal reasons for repudiating that consciousness and the traditional theoretical concern with it. The following passages reject the notion of free will.

The history of moral valuations is the history of an error, the error of responsibility, which is based on the error of the freedom of the will.

Consciousness of guilt, after the deed, is not necessarily reasonable, indeed it is assuredly not reasonable, for it is based upon the erroneous presumption that the action need not have inevitably followed. It is only because man *believes* himself to be free, not because he *is* free, that he experiences remorse and pricks of conscience. This ill-humor is a habit that can be broken off. In many people it is entirely absent in connection with actions where others experience it. It is a very changeable thing, and one which is connected with the development of customs and culture, and probably only existing during a comparatively short period of the world's history. Nobody is responsible for his actions, nobody for his nature; to judge is identical with being unjust. This also applies when an individual judges himself.

People who are cruel must be accounted for: they themselves are as little responsible as is a block of granite for being granite.

What is volition? We laugh at a man who, when the sun is rising, says "It is my will that the sun shall rise" or at him who, unable to stop a wheel, says "I wish it to roll" or at him, who thrown in a wrestling match, says "I wish to lie here." But do we not act like one of these whenever we use the expression "I wish"?

If only those actions are moral which spring from our own free will, then there are no moral actions at all.

We do not complain of nature as immoral because it sends a thunderstorm and soaks us. Why do we call those who injure us immoral? Because in the latter case we take for granted a free will functioning voluntarily; in the former we see necessity. But this distinction is an error. Thus we do not call even intentional injury immoral in all circumstances; for instance, we kill a fly unhesitatingly and intentionally, only because its buzzing annoys us; we punish a criminal intentionally and hurt him in order to protect ourselves and society.

In looking at a waterfall we imagine that there is freedom of will in the countless turnings, twistings, and breakings of the waves; but everything is compulsory, every movement can be mathematically calculated. So it is also with human actions. The one who acts labours under the illusion of voluntariness; if the world's wheel were to stand still for a moment and an all-knowing calculating reason were there to make use of this pause, it could foretell the future of every creature to the remotest times, and mark out every track upon which that wheel would continue to roll. The delusion of the acting agent about himself, the supposition of a free will, belongs to this mechanism which still remains to be calculated.

The complete irresponsibility of man for his actions and his nature is the bitterest drop which he who understands must swallow if he was accustomed to see the patent of nobility of his humanity in responsibility and duty. All his valuations, distinctions, disinclinations, are thereby deprived of value and become false. His deepest feeling for the sufferer and the hero was based on an error; he may no longer either praise or blame, for it is absurd to praise and blame nature and necessity. In the same way as he loves a fine work of art, but does not praise it, because it can do nothing for itself, so must he regard his own actions and those of mankind. He can admire strength, beauty, but must find no merit therein. The torments of the sick person who thirsts after recovery, are all equally as little merits as those struggles of the soul . . . in which we are torn . . . by different impulses. . . .

QUESTIONS

1. Elucidate: "Morality can often paralyze the critical will."
2. What would Nietzsche say to the person who said: "An act is right if, and only if, it is according to conscience"?
3. Traditional moralists have sought to give a "basis" to morality.

What does that mean? Use Paley, Bentham, or Kant as an example. What is Nietzsche's objection?

4. What does Nietzsche mean by a science of morals? What, for some time to come, must a science of morals set itself to do?

5. Why does a science of morals require a position "beyond good and evil"?

6. Why has a science of morals little to learn from historians of morality?

7. Reduce Nietzsche's thesis about morality—"obedience to custom"—to three essential claims. If Nietzsche's thesis is granted, could a moral judgment ever be passed upon customs?

8. Study carefully the two paragraphs beginning "There are two classes of people . . ." and "There are no such things . . ." (on page 101). They are important. Be sure that you understand them.

9. There is no universally recognized goal. Therefore, according to Nietzsche, what? If there were, however, then what? What goal did Nietzsche propose? Why did it call for an *interims-ethik*?

10. State Nietzsche's views on free will. What is the relation of these to his break with traditional moral philosophy?

2. DEWEY

John Dewey is one of America's most stimulating and influential philosophers. In the wide sense of the word, he was a student and critic of morals. He was born in 1859 and died in 1952, aged ninety-three. If you had called on him, you would have found him easy to talk to and an interested listener. You would have come away feeling important. If you had explained that you wanted him to speak about the question put to Paley, Bentham, and Kant—"What acts do you consider it, under assignable circumstances, wrong to do?"—you would, I think, have gotten an answer. If you had followed your question with an intelligent proposal for reducing the number of such acts, you would, I think, have found Mr. Dewey even more interested. Judging by his writings, it is safe to say that intelligent proposals for improving the conditions of human living, thereby improving that living itself, meant more to Mr. Dewey than any other single thing. If, however, you had gone on to ask, "What fact, common to all your cases of wrongdoing, is the reason for calling them cases of wrongdoing?"—you might have found yourself being looked at somewhat quizzically. Mr. Dewey would be entitled at that point to ask whether you were not familiar with his essays and chapters on that question, because he has written on it often and at great length, repudiating not only the question but the state of mind it implies. He has repeatedly insisted that there is no one fact or group of facts common to all cases of wrongdoing, and no one fact or group of facts common to all cases of right doing. He has repeatedly denied that there is any single principle of morality, illustrated by all right acts and violated by all wrong acts. In this he has explicitly separated himself from all such traditional moralists as Paley, Bentham, or Kant. Even more emphatically, however, he has criticized the state of mind which finds this question interesting and important. For Mr. Dewey it is neither. It is not only mistaken; it is also merely academic and ivory-tower. The question is misleading, and concern with it is wrong-headed. The important question is, how are the ills of humanity to be intelligently reduced? Concern with that is rightheaded.

General Position. Mr. Dewey's critique of traditional moral philosophy has formed part of his wider critique of traditional philosophy in general. This we must get clear, even at the cost of a considerable detour. For nearly half a century Mr. Dewey has been demanding—and proposing—what he calls "reconstruction in philosophy." His reconstruction in ethics is part of this more inclusive program. The argument gets under way in the form of a historical theory concerning the origin of western philosophy in the ancient world. I think it is well to begin at this point because what you find Mr. Dewey saying, in the end, is something like this: "You see how philosophy began. You see how regrettable its beginnings were. It has never wholly changed its ways. Meanwhile man's other interests have been changing their ways. Philosophy is thus in a very 'unreconstructed' condition."

The historical theory is this: Early in the history of western civilization there occurred a growth of factual, empirical, com-

mon-sense knowledge of nature and her ways. This early
"natural knowledge" was not yet science, but it was destined
to become so. It was the body of usable knowledge worked out
by men who had to deal with nature as a material order—
hunters, farmers, sailors, warriors, and so forth. This early slow-
growth body of factual, empirical, common-sense knowledge
of nature and her ways occurred in a society whose dominant
mores and institutions came from a yet earlier time. These
mores and institutions therefore did not reflect the outlook, the
point of view, of the growing body of natural knowledge.
They would not have been what they were if they had
taken shape along with or subsequent to the increase in natural
knowledge. The "lagged" over from one culture to another.

You had therefore an early and radical dislocation between
the point of view embodied in the mores and institutions, and
the point of view embodied in the growing natural knowledge.
Philosophy arose as the attempt to deal with this dislocation.
Her method of dealing with it was unfortunate from the start.
She should have familiarized people with the point of view and
the method of thinking which was resulting in the growth of
natural knowledge, explained it to them, convinced them of
its value, and extended this method from the study of nature to
the study of human nature and society, thus bringing about a
revision of the mores and institutions so that they would reflect
the point of view of the new natural knowledge. This would
have been timely, but this she did not do.

Instead, philosophy set herself to preserve, to perpetuate, to
sanctify those mores and institutions. This task she took over
from primitive religion. She set herself to "rationalize" the
mores and the institutions when they needed criticism and revision. In doing this she became the mouthpiece of those
persons in society (kings, nobles, priests, and so forth) who had
vested interests in the old order, who stood to lose wealth and
power and position and prestige if the needed revisions were
put through. She was thus the rationalizer for the reactionary.

Plato, in contrast to Protagoras and the sophists, is exhibit *A* in Mr. Dewey's case against traditional philosophy. Plato shows what she began as, and what, in many essential respects, she continued to be. He gave to western philosophy its characteristic concerns. Thus, much of western philosophy has been "apologetic" in character. You find this in Greek philosophy; in Catholic philosophy; in modern metaphysical idealism. Again, philosophy has cultivated argument, refutation, demonstration, system, and similar procedures which involve a great show of definition, reasoning, and logic. These procedures stand in sharp contrast to "inquiry," the method by which men go about extending their everyday knowledge of nature and her ways. Again, philosophy has nearly always sponsored some sort of "two-world" theory, a here-and-now in contrast to a Beyond, a natural in contrast to a supernatural, appearances in contrast to reality, an everyday world in contrast to a transcendental world. This befits her as heir and assign of primitive religion, and as advocate for mores and institutions which require powerful sanctions to offset the demands which they make upon ordinary belief and desire. Again, philosophy has traditionally gone in for certainties in contrast to probabilities, for eternal and immutable truths, for ultimates and first principles. Mr. Dewey sees in this a kind of compensatory desire on the part of philosophy to make up in impressiveness what she lacks in usefulness; and to acquire the kind and degree of finality that would befit her as guardian of traditional beliefs, mores, and institutions which had lagged over from an earlier culture. Again, philosophy has created and sustained her own "opposition," her skeptics, empirics, materialists, positivists, and the like. These do not show her setting about the business of reconstruction. They are merely parasitic upon her traditional assignment. Take away her characteristic doctrines and procedures, and these intellectually left-wing antibodies would perish for lack of something to feed on. In this sense, Hume's skepticism, for example, is no better than Berkeley's idealism. Again, as a kind of escape from pomposity and futility, philosophy has generated a vast amount of technicality. This gives her a jargon which marks her off from the common man, and enables her to invite comparisons between herself and well-developed bodies of natural and historical knowledge.

You have, then, Mr. Dewey's picture of how philosophy got off to a bad start. No essential changes occurred through the balance of Greek times, Roman times, Christian times, or medieval times. From Plato to Aquinas philosophy continued to run interference for or be preoccupied with beliefs, mores, and institutions which do not reflect the interests and methods which produce ordinary natural knowledge. Then once again, and this time more seriously, philosophy was given a second chance to mend her ways, to clean house, to institute what Mr. Dewey calls a "reconstruction." This occurred incidental to the coming of the modern world, during the last three or four centuries.

Philosophy was again confronted with a chance and a choice. Would she cease from being the handmaid, the ancilla, of beliefs, mores, and institutions which do not reflect a scientific interest in nature? Would she undertake to remake the popular mind and popular loyalties? Would she press for the extension of the new methods from the study of nature to the study of human nature and society? To the degree that she would undertake to do these things, she belonged on board, as the good ship "Modern World" pulled away from medival Europe.

The situation which calls for a reconstruction in philosophy has been produced, Mr. Dewey says, by three major revolutions—the scientific revolution, the industrial or technological revolution, and the political revolution. These three revolutions define Mr. Dewey's world. The first revolution—symbolized by such names as Copernicus, Newton, and Darwin—represents, by contrast with what preceded it, a radically revised conception of nature and man's place in nature. It is the outcome of scientific method applied to the study of nature and man's place in nature. This revolution is the thing which T. H. Huxley celebrated for Victorian England. It has vastly increased our power to predict and control processes going on around us. The second revolution is the application of scientific knowledge and scientific method to the production of wealth. It is "technology" in contrast to science, although Mr. Dewey would insist that there is no sharp distinction between the two. It represents, by contrast with what preceded it, a radically increased productivity. An economy which has undergone this revolution possesses a vastly increased productivity, a vastly increased power to produce. It is the thing which economists since Adam Smith have been analyzing and describing, and inventors and entrepreneurs since James Watt have been bringing to pass. It has vastly increased our power to use and transform Nature to our own ends. The third revolution is the introduction of the idea of democracy into political and social organization and control. This idea is not easy to express in words that are both simple and adequate. You cannot equate it with any of the political or social arrangements which men have adopted in its name. Thus you cannot equate the idea of democracy with representative government, nor universal suffrage, nor freedom of speech, nor abolition of slavery, nor government regulation of the economy, nor equality before the law. It is all of these things but it is always something more. These are ways in which men who have understood the democratic idea have sought to enact it. It is symbolized by such dates as 1776, 1789, and 1848. It is the notion of community self-government. It is the institutionalizing of the notion of the brotherhood of man. It is expressed in such phrases as "life, liberty, and the pursuit of happiness," and "liberty, equality, fraternity." It is, in respect to legal organization, the idea that a law is just if, and only if, it can say to the citizen, "I am what you ask of others; I am therefore what you ought to ask of yourself." It fought its way into history against the opposition of old regime absolutisms; and it is fighting to stay in history against latter-day totalitarianisms. It is the thing we all know about and believe in. It is the thing Mr. Dewey calls the "idea of democracy," and its introduction, "the political revolution."

You have then the conception of the modern world ushered in by these three revolutions, and marked by changes produced by the continuing presence of science, technology, and democracy. You do not need Mr. Dewey to tell you that this modern world is one of great promise; and, that, since its arrival, it has been fraught with great tensions. This is the world which struggled into being during the last few centuries, which plunged into a world war in 1914, and which has not seen any real peace and quiet since. This is the world within which Mr. Dewey has been calling for a "reconstruction in philosophy."

Mr. Dewey's picture of philosophy in the modern world is more complex than his picture of philosophy in the ancient and medieval world. Some distinctions are necessary. Among modern philosophers he recognizes two groups and calls for a third. There are those who have remained untouched in all essential matters. These are modern vehicles of philosophy in the traditional sense, the "unreconstructed" descendants of Plato, Aristotle, Plotinus, Augustine, Aquinas, and the rest. These include speculative metaphysicians of any and every stripe. They are wasting their own time, and Mr. Dewey would like it to stop at that. There are, secondly, those who have taken seriously the scientific picture of nature, and have undertaken to present the viewpoint and method of science to all comers, as the only way of getting to know more and more about nature and her ways. Mr. Dewey's great enthusiasm here is Francis Bacon. This second group represents an early and necessary stage of reconstruction. Mr. Dewey venerates and commends their efforts, but, when he calls for "reconstruction" he does not want merely more of them. The third group, who do not yet exist, or who exist in such small numbers as to be almost negligible, are those who will force the extension of scientific method from the study of nature to the study of human nature and society, who will thus turn upon mores and institutions the kind of inquiry and criticism needed to bring them into line with the world which has been produced by natural science and technology.

The following set of brief passages are quoted from Mr. Dewey's 1931 essay "Science and Society":

The significant outward forms of the civilization of the western world are the product of the machine and its technology. Indirectly, they are the product of the scientific revolution which took place in the seventeenth century. In its effect upon men's external habits, dominant interests, the conditions under which they work and associate, whether in the family, the factory, the state, or internationally, science is by far the most potent social factor in the modern world. It operates, however, through its undesigned effects rather than as a transforming influence of men's thoughts and purposes. This contrast between outer and inner operation is the great contradiction in our lives. Habits of thought and desire remain in substance what they were before the rise of science, while the conditions under which they take effect have been radically altered by science. . . .

Science through its applications is manufacturing the conditions of our institutions at such a speed that we are too bewildered to know what sort of civilization is in process of making. . . .

Science is strictly impersonal; a method and a body of knowledge. It owes its operation and its consequences to the human beings who use it, to the purposes and desires which animate these human beings. It lends itself with equal impartiality to the kindly offices of medicine and hygiene and the destructive deeds of war. It elevates some through opening new horizons; it depresses others by making them slaves of machines operated for the pecuniary gain of owners. . . .

In the degree in which we realize this fact, we shall devote our attention to the human purposes and motives which control its application. Science is an instrument, a method, a body of technique. While it is an end for those inquirers who are engaged in its pursuit, in the large human sense it is a means, a tool. For what ends shall it be used? Shall it be used deliberately, systematically, for the promotion of social well-being, or shall it be employed primarily for private aggrandizement, leaving its larger social results to chance? Shall the scientific attitude be used to create new mental and moral attitudes, or shall it continue to be subordinated to service of desires, purposes and institutions which were formed before science came into existence? Can the attitudes which control the use of science be themselves so influenced by scientific technique that they will harmonize with its spirit? . . .

Science itself is an instrument which is indifferent to the external uses to which it is put. Steam and electricity remain natural forces when they operate through mechanisms; the only problem is the purposes for which men set the mechanisms to work.

We are forced to consider the relation of human ideas and ideals to the social consequences which are produced by science as an instrument.

The problem involved is the greatest which civilization has ever had to face. It is, without exaggeration, the most serious issue of contemporary life. Here is the instrumentality, the most powerful, for good and evil, the world has ever known. What are we going to do with it? Shall we leave our underlying aims unaffected by it, treating it merely as a means by which uncooperative individuals may advance their own fortunes? Shall we try to improve the hearts of men without regard to the new methods which science puts at our disposal? There are those, men in high position in church and state, who urge this course. They trust to a transforming influence of a morals and religion which have not been affected by science to change human desire and purpose, so that they will employ science and machine technology for beneficent social ends. But there is another alternative: to take the method of science home into our own controlling attitudes and dispositions, to employ the new techniques as means of directing our thoughts and efforts to a planned control of social forces.

The technologies of industry have flowed from the intrinsic nature of science. But the pecuniary aims which have decided the social results of the use of these technologies have not flowed from the inherent nature of science. They have been derived from institutions and attendant mental and moral habits which were entrenched before there was any such thing as science and the machine. In consequence, science has operated as a means for extending the influence of the institution of private property and connected legal relations far beyond their former limits.

Here lies the heart of our present social problem. Science has hardly been used to modify men's fundamental acts and attitudes in social matters. It has been used to extend enormously the scope and power of interests and values which anteceded its rise. Here is the contradiction in our civilization. The potentiality of science as the most powerful instrument of control which has ever existed puts to mankind its one outstanding present challenge.

The anarchy called natural law and personal liberty still operates with success against a planned social use of the resources of scientific knowledge. . . . We have an extensive and precise control of physical energies and conditions, and in which we leave the social consequences of their operation to chance, laissez-faire, privileged pecuniary status, and the inertia of tradition and old institutions. . . . The outer arena of life has been transformed by science. The effectively working mind and character of man have hardly been touched.

If both democracy and capitalism are on trial, it is in reality our collective intelligence which is on trial. We have displayed enough intelligence in the physical field to create the new and powerful instrument of science and technology. We have not as yet had enough intelligence to use this instrument deliberately and systematically to control its social operations and consequences.

What stands in the way is a lot of outworn traditions, moth-eaten slogans and catchwords, that do substitute duty for thought, as well as our entrenched predatory self-interest. We shall only make a real beginning in intelligent thought when we cease mouthing platitudes; stop confining our ideas to antitheses of individualism and socialism, capitalism and communism, and realize that the issue is between chaos and order, chance and control: the haphazard use and the planned use of scientific techniques.

About physical conditions and energies we think scientifically; at least, some men do, and the results of their thinking enter into the experiences of all of us. But the entrenched and stubborn institutions of the past stand in the way of our thinking scientifically about human relations and social issues. Our mental habits in these respects are dominated by institutions of family, state, church, and business that were formed long before men had an effective technique of inquiry and validation. It is this contradiction from which we suffer today.

It is impossible to overstate the mental confusion and the practical disorder which are bound to result when external and physical effects are planned and regulated, while the attitudes of mind upon which the direction of external results depends are left to the medley of chance, tradition, and dogma. It is a common saying that our physical science has far outrun our social knowledge; that our physical skill has become exact and comprehensive while our humane arts are vague, opinionated, and narrow. The fundamental trouble, however, is not lack of sufficient information about social facts, but unwillingness to adopt the scientific attitude in what we do know.

The great scientific revolution is still to come. It will ensue when men collectively and cooperatively organize their knowledge for application to achieve and make secure social values; when they systematically use scientific procedures for the control of human relationships and the direction of the social effects of our vast technological machinery. Great as have been the social changes of the last century, they are not to be compared with those which will emerge when our faith in scientific method is made manifest in social works.

The story of the achievement of science in physical control is evidence of the possibility of control in social affairs. It is our human intelligence and human courage which are on trial; it is incredible that men who have brought the technique of physical discovery, invention, and use to such a pitch of perfection will abdicate in the face of the infinitely more important human problem.[2]

Criticism of Fixed Ends. The following passages from Mr. Dewey's *Reconstruction in Philosophy* and *Human Nature and Conduct* state his repudiation of our central problem—his break with traditional moral philosophy—and give some of his reasons for so doing. The first passage contains the heart of the matter; the rest provide reasons for and commentary upon what is therein proposed. This first passage should be studied carefully. It says that ethical theory began among the Greeks, that its beginnings were motivated in a certain way, and that in consequence it has been committed ever since to the notion that there is some ultimate good, or end, or law, by reference to which conduct is judged right or wrong. Mr. Dewey refers to this notion as "the theory of fixed ends." The passages follow-

---

[2] From *Philosophy and Civilization* by John Dewey, copyright 1931, reprinted by permission of G. P. Putnam's Sons.

ing, then, contain a statement and criticism of that theory.

It will be noted that the theory of fixed ends defines an area of agreement among many moralists who are otherwise sharply opposed to each other: Paley would subscribe to the theory, but so also would Bentham and Kant. Mr. Dewey is skeptical that disagreement about what the fixed end is can ever be overcome, even though it implies agreement that there is a fixed end. Paley, Bentham, and Kant would never reach agreement as to what the fixed end is, although their disagreement implies that there is a fixed end. Mr. Dewey therefore proposes that the theory of fixed ends be itself abandoned. It is a persistent primary agreement which underwrites persistent secondary disagreements. The way to get rid of the secondary disagreements is to abandon the primary agreement. The crucial first passage is this:

Ethical theory began among the Greeks as an attempt to find a regulation for the conduct of life which should have a rational basis and purpose instead of being derived from custom. But reason as a substitute for custom was under the obligation of supplying objects and laws as fixed as those of custom had been. Ethical theory ever since has been singularly hypnotized by the notion that its business is to discover some final end or good or some ultimate and supreme law. This is the common element among the diversity of theories. Some have held that the end is loyalty or obedience to a higher power or authority; and they have variously found this higher principle in Divine Will, the will of the secular ruler, the maintenance of institutions in which the purpose of superiors is embodied, and the rational consciousness of duty. But they have differed from one another because there was one point in which they were agreed: a single and final source of law. Others have asserted that it is impossible to locate morality in conformity to law-giving power, and that it must be sought in ends that are goods. And some have sought the good in self-realization, some in holiness, some in happiness, some in the greatest possible aggregate of pleasures. And yet these schools have agreed in the assumption that there is a single, fixed and final good. They have been able to dispute with one another only because of their common premise. The question arises whether the way out of the confusion and conflict is not to go to the root of the matter by questioning this common element.[3]

Mr. Dewey has made a radical claim; namely, that moralists from Socrates to Bentham were mistaken in their common assumption of a theory of fixed ends. The question therefore arises, why did so many distinguished thinkers make this mistake? If you accuse one eminent predecessor of confusion, you may not feel called upon to account for his lapse. But if you accuse *all* your eminent predecessors of confusion, you must proceed more deliberately: a lack on so grand a scale demands to be accounted for. One way to account for it is to trace it to some more primary, more radical, more fundamental confusion. Mr. Dewey's problem can be stated this way: when philosophers from Socrates to Bentham thought about morality, why were they misled into the theory of fixed ends? What more fundamental assumption was clouding their philosophical eye, distorting their philosophical vision, inclining them to subscribe to that gratuitous and conflict-generating theory? Mr. Dewey's explanation attempts to go to the root of the matter. His predecessors were misled into the theory of fixed ends in morals because they already adhered to the theory of fixed principles in nature; and they adhered (mistakenly) to the theory of fixed principles in nature, because they already adhered to the theory of fixed truth as the proper object of thought and knowledge. Why did they adhere (mistakenly) to this theory of fixed truth? Because they desired certainty, and believed that unless there was a fixed truth there would be nothing to be certain about. If, therefore, we would cease to desire certainty, we would not need to retain the theory of fixed truth. Then we could abandon the theory of fixed principles in nature. Then we could abandon the theory of fixed ends in morals. Then we could dissolve (not solve) the confusions and conflicts in ethical theory. Thus Mr. Dewey:

[3] Passages in this section are from *Reconstruction in Philosophy* by John Dewey, copyright 1920 by Henry Holt and Company, copyright 1948 by John Dewey; and from *Human Nature and Conduct* by John Dewey, copyright 1922 by Henry Holt and Company, copyright 1950 by John Dewey.

Why have men become so attached to fixed, external ends? The acceptance of fixed ends in themselves is an aspect of man's devotion to an ideal of certainty. This affection was inevitably cherished as long as men believed that the highest things in physical nature are at rest, and that science is possible only by grasping immutable forms and species: in other words, for much the greater part of the intellectual history of mankind. Only reckless skeptics would have dared entertain any idea of ends except as fixed in themselves as long as the whole structure of science was erected upon the immobile. Behind, however, the conception of fixity whether in science or morals lay adherence to certainty of "truth," a clinging to something fixed, born of fear of the new and of attachment to possessions. . . . Love of certainty is a demand for guarantees in advance of action. Ignoring the fact that truth can be bought only by the adventure of experiment, dogmatism turns truth into an insurance company. Fixed ends upon one side and fixed "principles"—that is authoritative rules—on the other, are props for a feeling of safety, the refuge of the timid and the means by which the bold prey upon the timid.

When the consciousness of science is fully impregnated with the consciousness of human value, the greatest dualism which now weighs humanity down, the split between the material, the mechanical, the scientific and the moral and ideal will be destroyed. Human forces that now waver because of this division will be unified and reinforced. . . . The vexatious and wasteful conflict between naturalism and humanism is terminated.

When men believed that fixed ends existed for all normal changes in nature, the conception of similar ends for men was but a special case of a general belief. . . . When the notion was expelled from natural science by the intellectual revolution of the seventeenth century, logically it should also have disappeared from the theory of human action. But man is not logical and his intellectual history is a record of mental reserves and compromises. He hangs on to what he can in his old beliefs even when he is compelled to surrender their logical basis. So the doctrine of fixed ends-in-themselves at which human acts are—or should be—directed and by which they are regulated if they are regulated at all persisted in morals, and was made the cornerstone of orthodox moral theory.

In morals now, as in physical science then, the work of intelligence in reaching such relative certainty, or tested probability, as is open to man is retarded by the false notion of fixed antecedent truths. Prejudice is confirmed. Rules formed accidentally or under the pressure of conditions long past, are protected from criticism and thus perpetuated. Every group and person vested with authority strengthens possessed power by harping upon the sacredness of immutable principle.

Mr. Dewey's proposal is clear: let moralists abandon the traditional theory of fixed ends. His explanation of why they were misled into adopting it is clear: they desired certainty in moral judgments. This explanation carries the supplementary proposal that they abandon the desire for certainty—a large order, about which Mr. Dewey wrote an entire book, *The Quest for Certainty,* in which he traced many philosophical ills to that quest and urged philosophers to abandon it. One of Mr. Dewey's inducements to abandon the theory of fixed ends is the dissolution (not solution) of traditional controversy in moral philosophy:

More definitely, the transfer of the burden of the moral life from following rules or pursuing fixed ends . . . eliminates the causes which have kept moral theory controversial, and which have also kept it remote from helpful contact with the exigencies of practice. The theory of fixed ends inevitably leads thought into the bog of disputes that cannot be settled. If there is one *summum bonum,* one supreme end, what is it? To consider this problem is to place ourselves in the midst of controversies that are as acute now as they were two thousand years ago. Suppose we take a seemingly more empirical view, and say that while there is not a single end, there also are not as many as there are specific situations that require amelioration: but there are a number of such natural goods as health, wealth, honor or good name, friendship, esthetic appreciations, learning and such moral goods as justice, temperance, benevolence, etc. What or who is to decide the right of way when these ends conflict with one another, as they are sure to do? Shall we resort to the method that once brought such disrepute upon the whole business of ethics: Casuistry? Or shall we have recourse to what Bentham well called the *ipse dixit* method: the arbitrary preference of this or that person for this or that end? Or shall we be forced to arrange them all in an order of degrees from the highest good down to the least precious? Again we find ourselves in the middle of unreconciled disputes with no indication of the way out.

The dissolution (not solution) of traditional controversy in moral philosophy is, up to a point, an advantage, an inducement. But it is a negative sort of advantage. Suppose the quest for certainty and the theory of fixed ends are abandoned. Then what? Less argument among moralists. But for Mr. Dewey, who holds such argument in contempt, a more positive advantage would be needed. As I read him, the positive inducement is that if these abandonments are made, argument will be replaced by inquiry. Moralists will argue less (or not at all) about wrongness in principle, and begin inquiring into what specific wrongs exist and how to get rid of them. As Mr. Dewey remarks somewhere, medical science aims to diagnose and cure specific ills of the body physical: would we have it set up endless argument about defining illness in principle? Let moralists take the hint; let moral philosophy become moral science:

It is worth noting that the underlying issue in ethics is, after all, only the same as that which has been already threshed out in physical inquiry. There too it long seemed as if rational assurance and demonstration could be attained only if we began with universal conceptions and subsumed particular cases under them. The men who initiated the methods of inquiry that are now everywhere adopted were denounced in their day (and sincerely) as subverters of truth and foes of science. After all, then, we are only pleading for the adoption in moral reflection of the logic that has been proved to make for security, stringency and fertility in passing judgments upon physical phenomena.

Morals is not a catalogue of acts nor a set of rules to be applied like drugstore prescriptions or cook-book recipes. The need in morals is for specific methods of inquiry and of contrivance: Methods of inquiry to locate difficulties and evils; methods of contrivance to form plans to be used as working hypotheses in dealing with them. And the pragmatic import of the logic of individualized situations, each having its own irreplaceable good and principle, is to transfer the attention of theory from preoccupation with general conceptions to the problem of developing effective methods of inquiry.

But the experimental logic when carried into morals enforces the moral meaning of natural science. When all is said and done in criticism of present social deficiencies, one may well wonder whether the root difficulty does not lie in the separation of natural and moral sciences. When physics, chemistry, biology, medicine, contribute to the detection of concrete human woes and to the development of plans for remedying them and relieving the human estate, they become moral; they become part of the apparatus of moral inquiry or science. The latter then loses its peculiar flavor of the didactic and pedantic; its ultra-moralistic and hortatory tone. It loses its thinness and shrillness as well as its vagueness. It gains agencies that are efficacious. But the gain is not confined to the side of moral science. Natural science loses its divorce from humanity; it becomes itself humanistic in quality. It is something to be pursued not in a technical and specialized way for what is called truth for its own sake, but with the sense of its social bearing, its intellectual indispensableness. It is technical only in the sense that it provides the technique of social and moral engineering.

When the consciousness of science is fully impregnated with the consciousness of human value, the greatest dualism which now weighs humanity down, the split between the material, the mechanical, the scientific and the moral and ideal will be destroyed. Human forces that now waver because of this division will be unified and reinforced. . . . The vexatious and wasteful conflict between naturalism and humanism is terminated.

The advantages pile up: by abandoning the mistaken theory of fixed ends you dissolve (not solve) much traditional controversy, you replace argument by inquiry, you make it possible for moral science to replace moral philosophy. But this is not all. You put the ax to the theological problem of evil, and you replace optimism and pessimism by meliorism:

Although the bearing of this idea upon the problem of evil and the controversy between optimism and pessimism is too vast to be here discussed, it may be worth while to touch upon it superficially. The problem of evil ceases to be a theological and metaphysical one, and is perceived to be the practical problem of reducing, alleviating, as far as may be removing, the evils of life. Philosophy is no longer under obligation to find ingenious methods for proving that evils are only apparent, not real, or to elaborate schemes for explaining them away or, worse yet, for justifying them. It assumes another obligation:—that of contributing in however humble a way to methods that will assist us in discovering the causes of humanity's ills.

Pessimism is a paralyzing doctrine. In declaring that the world is evil wholesale, it makes futile all efforts to discover the remediable causes of specific evils and thereby destroys at the root every attempt to make the world better and happier. Wholesale optimism, which has been the consequence of the attempt to explain evil away, is, however, equally an incubus. After all, the optimism that says that the world is already the best possible of all worlds might be regarded as the most cynical of pessimisms. If this is the best possible, what would a world which was fundamentally bad be like?

Meliorism is the belief that the specific conditions which exist at one moment, be they comparatively bad or comparatively good, in any event may be bettered. It encourages intelligence to study the positive means of good and the obstructions to their realization, and to put forth endeavor for the improvement of conditions. It arouses confidence and a reasonable hopefulness as optimism does not. For the latter in declaring that good is already realized in ultimate reality tends to make us gloss over the evils that concretely exist. It becomes too readily the creed of those who live at ease, in comfort, of those who have been successful in obtaining this world's rewards. Too readily optimism makes the men who hold it callous and blind to the sufferings of the less fortunate, or ready to find the cause of troubles of others in their personal viciousness. It thus co-operates with pessimism, in spite of the extreme nominal differences between the two, in benumbing sympathetic insight and intelligent effort in reform. It beckons men away from the world of relativity and change into the calm of the absolute and eternal.

It should be clear that American Pragmatism has close affiliations with English Utilitarianism. Between Jeremy Bentham and John Dewey there is an area of community. Mr. Dewey emphasizes this. It is therefore interesting to note that he goes out of his way to insist that even so enlightened a movement as Utilitarianism was infected by its adherence to the ill-starred theory of fixed ends. I think Mr. Dewey's criticism of Utilitarianism is valuable by way of conclusion because it shows unmistakably that he means what he says when he objects to the theory of fixed ends:

Upon the whole, utilitarianism has marked the best in the transition from the classic theory of ends and goods to that which is now possible. It had definite merits. It insisted upon getting away from vague generalities, and down to the specific and concrete. It subordinated law to human achievement instead of subordinating humanity to external law. It taught that institutions are made for man and not man for institutions; it actively promoted all issues of reform. It made moral good natural, humane, in touch with the natural goods of life. It opposed unearthly and other worldly morality. Above all, it acclimatized in human imagination the idea of social welfare as a supreme test. But it was still profoundly affected in fundamental points by old ways of thinking. It never questioned the idea of a fixed, final and supreme end. It only questioned the current notions as to the nature of this end. . . .

Utilitarian ethics thus afford a remarkable example of the need of philosophic reconstruction which these lectures have been presenting. Up to a certain point, it reflected the meaning of modern thought and aspirations. But it was still tied down by fundamental ideas of that very order which it thought it had completely left behind: the idea of a fixed and single end lying beyond the diversity of human needs and acts rendered utilitarianism incapable of being an adequate representative of the modern spirit. It has to be reconstructed through emancipation from its inherited elements.

Recapitulation. The essentials of Mr. Dewey's position are as follows: Traditional ethical theories have proposed to judge and guide action by reference to some fixed law to be followed or some fixed end to be achieved. This common premise has led to endless argument, both within each type ("What is the law in question?") and between types ("Is it a law or is it an end?"). If this common premise were abandoned, the argument would stop, having nothing to go on. This common premise, whether fixed law or fixed end, has led to argument, dispute, controversy, instead of inquiry; argument over the nature of right and wrong instead of inquiry into the conditions which promote right and reduce wrong. If moral philosophy ceased to be argument and became inquiry it would become moral science, that is (on the analogy of medical science), the scientific way of righting human wrongs. Such a shift from moral philosophy to moral science would liquidate many traditional "problems," for example, the problem of evil, or the dispute between optimism or pessimism. Evil as a fact to be accounted for would be replaced by evil as a fact to be dealt with, alleviated. The question whether things are as good as they can be (optimism) or as bad as they can be (pessimism) would be replaced by the question "How are things to be made better than they are?" (meliorism). Among traditional ethical theories, Utilitarianism is least objectionable. It did direct inquiry into the causes and conditions which produce happiness and reduce unhappiness. However, even Utilitarianism is tainted: it presupposes the theory of fixed ends, in this case "the greatest happiness of the greatest number." Traditional ethical theory invites comparison with traditional (pre-scientific) theory of nature: both work with the notion of "fixed." In modern scientific theory of nature there are no fixed truths, only hypotheses possessing varying degrees of probability, only continuous criticism and revision. When moral philosophy has become moral science, it too will consist only of hypotheses subject to continuous criticism and revision; hypotheses concerning the causes which promote right and reduce wrong. When men enter into the possession and use of such human knowledge humanly arrived at, they will become genuinely modern.

Comment. What shall we say to Mr. Dewey? Indeed, what *can* we say? He is less noisy and less colorful than Nietzsche but in the end his criticisms are more devastating. If you have a fondness for traditional philosophy—defining terms, propounding arguments, instituting distinctions, formulating principles, diagnosing presuppositions—you tend either to dismiss

Mr. Dewey as carping and illiberal, or you feel the sting of his persistent and quiet-spoken rebuke. Either outcome would be unhappy. As you read through his books, it becomes abundantly clear that Mr. Dewey is not carping and not illiberal. He is tolerant and wise and humane. He has enlightened sympathy for all who suffer from preventable ills whether of body or mind. As an educator he has worked and taught others to work against ignorance and narrowness and shallowness and superstition. For better than half a century his writings and influence have put the world in his debt.

And yet, the uneasiness persists. Mr. Dewey's proposal to ban philosophy is in the end no more convincing that Plato's proposal to ban the poets. When asked, along with Charles Beard and the editor of the Atlantic Monthly, to name the books which in his judgment had contributed most heavily to form the outlook of the twentieth century, Mr. Dewey placed Edward Bellamy's *Looking Backward* near the top of his list. Bellamy's utopian romance presents a tidied-up world. And it is a tidied-up world which Mr. Dewey would get for us, or have us get for ourselves, if he had his way. That is all to the good, but it is not enough. It is no accident that the word *philosophy* contains the Greek words for love and wisdom. Love is a passion, and it often both demands and produces an untidy world. We owe much great philosophy to ingredients in the human world which Mr. Dewey, like Plato and Bellamy, would do away with. Mr. Dewey does not say that philosophy causes those ingredients; but since it does nothing to remove them, and since they provide often the occasion for it, he would have men spend on them the energy they spend on it. But this they will not do, and Mr. Dewey, it seems, should know better than to suggest that they should. If, in this matter, he is up against a deep human passion, he will not get a hearing. Philosophy announces itself as the love of wisdom. Now wisdom is a knowledge of the good for man. This does not mean a knowledge of what conditions will produce the good for the man. It means a knowledge of the nature of that good itself. This is not to be had by the methods which make for a mastery over nature. In this sense, it is not an example of Francis Bacon's "Knowledge is power." It is deepened self-knowledge, and it comes through reflections, not investigation. What Mr. Dewey belittles as mere "definition and argument" is reflection's way of going about its job. Reflection can be soliloquy, but it does not have to be; and once it breaks through the walls of soliloquy, it becomes argument. There is a certain attraction to Mr. Dewey's vision of moral philosophy transformed into moral science; but it is not the attraction you feel in the pages of the great moralists. A world which would satisfy Mr. Dewey's crusading spirit is no substitute for the world you find in Plato's *Apology* or Kant's *Groundwork* or even Nietzsche's *Zarathustra*. It is as much the mark of wisdom to reflect upon the nature of man, and the human predicament which embodies it, as it is to attack that predicament with a view to straightening it out.

QUESTIONS

1. What is Dewey's historical theory concerning the origin of philosophy?

2. What did he mean by "reconstruction" in philosophy?

3. Name three revolutions which have produced a demand for a reconstruction in philosophy.

4. Distinguish the theory of "fixed ends" from the theory of "fixed law," in traditional moral philosophy.

5. How, according to Dewey, did those notions get into traditional moral philosophy?

6. The theory of fixed ends and the theory of fixed laws give rise to two kinds of endless argument. Explain.

7. These arguments deal with questions that cannot be solved but can be dissolved. Illustrate.

8. Dewey would replace argument about what by inquiry into what?

9. If that is done, moral philosophy would become moral science. Explain.

10. Discuss the bearing of the change from moral philosophy to moral science on the traditional problem of evil; on the traditional argument between optimism and pessimism.

11. Why, among traditional ethical theories, does Utilitarianism look least bad to Mr. Dewey?

12. Show wherein Utilitarianism is still "traditional."

13. Explain the point which separates Dewey from such traditional moralists as Paley, Bentham, Kant.

14. Contrast Dewey's "moral science" with Nietzsche's "natural history of morals," as proposed substitutes for traditional ethical theory.

3. AYER

Recapitulation. We began by posing a question: "What fact, common to all your cases of wrongdoing, is your reason for calling them cases of wrongdoing?" An answer to that question constitutes an essential portion of traditional ethical theories; so much so, indeed, that it would not be misleading, when speaking of a traditional moralist, to say that his answer to that question *was* his ethical theory. We put that question to Paley, Bentham, and Kant. Their answers did not agree. The only point of agreement was their acceptance of the question as central, answerable, and meaningful. Their disagreements are an example of controversy *within* traditional theories.

We moved forward to three modern moralists, Nietzsche, Dewey, and now Ayer. Here we encountered an important difference. This second group repudiate our original question as not central, or not answerable, or not meaningful. Controversy here does not fall *within* traditional theory. It occurs in relation to traditional theory, involving a repudiation of that theory. Instead of proposing an answer *to* our original question, these moralists propose a theory *about* that question: Nietzsche, that it presupposes that there is one morality, when there are many; Dewey, that it presupposes the notion of fixed ethical ends, when there are none; and now Ayer, that it presupposes that ethical terms are meaningful, when they are not. Of the three attempts to liquidate traditional ethical theory, this last is the most radical and (currently, at least) the most hotly disputed. Neither Nietzsche nor Dewey goes quite so far as to suggest that the trouble with traditional ethical theories is that they propose answers to a meaningless question. If Paley, Bentham, and Kant could listen in on Nietzsche, Dewey, and Ayer it is likely that they would receive the biggest jolt from this so-called "meaningless" theory of ethical terms. What does this theory say about ethical terms? Why does it say it? What consequences follow?

The Emotive Theory.[4] The position in question is known as the emotive theory of ethical terms and the judgments in which they occur. In the sentence, "Under assignable circumstances it is wrong to steal," the word "wrong" is a term and the sentence in which it occurs is a judgment. Instead of "terms" one sometimes speaks of "concepts." This difference in language makes no difference in what the emotive theory says about terms and the judgements in which they occur. Let us use the word "concept" and speak of moral concepts and the moral judgments in which they occur. We can then formulate the emotive theory as follows: moral concepts are pseudo concepts, and the judgments in which they occur are pseudo judgments. Now, what does that mean?

Concept. If "wrong" is a pseudo concept, we may begin by asking, what is a concept? That would make clear what, on the emotive theory, "wrong" is not. The dictionary states that a concept is a predicate of a possible judgment. Thus, to select something which the emotive theory would not denounce as pseudo, consider "blue" or "triangle" or "heavier than two pounds." These are concepts, predicates of possible judgments, for example, "The sky is blue"; "The figure is a triangle"; "The package is heavier than two pounds." The word "concept" is derived from two Latin words, *con* and *capio* meaning "with, by means of" and "seize, grasp." By the time this reaches ordinary English usage, you have a metaphor, but a metaphor the intent of which is clear. A concept is an idea with which, by

---

[4] Material in this section is taken from the author's Knoles Lectures ("Science as a Goad to Philosophy") delivered at the College of the Pacific, 1953; and from the author's article, "Meanings: Emotive, Descriptive and Critical," published in *Ethics*, 1949.

means of which, you seize or grasp something. Thus, by means of the concept "blue" you grasp the color of the sky; by means of the concept "triangle" you grasp the shape of the figure. These matters which you grasp (blue color, triangle shape) are "properties" respectively of the sky and the figure. Now, you can grasp these properties of the sky and the figure because they have them, because these properties are there. If the sky did not have any color, you could not grasp it with the concept "blue," because there would not be any color there to grasp. If the figure did not have any shape, you could not grasp it with the concept "triangle" because there would not be any shape there to grasp. Thus "black" can function as a genuine concept apropos of my pen because my pen has or can have the property black. And a judgment in which this concept occurred, for example, "My pen is black," would be a genuine judgment. It would ascribe an actual or possible property to my pen. If I judge that my pen is black, and it is black, then my judgment is also true. But its being a genuine judgment does not depend on its being true. It it were false, it would not therefore be pseudo. If I judge that my pen is black, and it is not, there is still judgment but it is false. The point is that, in pens, the color black is an actual or possible property. So long as this is so, "black" is a genuine concept, even though it should occur in a false judgment. A concept, then, is an idea which enables you to grasp some actual or possible property. What, then, is a pseudo concept?

Pseudo Concept. It should be clear that a pseudo concept is not a genuine concept that has been mistakenly used in a false judgment. If my pen is black and I mistakenly judge that it is not black, there is a false judgment, but "black" does not function here as a pseudo concept. It is a genuine concept mistakenly applied. You can go even further. The sentence "The square root of nine is dark green" is not only false, it is also preposterous. But even there, the concept "dark green," although used preposterously, is still a concept; it is not, even there, a pseudo concept. The fact that the square root of nine does not, and could not, have the property dark green, is not enough to make "dark green" a pseudo concept, because there are things (pencils, for instance) which have or could have the property dark green. So long as there is, or could be, anything anywhere any time which has or could have a certain property, then the concept corresponding to that property is not an example of what the emotive theory means by a pseudo concept. When therefore it says that moral concepts (right–wrong, and so on) are pseudo concepts, it is using strong language. For an idea to function as a pseudo concept, the user of the idea must be exceedingly, indeed almost incredibly, confused. I say "almost incredibly confused" and not "incredibly confused," because, if the emotive theory is correct in its diagnostic claim, then most people are that confused; and if most people are in a certain condition, it ill-behooves us to find this fact incredible.

In the sentence "Under assignable circumstances killing is wrong and ought to be stopped," there are two moral concepts, "wrong" and "ought." The emotive theory says they are pseudo concepts; and the judgment in which they occur, a pseudo judgment. This means that the person who uttered the sentence is under the radical illusion or delusion that wrongness and oughtness are or could be properties of something, in this case of acts, and specifically the act of killing. Whereas, if the emotive theory is true, wrongness and oughtness are not and could not be properties of anything anywhere any time. A person who made that pseudo judgment would be under a very serious misapprehension. His mistake would not consist in supposing that killing is wrong when it is right. It would go deeper than that. His mistake would consist in supposing that "wrong" is a concept when it is a pseudo concept, that wrongness is or could be a property when it is not and could not be.

To say that moral concepts, and the judgments in which they occur, are pseudo, tells us what they are not, namely not concepts or judgments. But it does not tell us what they are. The answer to this question is the second half of the emotive theory. It is to this effect: Moral concepts and the judgments in which they occur are effecters or vehicles. They enable us to do some-thing, although, as we have seen, they do not enable us to designate properties or make judgments. They enable us to express or excite feeling or emotion or attitude. Thus the judg-ment "Killing is wrong" does not say anything about the act of killing, does not affirm a belief about killing. What it does is to express feeling or emotion or attitude, presumably the feeling or emotion or attitude of disapproval. The word "ouch" uttered by a person in pain would be a simpler example of the point. So uttered, the word "ouch" does not say anything, does not make a judgment. It expresses a feeling, or an emotion. If the set of words "Killing is wrong" does nothing but express a feeling, even though it has the grammatical form of a judgment, you cannot say that it is true or false. You can say that it is success-ful or unsuccessful, that by means of it you either do or do not succeed in expressing your feeling. If you have strong feelings on the subject of murder, and the judgment "Murder is wrong" enables you to express those feelings, get them off your chest, then you can say that the utterance is successful. What you cannot say is that it is true, because to say that would be to mistake it for a judgment.

Cognitive *vs.* Emotive Meaning. The emotive theory, then, makes two principal claims: first, that moral concepts and the judgments in which they occur are pseudo; second, that they express or excite emotion, feeling, attitude. There is a third somewhat derivative point, namely, the notion of "emotive meaning." The theory claims that moral concepts and judg-ments have "emotive" meaning. This is a double claim, involv-ing a denial and an assertion. When you speak of the "meaning" of a concept, at least part of what you refer to is something actual or possible which the concept enables you to grasp. Thus the meaning of the concept black is, in part at least, the partic-ular color which the concept enables you to grasp or designate. This you could call its "cognitive" meaning, because by means of it you are able to state what you know or cognize about an object, for example, that it is black. Now any genuine concept has this kind of "cognitive" meaning, meaning that enables you to know or state what you know. But it is clear that no pseudo concept could have this kind of meaning, because, being only a pseudo concept, it doesn't refer to anything in the sense of predicating or affirming a belief about that thing. You could not use a pseudo concept to know or state what you know because there is, by hypothesis, nothing there to know or make statements about. In this cognitive sense of meaning, therefore, a pseudo concept has no meaning. It is meaningless. The emotive theory, therefore, speaks of moral concepts and judgments as "meaningless," intending to convey that they are devoid of "cognitive" meaning in the sense explained above. Moral concepts are thus meaningless in the sense that there is nothing about anything that you can know or state by means of them. That is the denial part. There is, however, another sense of "meaning," another kind of meaning, namely "emotive" meaning in contrast to "cognitive" meaning. And in this sense, moral concepts and judgments have meaning, are meaningful. The term "meaning" has two or more kinds of meanings. One of these is cognitive and one emotive. You can put the matter this way: the concept "black" has cognitive meaning because, and only because, there are objects which have or could have the property black; whereas the concept "right" does not have cognitive meaning because, and only because, there is nothing which has or could have the property "right." However, while the concept "right" cannot be used to refer to anything, it can be used to express or excite feelings, emotions, attitudes. Now these things which it can express or excite are its emotive meaning. A concept's emotive meaning is the feeling or emotion which it enables you to express or excite. Given this distinction you could say that a concept which possessed only cognitive meaning was emotively meaningless; and that one which possessed only emotive meaning was cognitively meaningless. The theory in question says that moral concepts and judgments have emotive meaning but are cognitively meaningless.

Not Ayer Alone. The theory that moral concepts—for example, right–wrong, good–evil, virtue–vice, ought–ought not —are meaningless, has been propounded most forthrightly by Professor A. J. Ayer in his truculent and lively little book, *Language, Truth and Logic*. But Mr. Ayer does not stand alone in this matter. Others have staked out the same claim. My suggestion is that we work up to Mr. Ayer by noting what some of these others have said.

Carnap. If the reader will secure a copy of Professor Rudolph Carnap's small volume, *Philosophy and Logical Syntax* (1935), and turn to page 24, he will find Professor Carnap speaking as follows: ". . . the value statement, 'Killing is evil,' although . . . merely an expression of a certain wish, has the grammatical form of an assertive proposition. Most philosophers have been deceived by this form into thinking that a value statement is really an assertive proposition, and must be either true or false." Read on for the next couple of paragraphs, in which Professor Carnap rounds out his statement of the emotive theory of ethical judgments.

There is no ambiguity in Professor Carnap's formulation of the point. He takes the sentence "Killing is evil," and makes a number of claims about it. Thus, although the sentence has the grammatical form of an assertion, it is not an assertion but the expression of a wish. Most philosophers (the traditional ones), misled by the grammatical form into thinking that it was an assertion, were further misled into thinking that it was either true or false, when in fact it is neither. These two mistakes led them into a third, namely, giving reasons for their belief that killing is evil, and trying to disprove the belief that killing is not evil. They were mistaken in all of this, because the sentence "Killing is evil" does not assert anything, is neither true nor false, can be neither proved nor disproved, is not verifiable, and considered as a theory, has no sense. And these restrictions apply to all other value statements.

Russell. If the reader will obtain a copy of Bertrand Russell's little book, *Religion and Science* (1935), on page 236 (Chapter 9) he will find Mr. Russell saying the following: "If, now, a philosopher says 'Beauty is good,' I may interpret him as meaning either 'Would that everybody loved the beautiful'—or 'I wish that everybody loved the beautiful.'—The first of these makes no assertion. . . ." Read on for the next couple of pages.

Mr. Russell's claim is as clear-cut as Mr. Carnap's. You may, he says, interpret the sentence "Beauty is good" in two ways, namely, as expressing a certain wish, or as making the assertion that you do have that wish. If you take it as expressing a wish, then it asserts nothing, is neither true nor false, and can have no evidence for or against it. If however you take the sentence ("Beauty is good") as asserting that you do have that wish, then it does make a statement, does assert something, is either true or false, and can have evidence for or against it. But, so construed, the sentence is not an assertion about either beauty or goodness, but about yourself, about your state of mind. The sentence "Beauty is good" seems to say that beauty is good. What it really says, if construed as an assertion, is that you have a certain wish about beauty. Evidence for or against this assertion would not come from either aesthetics or ethics. It would come from your biography or psychology. Construed as a wish, the sentence "Beauty is good" comes from ethics, but it does not say anything; it merely expresses a desire.

Richards. The following passage from I. A. Richards' *Meaning of Meaning* introduces the diagnostic word "emotive." This gives the passage importance, because the theory about moral concepts currently propounded by Carnap, Russell, Feigl, Ayer, and others is often referred to as "the emotive theory." Mr. Richards is speaking of the term "good." He says:

Thus when we do so use it (the word good) in the sentence "this is good" we merely refer to *this*, and the addition of "is good" makes no difference whatever to our reference. . . . It serves only as an emotive sign expressing our attitude to this. . . .

Mr. Richards' point could be illustrated. Suppose you are talking about shared affection, in contrast, say, to mutual hatred. You think the latter is bad and the former good. And so, referring to them, you say "This is good, whereas that is bad." Now consider the words which refer to shared affection, namely, "This is good." Your word "this" clearly refers to shared affection. You might think that your word "good" also referred to shared affection. But if you did, you would, according to Mr. Richards, be mistaken. Your "this" is all right. It makes sense. It says something. Its presence in your sentence, in contrast, say, to the word "that," makes a difference. Not so the word "good." It does not enable you to say anything about shared affection. It is not therefore useless, but it does not have the use you might think it has. It functions as an emotive sign. It expresses your emotional attitude toward shared affection. It may operate also to evoke a similar attitude in other persons, or perhaps to incite them to do something. The one thing it does not do is to enable you to say of shared affection that it is good.

Feigl. The following passage from Professor Herbert Feigl makes the same point in reference to the New Testament injunction, Do unto others as you would have them do unto you. Speaking of this commandment, Mr. Feigl says it

. . . simply means: "Would that everybody behaved toward his fellowmen as he expects them to behave toward him." This sentence . . . could not possibly be deduced from facts only; it is neither true nor false. Absolute values as well as categorical imperatives can be expressed only in emotive language.

If you adhere strictly to Mr. Feigl's words, you do not have a clearcut formulation of the characteristic denials made by the emotive theory of ethical terms. Those denials are clearest when made apropos of a sentence which has the grammatical form of an assertion or statement, for example, Killing is evil; Beauty is good; Stealing is wrong. These sentences have the grammatical form of an assertion. The emotive theory denies that they are assertions, and says that they are expressions of emotion or attitude and are therefore neither true nor false. Now the Golden Rule does not have the grammatical form of an assertion. It has, instead, the grammatical form of an injunction, a command, an imperative, a "do this." You can therefore, without appearance of a paradox, say of the Golden Rule that it is neither true nor false, since a command, qua command, does not pretend to be either true or false. If you utter, as a command, the sentence "Women and children first!" your words do not have the grammatical form of an assertion and hence do not claim to be either true or false. If, however, you were to utter the sentence "Under these circumstances the right thing to do is to let women and children go first," your words would have the grammatical form of an assertion and hence would, according to traditional ethical theory, be either true or false. At this point the emotive theory could enter its characteristic denials. To bring this out, one would therefore have to propose the Golden Rule as an assertion: "It is always and everywhere right to do unto others as you would have them do unto you." Now I think Mr. Feigl would say of this assertion what he says of the Golden Rule in its usual imperative form: it has its accent in emotional appeal. It could not be deduced from facts only. It is neither true nor false. Its point cannot be conveyed in statement language but only in emotive language.

Ayer. Professor Ayer propounded his emotive theory of moral concepts and the judgments in which they occur, in his 1936 publication *Language, Truth and Logic*. The book has been widely read and hotly disputed. Mr. Ayer has a fresh and emphatic manner of expressing himself. The reader should secure a copy of Professor Ayer's lively little book and turn to Chapter 6, "Critique of Ethics and Theology." The doctrine is there set forth in a dozen pages. These pages bear careful and repeated reading. They have the essence of the matter in them. Having given Professor Ayer a hearing, ask yourself what he has said.

Begin with the negative side of the doctrine: moral concepts are pseudo concepts; that is, they appear to be concepts, but in reality they are not. They appear to have (cognitive) meaning, but in reality they do not. The judgments in which they occur are pseudo judgments. Since they are not judgments and do not have any (cognitive) meaning, they are neither true nor false,

probable nor improbable. The task of an ethical theory is simply
to say these things about moral concepts and the judgments in
which they occur; anything beyond that belongs in anthropology, sociology, psychology or psychoanalysis. What is here said
about moral concepts applies also to aesthetic concepts.

On its positive side the doctrine claims that moral concepts
and the judgments in which they occur express or arouse feeling. This is not to be confused with subjectivism. According to
subjectivism moral concepts are meaningful and moral judgments are either true or false; whereas according to emotivism
they are neither.

The reader should not be misled by the common ambiguity
of the words "feel" and "feeling." In one sense of those words, a
judgment in which they occurred would be meaningful and
could be either true or false. For example: "I feel that we are
going to need more money than that," or "I have the feeling
that you will miss your train if you do not hurry." In these statements the words "feel" and "feeling" have some such meaning
as "believe" or "am of the opinion that." Hence it makes good
sense to say either that it is true that I feel this, or that what I
feel is true. This use of the words is to be distinguished from
Mr. Ayer's use. You come closer to what Mr. Ayer has in mind
if you say "I feel anger" or "I feel tired." Here it makes good
sense to say that it is true I feel anger or feel tired. But it does
not make good sense to say that *what* I feel is either true or
false, that is, to say that either anger or tired are either true or
false. They are *feelings,* not judgments. They have no meaning
of the kind that judgments claim to have. They are neither true
nor false. Now, when Mr. Ayer says that ethical terms and the
judgments in which they occur express or arouse feeling, he
means "feeling" in this *second* sense, in the sense of "emotion."
In this sense, if words express or arouse feeling or emotion, they
are, qua expressing or arousing, neither true nor false. They
may be successful or unsuccessful, in expressing or arousing the
emotions in question, but that is not to be confused with trueness or falseness.

Comment. Emotivism is unique among ethical theories: its hand is against every other theory in a way that is not true of any other theory. No other ethical theory claims that moral judgments are pseudo, meaningless, neither true nor false. Nietzsche's immoralism did not go that far, nor does Mr. Dewey's repudiation of fixed ethical ends; whereas emotivism outlaws them all. It completes, for those who accept it, the liquidation of traditional ethical theory, and, as though to make sure of it, liquidates all other ethical theories as well.

Criticism. Is the emotive theory itself open to criticism? If so, at what points or along what lines? There are in general two ways of criticizing a theory. One is to inspect the reasons offered in support of the theory, and to show that they need not or cannot be admitted; or that even if admitted, they do not justify the theory in question. Suppose a man claims that the existence of a benevolent power outside of nature can be proved by the occurrence of miracles. You might argue that miracles do not occur, or that even if they do occur they do not justify the claim that any such power exists. The second method is to inspect the consequences which would follow if the theory were admitted, and to show that they cannot be admitted, that they are too high a price to pay for the theory in question. The first would be criticism directed at the grounds of a theory; the second, criticism directed at the consequence of a theory. Is the emotive theory open to criticism along either of these lines?

Suppose you come at it by way of its consequences. You could point out that if the theory is true, then almost all moralists from Socrates to G. E. Moore have been guilty of one and the same colossal blunder, namely, thinking that moral judgments are cognitively meaningful. "That," you might say, "I find incredible. That is too high a price to pay for the theory in question." You could point out that if the theory is true, then no act can ever be criticized or justified in moral terms since criticism and justification do not mean simply expressing or arousing feeling. Thus nothing could be said for honesty or justice or against dishonesty or injustice, since that sort of judgment does not mean simply expressing or arousing feeling. "That," you might say, "I find incredible. That is too high a price to pay for the theory in question." You could point out that if the theory is true, then what is traditionally and properly called "skepticism" with respect to moral judgments cannot be said to occur. This would hold for particular moral judgments ("I doubt that you did the right thing last week"), and general moral judgments ("I doubt that stealing is wrong"). Now, the skeptic is an ancient and honorable fellow, who, it would seem, must needs be provided for. But emotivism makes skepticism impossible because meaningless. "That," you might say, "I find incredible. That is too high a price to pay for the theory in question." You could point out that if the theory is true, then there is only one possible criticism to be made of any ethical theory and only emotivism can make it. Thus Bentham cannot criticize Paley, Kant cannot criticize Bentham, and Dewey cannot criticize any of the three of them, unless what each says of the other or others is simply this: "You mistakenly suppose that moral judgments are judgments, whereas they are not." Any other criticism would be irrelevant. "That," you might say, "I find incredible. That is too high a price to pay for the theory in question." And so it might go. In each case you would be objecting to the theory because of its consequences.

Now, how about its reasons?

What reasons are there for believing that all of a moralist's terms are simply emotive? I have yet to encounter a good reason for any such claim. Take the statement, "The key words in any moral judgment, or in any statement of the principle of morality, have emotive meanings only." What is the character of such an assertion? Is it an induction from instances? If so, what do you do with the person who says that it does not give an accurate account of his thinking? If he says that he does not use these terms emotively, are you going to tell him that he does not know his own mind? That would be intolerably presumptuous. Is it a definition? If nominal, the statement is trivial; if real, the statement is dogmatic, unless accompanied by reasons, and is amply met by sheer denial or counterassertion. Is it what Kant would have called "synthetic a priori"? That is, is there a necessary connection, not analytic in character, between a judgment's being ethical and being emotive? I doubt that people who hold the emotive theory of ethical meanings would be caught dead offering any such account of their characteristic claim. Is it a tautology? If so, it is one of the most fantastically untautologically worded tautologies I have ever encountered. This does not prove that it is not a tautology, but it ought, in all conscience, to suggest that the tautology hypothesis is not supported by any open-and-shut case. Is it an example of what it claims ethical judgments to be? That is, is the emotive theory of ethical meanings itself an instance of the emotive use of language? I have sometimes thought so, in my less charitable moments. If it is, it is neither true nor false and is hoist with its own petard.

One is brought back again to the original question: what reason could a man have for claiming that the key words in any moral judgment, or in any statement of the principle of morality, have emotive meanings only? If he says, "I say so because I do not know what else to call them," we may sympathize with him but remind him that his limitations do not entitle him to propound so odd a thesis. If he says, "I say so because I myself use all ethical terms in an emotive sense, and I infer from that that other persons do, or should do, likewise," we may ask him why he always uses ethical terms in an emotive sense and why he thinks that others therefore do or ought to do likewise. If he says, "I say so because there is no unanimity among moralists," we may recognize the truth of what he says but question it as a reason for his claim. You can say the same thing about logicians: there is often no unanimity among them. Yet does this fact incline people to say that logicians study only emotive meanings? The fact that two people mean different things when they use the same word does not prove that either of them is using the word in an emotive sense. If he says, "I say so because eventually ethical terms become ultimate terms.

incapable of further analysis or further justification," we may agree with him but see in this no grounds for saying that they therefore have only emotive meanings. Ethical terms are not alone in that boat. The same reasoning would lead one to insist that the terms used in logic, when they are ultimate, are also only emotive. If he says, "I say so because they are often patently used in an emotive sense, and from that I infer that they are always so used," we can again agree with him but point out that though many of a logician's key terms are often so used, no one infers from that that they are always so used; and we can ask him why he picks on ethical terms for such a deflating generalization. If he says, "I say so because since they are not verifiable, they must be emotive," we must ask him in what sense they are not verifiable. If you know what you mean by "tall," you can verify the statement that Tommy is tall. If you know what you mean by "good," you can verify the statement that Tommy is good; or that Tommy is a fallacious reasoner when it comes to syllogisms. And this verification is not "private," in the sense of idiosyncratic: it will be as widely "public" as those who go along with you in what you mean by your claims about Tommy. In this, it differs only in degree from any verification. And in any case, to make too much of this point would force the emotive theory to adopt the argument from *consensus gentium,* and I assume it would as soon have the measles.

I have been casting about for reasons that might be offered for the doctrine that, as normally used, ethical terms have only emotive meanings. Let me quote again the forthright statement of this singular doctrine from one who professes to believe it: "Ethical philosophy consists simply in saying that ethical concepts are pseudo-concepts. The further task of describing the feelings that ethical terms are used to express and evoke is a task for the psychologist." It seems to me that one who would make that statement must have either a good reason or a strong motive for so doing. Suppose I were to say, "The business of a philosophically minded logician is simply to say that all concepts studied by logic are pseudo concepts." That would be regarded as a somewhat paradoxical statement, even by a person who would authorize a similar statement about ethical concepts. My question is "Why?" The root situation that generates logic is that men believe and that upon occasion they want their beliefs to be true. The root situation that generates ethics is that men act and that upon occasion they want their acts to be right. Logicians and moralists have in their keeping the key terms in which one proposes discourse about these matters. Why should it be said that the terms which define the moralist's concern are emotive, whereas the terms which define the logician's concern are not? I have canvassed most of the reasons advanced by those who thus discriminate against the moralist, and I am not convinced by any of them. I shall indicate briefly what seems to be the strongest reason and what I think is wrong with it.

You begin with the notion of "fact," one of the great undefined and possibly indefinable terms in the vocabulary of rational animals. Suppose you discover that cheating among freshmen is rare. You speak of this as a fact and no one challenges your use of the term. No one suggests that this is a state of affairs to which the concept of "fact" is not applicable. No one suggests that to say this is a "fact" is as inappropriate as to say that the square root of −1 is green. No one suggests that, in saying cheating among freshmen is rare, you are adding nothing to the statement that cheating occurs among freshmen. There is, apparently, something about rareness which, when it occurs, entitles it to be referred to as a "fact." If you formulate your discovery as a hypothesis and say that it is probably "true," no one will protest that use of the word "true," even though someone might deny that your hypothesis was true. So long as what you want to say about cheating among freshmen is that it is "rare," you can get away with the term "fact" and the term "true."

Suppose, however, after additional investigation and reflection you come to the further conclusion that, under assignable circumstances, cheating among freshmen is wrong and ought to stop or be stopped. It is at this point that you are in danger of a run-in with the doctrine that all ethical terms are emotive. In your new conclusion you have two such terms, namely, "wrong" and "ought." The presence of these terms, emotivism says, bars you from applying the word "fact" to what you are talking about or the word "true" to what you are saying. You may not say, for instance, "The fact is, cheating among freshmen is wrong"; nor may you say, "It is true that cheating among freshmen is wrong." There is, in these respects, a radical difference between rareness and wrongness. You can predicate the one as a "fact" and speak of your predication as "true"; in the case of the other, you cannot. There is something about wrongness that makes it misleading to speak of wrongness as a "fact." At this point the emotive theory delivers its characteristic pronouncement: "If you are not stating a fact (and wrongness is never a fact about any act), then you are expressing or arousing a feeling. If you are not stating, then you are emoting. If you are expressing or arousing a feeling, then you cannot speak of what you are doing as either true or false; although you may speak of it as successful or unsuccessful, depending on whether you do or do not manage to express or arouse the feeling in question."

Now, all of this appears to depend upon an unavowed definition of the concept of "fact." I do not know what this definition is. I have looked in vain for any definition of "fact" in the writings of the friends of emotive meaning. I suspect that I could not agree with it as a definition, if I did know it. Relatively little attention is paid to the question, "What do you claim something as, when you claim it as a 'fact'?" particularly by those who are sure that wrongness is never a fact about any act, whereas rareness sometimes is.

Another point. Emotivism authorizes the statement "Wrongness is never a fact about any act." This statement presupposes some answer to the question, "What is a fact?" A definition of "fact" forces the reduction of ethical terms to emotive. I am not in a position to criticize this definition because, as I said, I do not know it. But I can ask this question, "Does this definition of 'fact' also force the reduction of logical terms to emotives? If it follows from the nature of fact that neither rightness nor wrongness is ever a fact about any act, does it also follow that neither trueness nor falseness is ever a fact about any belief?" If so, I have nothing more to say. If not, then my question is, "Why not?" If the wrongness of an act can never be a "fact," how can the trueness of a belief ever be a "fact"? If it cannot, then does the term "true" become emotive?

My own suggestion is that "true" and "false" and their derivatives are not emotive terms but critical terms; that their primary function is not to express or arouse feeling but to serve as vehicles of criticism. I would add only that, in my opinion, the same holds of "right" and "wrong" and their derivatives.

A term is used "emotively" when it is used either to express or to arouse feeling. To verify that a term is being used emotively, one must know that in using it one intends either to express or to arouse feeling or know that about someone else's use of it. Unless we can interrogate ourselves or others and have good reason to trust the answers, it is not clear how we could ever know that any term was being used in an emotive sense. Whether a term is being used emotively depends upon what the user intends when he utters it. If he intends either to express or to arouse feeling, then his use of it is emotive; if he does not, then it is not. To use words emotively is often a difficult and hazardous undertaking. Great masters of the emotive use of language are rare, but they do exist.

A term is used descriptively when it is used to describe something. The distinction between using a word emotively and using it descriptively not only is obvious but also is so great that there is on most occasions no good reason for confusing the two. If you have feelings and use words to express them, that is one thing; if something has a describable character and you use words to describe it, that is another thing.

The notion of a description can be illustrated. You can describe the shape of a room, the sound of a voice, the color of new-fallen snow, the taste of a dill pickle, the behavior of a child learning to walk, the size of the library, and so on. It should be noted that you can describe feelings, too; that to describe a feeling is not the same thing as to express it. I see no way of stating in principle which words can function only descriptively, but I can name many words which are frequently so used—white, long, hot, tall, green, sour, heavy, slow, translatable, kinky, cheerful, complex, and so on, indefinitely.

I would repeat: one important difference between emotive and descriptive use of language is the difference in *intention*. The discourse of a man using language emotively, using it to express or to arouse feelings, differs in intention from the discourse of a man using language descriptively to convey descriptive meanings. I can conceive of a person's being so naive, so lacking in self-knowledge, that he could not tell whether he was "emoting" or describing or even which he was intending to do; but that circumstances is rare and ought not, I think, to be made the basis for any theory about what kinds of discourse are in principle emotive and what kinds are in principle descriptive.

The emotive theory of moral concepts is that they express or arouse feelings or emotions, and that they do nothing else. They do not possess descriptive meanings. Sometimes the animus is primarily negative, namely, to insist that ethical meanings are not descriptive; and, then, as though in answer to the question, "If not descriptive, what are they?" to use the hypothesis, "They must be emotive." Sometimes the animus is primarily positive, namely, to insist that ethical meanings are emotive; and, then, as though in answer to the question, "If they are emotive, what is it that they are not?" to urge the hypothesis, "They are not descriptive." Either way there is a tacit assumption that emotive and descriptive constitute an exhaustive disjunction, that if a meaning is not the one, then it is the other, and vice versa.

Now, I want to suggest a third alternative, namely, "critical." I want to speak of critical meanings and to distinguish them from both emotive and descriptive meanings. My intentions are not wholly innocent: I have never been willing to accept the alternative that they are descriptive. It seems to me that ethical meanings, in their primary intention, are neither emotive nor descriptive. I have therefore felt the need for some third alternative. It used to be said that they are "normative," but nowadays that word is under a cloud. No one uses the term "normative" any more, at least in a tone of voice that would indicate that he meant business; so I am going to use the term "critical" and contrast it with both emotive and descriptive.

The term "critical" is used in many senses. I should like to draw attention to some of these before closing in on the sense in which it is used in the phrase "critical meanings." You will find one use in the sentence, "His illness reached the critical stage at midnight." The suggestion here is that a stage is "critical" if, after it has been reached and passed, you either get better or die. You will find a second use in the sentence, "Don't be so critical: try being constructive for a change." Here "critical" carries the sense of "fault-finding," or "merely fault-finding," in contrast to "helpfully suggestive." You will find a third use in the contrast between "critical" and "uncritical," as in the sentence, "Uncritical thinking will not get you as far in business as critical thinking." You will find a fourth use in the sentence, "He published a critical edition of Shakespeare's *Hamlet*." I am not too sure what the word "critical" means there. It does not mean "an edition containing all the criticisms." It may mean "an edition in which great care is taken to make sure that the text is a reliable copy of the original." You will find a fifth use of the word "critical" in the contrast between "critical" and "mechanical" as in the sentence, "The behavior of the earth in going around the sun is mechanical, whereas the behavior of the astronomer astronomizing about the earth going around the sun is critical." These five uses of the word "critical" are probably not all that an examination of ordinary usage would disclose. I do not think any of the five is an exact equal of the sense in which "critical" can be contrasted with both "emotive" and "descriptive." The word "critical" in that last sense means "used as a vehicle of criticism." When words are so used, their meanings are neither emotive nor descriptive. To criticize a piece of reasoning, for example, is not the same thing as to express or to arouse the feeling which the reasoning may inspire; nor is it the same thing as to describe the reasoning, as in such sentences as "The reasoning was brief," or "The reasoning was elegant," or "The reasoning was timely." Perhaps the use of the term "critical" which I am here proposing to contrast with "emotive" and "descriptive" would be "made with reference to a criterion." A criticism is a judgment made with reference to a criterion; a critical handling of something is a handling made with such reference. To think critically is to think with reference to a criterion which is involved. A proposition setting forth a criterion would be, to borrow Professor Collingwood's phrase, a criteriological proposition. A moral criticism would be a judgment presupposing some criteriological proposition setting forth the criteria with reference to which the judgment was made.

I would maintain that philosophy is the theory of criticism; that is, your philosophy is what you finally assert in order to elucidate your use of critical, in contrast to emotive or descriptive, language. So understood, it includes at least logic, ethics, and aesthetics.

Consider logic. A logician is called upon to elucidate terms which have what I should call "critical" meanings; such terms as true, false, valid, invalid, probable, improbable. It is his business to clarify the meanings of these and similar terms. These terms, when applied to different modes of statement and inference, are vehicles of criticism. It may well be that these and similar terms can be used emotively or even descriptively; I am not sure, but I am sure that they can be used, and usually are used, as vehicles of criticism. It seems to me that the burden of proof would rest with the person who claimed that these and similar terms never are or never should be so used as vehicles of criticism, but are or should be used only emotively or descriptively. And I must confess that I am puzzled to know what he would use for evidence. I am, therefore, going to assume that there is a critical, in contrast to either an emotive or a descriptive, use of language and that many of the words studied in logic, having application to statement and inference, do illustrate such use, do have critical meanings, are used as vehicles of criticism.

Now, emotivism claims that ethical terms possess only emotive meanings and that statements using ethical terms are therefore neither true nor false, since neither the expression nor the arousal of a feeling can be said to be true or false. In saying that they are emotive, it is meant that they are *not* descriptive. The game is at all costs to make the moralist admit that, qua moralist, nothing he ever says is true or false. This being so, the stakes are high: the terms "true" and "false" have enormous prestige, can, indeed, be used with great emotive intent. The moralist begins to see himself walled off with preachers, propagandists, orators, and other practitioners of "persuasive eloquence" and to conclude that his only reaccess to intellectual respectability is to give up being a moralist and settle for being an anthropologist, a psychologist, or a sociologist. I have, thus far, been endeavoring to slip through the horns of this dilemma, to suggest "critical" as an alternative to both emotive and descriptive. And I have been seeking to lend prestige to this third alternative by suggesting that no logician can afford to ignore it and settle for the choice between emotive and descriptive. His stock in trade is a group of words which, in their primary intention, are neither emotive nor descriptive but critical. If there were not this third alternative, then the logician, like the moralist, would have to choose between being a propagandist and being a psychologist. And that choice, I opine, would bring out the sweat on any self-respecting logician. No logician would like to admit that his terms can never be used to criticize statements and inferences but only to describe them. Nor would he like to admit that when he speaks, qua logician, nothing he ever says is true or false.

My strategy in all this rests on the conviction that if the moralist is no worse off than the logician, he can continue to do business at the old stand. Is this strategy well grounded in the mind's terrain? Our question can be put this way: Granted that there are critical meanings and that some terms about which logicians propose discourse have critical meanings, must you say that no other terms have critical meanings? If there is no such necessity, if there are other terms which possess critical meanings, must you say that none of these are ethical terms? I am, of course, interested in the reasons one would give for answering "Yes" to this second question.

QUESTIONS

1. Those who have formulated the emotive theory say that moral judgments are pseudo judgments. What does that mean? Why do they say that?

2. The emotive theory says that moral judgments are emotive. What does that mean? If they are emotive, then they (*a*) are neither true nor false; (*b*) cannot be either contradicted or agreed with; (*c*) cannot be either verified or refuted. Show why in each case.

3. Distinguish between emotivism and subjectivism. Which of those terms applies to Mr. Russell's position? Why does Mr. Ayer reject subjectivism?

4. Why would emotivism be opposed by Paley, Bentham, and Kant?

5. Could you make out a case for saying that *true* and *false*, like *right* and *wrong*, have only emotive meaning? Would the emotive theory welcome this addition to its territory?

6. Your textbook proposes a threefold distinction, namely, (*a*) emotive, (*b*) descriptive, (*c*) critical. Do you go along with this? If not, why not?

7. How would you account for the liveliness of the controversy which emotivism has stirred up for itself?

IV. The Free Will Problem

1. PRO AND CON [1]

A moral judgment presupposes a theory of right and wrong. Consider the judgment, "It was wrong of him to take that money." Suppose you are asked "Why?" You answer, "Because he stole it, and stealing is wrong." You are asked "Why?" again. You answer, "Because stealing militates against the greatest happiness of the greatest number, and to do that is wrong." You are asked "Why?" again. It may be that you are a utilitarian. In that case you will proceed no further. "That," you would say, "is my theory about right and wrong. Don't ask me to abandon that."

A moral judgment presupposes also a theory of the human will or of its expression in action. The point can be indicated by asking: "When you criticize a person for wrongdoing, do you presuppose that he could have done other than he did do?" The question could be sharpened: "If you condemn or punish a person for wrongdoing, do you presuppose that he could have done other than he did do?" The question could be disengaged from considerations of moral judgment, criticism, condemnation, or punishment: "Do you ever presuppose that anyone could ever at any time have done other than he did do?" If you do, you presuppose that he has what is traditionally called "free will" or "choice," that his act was not necessitated or "determined" in any manner that is incompatible with the claim

---

[1] Material used in sections 1 and 3 of this chapter is taken from the author's article, "The Critical and the Mechanical" (*Philosophical Review*, 1951); and from the author's Knoles Lectures ("Science as a Goad to Philosophy") delivered at the College of the Pacific, 1953.

that he could have done other than he did do. If, however, you presuppose that he could not have done otherwise, you are denying free will. This denial is sometimes called "determinism," meaning that the act was determined and therefore could not have been otherwise.

We have here a pair of incompatible presuppositions. If it is true that he could have done otherwise, then it cannot also be true that he could not have done otherwise, and vice versa. One presupposition ("could have") says that the human will is the locus of freedom; the other ("could not have") denies this, and says that it is the locus of necessity. The controversy between these two contradictory claims is of long standing. Our business in this chapter is to become familiar with what each side has to say for itself, its reasons for its claims. The question is not, "Do you presuppose or deny that a person could have done otherwise?" The question is, "What reason have you for believing that your presupposition or denial is true?" It is one thing to presuppose or deny, and another thing to justify the presupposition or denial. What reason can be given for affirming man's free will? What reason for denying it? We might add a third question to provide for the skeptic: What reason can be given for refusing to do either, for saying, "I am skeptical about the possibility of justifying either claim"?

We shall begin with determinism, the theory which says, "You being what you were, the circumstances being what they were, you could never at any time have done other than you did do. If you think you could have, you are mistaken."

Each of the following passages contains a denial of free will in man. The denial is usually accompanied by a reason. The passages should be read carefully and thought about. They will help to convince you that determinism is no fly-by-night affair, but a persistent and widely held belief. They are a cloud of witnesses, testifying on behalf of determinism. As you read them, ask yourself which you find the most convincing. If you side with determinism ("could not have done otherwise"), do you find your reasons set forth in any of these passages? If your reason is not to be found here, how would you formulate it? There are eleven passages.

[1] I conceive that nothing taketh beginning from itself, but from the action of some other immediate agent without itself. Therefore, when a man hath a will to something, to which before he had no will, the cause of his will is not the will itself but something else not in his own disposing. To deny necessity is to destroy the power and foreknowledge of God Almighty. For whatsoever God hath purposed to bring to pass by man, or foreseeth shall come to pass, a man might frustrate and make not come to pass if he have freedom from necessity. Then would God foreknow such things as never shall be, and decree such things as shall never come to pass. Because every act of man's will and every desire and inclination proceedeth from some cause, and that from some other cause, in a continual chain, it proceeds from necessity. To him that could see the connection of those causes, the necessity of all men's voluntary actions would appear manifest.

[2] A stone receives from an external cause, which impels it, a certain quantity of motion with which it will afterwards necessarily continue to move. Conceive if you please that the stone while it continues in motion thinks, and knows that it is striving as much as possible to continue in motion. This stone, inasmuch as it is conscious only of its own efforts, will believe that it is completely free, and that it continues in motion for no other reason than because it wants to. Such is the human freedom which all men boast they possess, and which consists solely in this, that they are conscious of their desire and ignorant of the causes by which they are determined. Man thinks himself free because he is conscious of his wishes and appetites, while at the same time he is ignorant of the causes by which he is led to wish and desire. There is in the mind no free will; but the mind is determined in willing this or that by a cause which is determined in its turn by another cause, and this by another, and so on to infinity.

[3] Is there any alternative to necessity and chance? Is chance anything but a name for our ignorance of the cause? Does not everything therefore happen by necessity? Of what use, then, to talk of a man having a "free" will?

[4] If a creature is made by God, it must depend upon God and

receive all its power from Him; with which power the creature can do nothing contrary to the will of God, because God is almighty. If the creature is thus limited in his actions, being able to do only such things as God would have him do, and not being able to refuse doing what God would have done, then he can have no such thing as liberty, free will, or power to do or refrain an action.

[5] "Free will" can merely mean chance. If it is not that, its advocates are at least incapable of saying what else it is. Considered either theoretically or practically, "Free will" is a lingering chimera. Certainly no writer who respects himself can be called on any longer to treat it seriously, though it will continue to flourish in popular ethics. As soon as its meaning is apprehended, it loses all its plausibility. But the popular moralist will always exist by not knowing what he means.

[6] The prediction of human conduct is not less sure than the prediction of physical phenomena. . . . We might with equal appropriateness describe the stone as free to fall, the moon as free to deviate under solar disturbances. . . . Such phraseology would be unmeaning and absurd, but not a whit more so than in the application to the mental sequence of voluntary action.

[7] The character of a man is the result of the organization he received at birth, and all the various circumstances that have acted upon it since. The Doctrine of Necessity means that a man could in no case have acted differently from the manner in which he did act, supposing the state of his mind and the circumstances in which he was placed to be the same.

[8] The first dogma which I came to disbelieve was that of freewill. It seemed to me that motions of matter were determined by the laws of dynamics and could not therefore be influenced by the human will, even in the instance of matter forming part of a human body.

[9] Homo sapiens asserts freewill. The mechanist . . . denies this; and to me this assertion of freewill has always seemed unfounded and unintelligible. Man responds quite mechanically, and only so, to all such stimuli as he is prepared or constructed to. These stimuli are chemical or perhaps electro-physical call-bells.

[10] All our actions are determined by causes. There is no room for freewill. There cannot be any responsibility. . . . An individual

can no more shape his own character than a tree can shape its branches. When we act we believe we are free. This belief is an illusion.

[11] All human conduct reduces to different kinds of electron-proton groupings. The scientific study of personality assumes that the physico-chemical continuum is the sole existential datum.

Comment. These eleven passages present impressive testimony on behalf of determinism. It is perhaps better to call them testimony than evidence. They testify to the fact, never unimportant in philosophy, that the belief is widely and persistently held by persons who have given thought to the matter. They present or suggest defences which the friends of determinism would offer on behalf of their belief. Some distinctions can be pointed out:

(1) Sometimes the defence is theological: God, being omnipotent, all-powerful, produces all events; and therefore no individual can be said to produce any. If you assert the omnipotence of God, you cannot also assert free will in man: the two are incompatible. Some have cut this Gordian knot by denying the omnipotence of God.

(2) Sometimes the defence is that every event has a cause, that a cause necessitates its effect, and that therefore a human act, being an event, is the effect of some cause which necessitated it. If you say that actions are caused and therefore necessitated, you cannot also say that man has a free will: the two are incompatible. Some have cut this Gordian knot by denying that causes produce, in the sense of necessitate, their effects.

(3) Sometimes the defence is that there is no free will in nature, that man is a part of nature, and that therefore there is no free will in man. If you say that nature is closed to freedom, and that man is a part of nature, you cannot also say that man is *not* closed to freedom; the two statements are incompatible. Some have cut this Gordian knot by denying that man is a part of nature, by giving him a status outside of nature, therefore not subject to nature's necessity.

(4) Sometimes the defence is that everything happens ac-

cording to mechanical laws, that human action is no exception to this rule, and that therefore human action happens according to mechanical laws. If you say that laws "govern" everything, you cannot also say that laws do not "govern" human action. This defence is sometimes augmented by the argument that if an event does not happen according to mechanical laws, it must happen by chance. This is supposed to throw a scare into you, since you would not care to admit that anything happens by chance. Some have cut this Gordian knot by saying that laws do not "govern": they merely describe. This gets rid of the necessity because no process is under any necessity of agreeing with its description. Others have cut the knot by denying that mechanical law and chance constitute between them an exhaustive disjunction. If there are moral laws as well as natural laws, you have a third alternative here. If, furthermore, chance is not the opposite of law but of intention, then the proposed disjunction between law and chance is misleading.

(5) Sometimes the defence is that an entity should not be claimed unless its existence and operation can be verified by sense experience; that no such verification of free will is possible; that, therefore, its existence and operation should not be claimed. You cannot see, taste, hear, smell, touch, weigh, measure, or photograph free will. What sense qualities do "free wills" have? Through which sense organs do you perceive them? This defence is sometimes augmented by the further claim that if you cannot thus verify the existence and operation of the referent of a term, then that term is meaningless. This is a more drastic claim. It is one thing to say that you should not claim free will unless you can verify your claim. It is more radical to say that your claim is meaningless unless you can verify it. Some have cut this Gordion knot by urging that determinism is not an hypothesis *in* science but a presupposition *of* science. A science does not verify its presuppositions. It makes them, and is thereby able to verify its hypotheses.

You will encounter these five lines of reasoning if you go among the friends of determinism and ask them to state their case. The defence will not stop at these five. If you asked them for a complete briefing you would get at least as many more. The point here is simply to indicate how many claims and counterclaims meet and cross in this question of man's free will. Before you are finished briefing yourself either pro or con, you will be working with such major distinctions as cause–effect, necessity–chance, hypothesis–presupposition, appearance–reality, description–prescription. When two views are contending for the right to say the last word about the human will the stakes are high. The commitments on both sides run wide and deep. If so acute a person as David Hume went out of his way to *dis*solve a problem, to demonstrate that it is a pseudo problem, it is safe to assume that there must be something *to* the problem. If such disparate persons as Kant and William James make common cause on behalf of a conviction, it is safe to assume that the conviction does not refer to trivial matters. If human nature is called upon to deny its freedom in the name of God and nature and science, you may be assured that its freedom is a pearl of great price.

How wide a net does this question cast? Does it catch the man who says, "I never criticize a person, myself or anyone else, for wrongdoing, so you cannot catch me with this free will–determinism question"? To catch a person who would evade our question in that way, we would have to disengage it from considerations of moral judgment, criticism, condemnation, punishment, and ask simply: "Do you ever presuppose that anyone could ever at any time have done other than he did do? Do you believe that all your beliefs and actions are the effects of causes which lie outside your control?" It is conceivable that a person might answer no to the first question and yes to the second. If he could stop the discussion at that point, he would evade our principal question; namely, "Is that presupposition true or false?" But it is difficult to see how he could stop the discussion at that point; and if he didn't, he would shortly find himself embroiled. We can say therefore that our question is one which almost no one can evade. It is almost universal in scope.

We have been considering the person who says, "I deny that anyone ever at any time could have done other than he did do," and adds, "I do so for the following reasons." Our claim is that he holds a theory about the human will, namely that it is not the locus of free will. Is this theory true or false? If it is false, how can that be shown? The lines of attack are two. There is the belief and its reasons. One line would be to inspect the reasons offered in support of the theory and to show that they need not or cannot be admitted, or that even if admitted they do not justify the theory in question. Again, there is the belief and its consequences. The second line of attack would be to inspect the consequences which follow if the theory is admitted, and to show of those consequences that they cannot be admitted, that they are too high a price to pay for the theory in question. Is determinism open to criticism along either of those two lines? Suppose you come at it by way of its consequences.

(1) If no one ever at any time could have done other than he did do, then we are under a peculiar illusion, what might be called the illusion of voluntariness. Often when we do something it seems to us that we could have done otherwise. "I did it voluntarily," we say. If determinism is true, we are mistaken: no act is ever voluntary, no matter how clearly it may seem to be so. Our sense that the act is voluntary is illusory. As Spinoza argued, if a stone hurled through the air were conscious, it would think it was moving of its own free will. Nietzsche pictures a man thrown in a wrestling match who should say that he was prostrate because he freely willed to be so. We would laugh at such a man. I, says Nietzsche, laugh at all men who say they do anything because they freely will to do so: the one who acts labors under the illusion of voluntariness. This illusion which a man has about his actions is in itself a mechanism which remains to be calculated. Even so resolute a person

as Fridtjof Nansen says, "In the moment when we act, we all of us believe that we are free. This idea is an illusion." If Nietzsche and Nansen are correct, an act may feel voluntary; but in fact it is not voluntary. Whether we accidentally fall off a ladder and land on a man's head or are pushed off or deliberately jump off because we intend to land on his head, in any case we could not have done otherwise. If we say that the situations *feel* different, that the one feels involuntary and the other feels voluntary, we are warned against inferring that they are different: both are "necessitated."

You can go further. Sometimes we say, "I couldn't help doing that. It was quite involuntary. At the moment I could not have done otherwise." Here you have the feeling of involuntariness. Now according to determinism you can say that this feeling of involuntariness is not illusory. If the feeling of involuntariness ever accompanies an act, then it tells us the truth about the act, and we are not under an illusion. If the feeling of voluntariness ever accompanies an act, then it does not tell us the truth about the act; it misleads us, and we are under an illusion. If determinism is true, we are saved from illusion if we trust the one feeling ("involuntariness") and distrust the other ("voluntariness"). That the two feelings are equally clear and strong is not relevant: determinism endorses the one but not the other.

To mitigate somewhat the paradoxical character of this outcome, determinism might say that voluntary acts do not *feel* like involuntary acts because our will is present in the one, but not in the other. Our will is expressed in our voluntary acts but not in our involuntary acts: this difference, it would say, explains why these two kinds of acts feel different. There is a difference and our feeling accurately reports it. The mitigation afforded by this, however, is apparent only: to concede the presence of our will in some acts and its absence from others leaves us where we were if you also insist that our will is not free, that we never could have willed other than what we did will.

The above considerations give rise to two questions. Are we

justified, aside from the demands of determinism, in believing that the sense of involuntariness is always veridical and the sense of voluntariness always illusory? If not, then we are called upon to hold this belief because determinism requires it, and for no other reason. This illusion of voluntariness is peculiar. Normally we are able to detect an illusion, to see that it *is* an illusion, because we are in a position to crack it, to dispel it. We discover that we have been under an illusion because we have been able to detect the illusion. If you are under the illusion that a tree stump is a policeman, there are ways of cracking the illusion. You would know that you had been under an illusion if you were able to dispel the illusion. But if the illusion that a tree stump was a policeman could not be detected, cracked, dispelled, how would you know that you were or had been under an illusion? Now, in the case of this illusion of voluntariness, how are we to crack it? I know of no way to sense directly the illusory character of the experience of voluntariness. Aside from the demands of determinism, how do we get to know that the experience of freedom is illusory? If by no other way, then we are called upon to believe that our experience of voluntariness is illusory because, and only because, determinism requires it.

(2) If no one ever could have done other than he did do, we are led to some questions centering in the notions of condemnation and punishment. Suppose one man wrongs another man. Under assignable circumstances we would condemn him for so doing, find him guilty, even punish him. Speaking of such treatment, we would say, "It was fair enough," "He had it coming to him," "It was merited," "He deserved it." We see justice in the idea that he be tried, condemned, punished. "There is no injustice in that," we say. You have here a number of related and humanly important notions: guilty, condemn, deserve, merit, punish, just, fair. Others could be added to the list. In using such language, in performing the acts to which they refer do we presuppose that the individual in question could have done other than he did do? It seems to me that the burden of proof

rests with the person who denies that we do; and it is difficult to see what he would use for evidence. Determinism of course does not deny that we do so presuppose; it merely claims that if we do, our presupposition is false, since no one ever can do anything other than he did do.

Friends of the theory might rally to its support by saying, "We condemn and punish, but in doing so we do not pre-suppose that the guilty person could have done otherwise. In-deed, we will go further; we presuppose that he could not have done otherwise." Or they might say, "We never condemn or punish, because we presuppose that no one ever can do other than he does do." These friends are paying the price which, in their judgment, determinism demands. The first condemn and punish, but do so without denying determinism. The second refrain from condemning and punishing because of what de-terminism affirms.

What about the rest of us? We condemn and punish, but on the assumption that the individual could have done other than he did do. We recognize the possibility of what is called "de-liberate wrongdoing," wrong acts which a man does but, as we say, "need not have done," that is, could have refrained from doing, could have done otherwise. We say that, under assig-able circumstances, there is no injustice in condemning and punishing for such acts. We further argue that one reason for denying any injustice is contained in the presupposition that the guilty person could have done other than he did do. We are therefore doubly at loggerheads with determinism. If we give in to it, we must then take either of two further steps. We must refrain from condemning and punishing, or we must admit that in doing these things we do not presuppose that the guilty person could have done other than he did do. To the degree that respect for determinism is the sole reason for making either of these concessions, then, in my opinion, the price comes too high.

(3) Suppose it is said that no one ever could do other than he did do, and we ask, "What reason is there for believing that

that statement is true?" Our question here invites the speaker to do some reasoning, to go through some reasoning processes, to consider some facts as premisses and show how you can reason from them to the conclusion that no one ever could do other than he did do. Now, what about these reasoning processes? Do they, too, fall under the ban of "could not have done otherwise?" When a man is reasoning, are we to understand that each step taken by his mind is as rigidly necessitated as the sequence of steps by which a stone rolls down a hill? Is a man reasoning no more "in charge" of what he is doing than, say, when he is falling through the air from a roof top? If he is "in charge" of acts performed with his mind (for instance, reasoning) but not "in charge" of acts performed with his body (for instance, striking someone over the head), then we seem to have a break in the rule about "could not have done otherwise." Is determinism prepared to acknowledge such an exception to itself? If so, why? If not, if a person is no more "in charge" in the one case than in the other, then is the reasoning trustworthy? Are we to say that a mental process is trustworthy simply because each stage is causally necessitated by what precedes it? If so, the processes of a sick or crazed or over-fatigued mind are as trustworthy as the processes of a healthy, alert, sensitized mind, since in both cases (the claim is) each stage is causally necessitated by what precedes it. But if the processes of a sane mind are no more trustworthy than the processes of an insane mind, why do we trust the man who reasons in support of the theory that no one ever could do other than he does do? His reasoning processes are no more binding than a series of hiccoughs. Does this amount to saying that you cannot give a reason for determinism which would *justify* a person in accepting it? If so, the theory is pricing itself out of the market. It explodes itself.

It has been remarked that a man is known by the dilemmas he keeps. Our present point could perhaps be used in illustration. Suppose a friend of determinism says, "The scientific point of view applied to human nature presupposes determinism in regard to human nature. If I give up determinism I must give up the idea of a science of human nature, give up the idea of making scientific judgments about human nature." That would be one half of the dilemma. The other half would be something to this effect: "The ethical point of view presupposes that freedom is a fact about human nature. If I give in to determinism, I must make no moral judgment about human nature." If this is a genuine dilemma, we must choose between making scientific judgments about human nature and making moral judgments about human nature. Having chosen, could we give any reason which would justify our choice? And could we give any reason which would justify us in calling it a "choice"?

QUESTIONS

1. An excellent essay by C.A. Campbell, "Is Freewill a Pseudo-Problem?" will be found in the journal *Mind* for 1951. Read it, paying particular attention to section 6.

2. W. E. Hocking's small book, *The Self: Its Body and Its Freedom,* contains an excellent chapter. Read it too.

3. Consider some action of your own. The question is raised whether you could or could not have done otherwise. Can you suggest any experiment which would enable you to settle that question?

4. Do you believe that all your beliefs and actions are determined by causes that lie outside your control?

5. We speak of abnormal psychology. How does it happen that we do not speak of abnormal physics? Has the answer to that question any bearing on the free will controversy?

6. It is said that "It takes a fact to raise a problem." What fact raises the free will problem?

2. WILLIAM JAMES ON FREE WILL

The friends of free will are interested in "Could have done otherwise" for two reasons: first, because they believe it is the truth about the human will; second, because they believe that it is a presupposition of moral judgments directed at human action. That is, when you criticize a person for wrongdoing you not only presuppose that he could have done other than he did do, you also believe that this presupposition is true. If you did not believe it true, it is not clear why you would make it. But the question remains, "Why do you believe it is true?" We are concerned in this section with an attempt to deal with this question, an attempt to bolster up the conviction that human nature is the locus of freedom, by the American psychologist William James.

William James is the author of a notable treatise, *The Principles of Psychology*, published in 1890. As a psychologist, he felt the pressure of this free will controversy. He knew that as a psychologist he was expected by many to deny free will. He nevertheless strongly affirmed it. Two convictions stand out as you read his book, namely, that man's will is both free and purposive. We are concerned with the "free" part, although, as the next section will suggest, the notions of free and purposive (in contrast to necessitated and mechanical) belong together. James was some ten years writing his book. During those years he published a number of papers in which separate points were worked out. One of these was his 1884 paper, "The Dilemma of Determinism." This paper, quotations from which are given below, contains a criticism of determinism and a defence of the belief in free will. It is worth its reading time. Aside from its warmth and color, it presents the point of view of a man who thought of himself as both a scientist and a moralist, and who did not hesitate, if the issue were so drawn, to find for the latter at the cost of the former. James says many things in the passages quoted from his paper, but among them is the point that if, as student of human nature, he must choose between making scientific judgments and moral judgments, he will choose the latter. His paper is intended to make this stand clear.

A common opinion prevails that the juice has ages ago been pressed out of the free-will controversy, and that no new champion can do more than warm up stale arguments which every one has heard. This is a radical mistake. I know of no subject less worn out, or in which inventive genius has a better chance of breaking open new ground.

My ambition limits itself to just one little point. If I can make two of the necessarily implied corollaries of determinism clearer to you than they have been made before, I shall have made it possible for you to decide for or against that doctrine with a better understanding of what you are about. And if you prefer not to decide at all, but to remain doubters, you will at least see more plainly what the subject of your hesitation is. I thus disclaim all pretension to prove to you that the freedom of the will is true. The most I hope is to induce some of you to follow my own example in assuming it true, and acting as if it were true.

The arguments I am about to urge all proceed on two suppositions: first, when we make theories about the world and discuss them with one another, we do so in order to attain a conception of things which shall give us subjective satisfaction; and, second, if there be two conceptions, and the one seems to us, on the whole, more rational than the other, we are entitled to suppose that the more rational one is the truer of the two.

If a certain formula for expressing the nature of the world violates my moral demand, I shall feel as free to throw it overboard, or at least to doubt it, as if it disappointed my demand for uniformity of sequence, for example; the one demand being, so far as I can see, quite as subjective and emotional as the other is. The principle of causality, for example, is a demand that the sequence of events shall some day manifest a deeper kind of belonging of one thing with another than the mere arbitrary juxtaposition which now phenomenally appears. It is as much an altar to an unknown god as the one that Saint Paul found at Athens. All our scientific and philosophic ideals are altars to unknown gods. Uniformity is as much so as is free will. If this be admitted, we can debate on even terms. But if any one pretends that while freedom and variety are, in the first instance, subjective demands, necessity and uniformity are something altogether different, I do not see how we can debate at all.

To begin, I suppose you acquainted with all the usual arguments on the subject. I cannot stop to take up the old proofs from causation, from statistics, from the certainty with which we can foretell one another's conduct, from the fixity of character, and all the rest.

But there are two *words* which usually encumber these classical arguments, and which we must immediately dispose of if we are to make any progress. One is the eulogistic word *freedom*, and the other is the opprobrious word *chance*. The word "chance" I wish to keep, but I wish to get rid of the word "freedom." Its eulogistic associations have so far overshadowed all the rest of its meaning that both parties claim the sole right to use it, and determinists today insist that they alone are freedom's champions. Old fashioned determinism was what we may call *hard* determinism. It did not shrink from such words as fatality, bondage of the will, necessitation, and the like. Nowadays, we have a *soft* determinism which abhors harsh words, and, repudiating fatality, necessity, and even predetermination, says that its real name is freedom; for freedom is only necessity understood, and bondage to the highest is identical with true freedom. Now, all this is a quagmire of evasion under which the real issue of fact has been entirely smothered. Freedom in all these senses presents simply no problem at all. But there *is* a problem, an issue of fact and not of words, an issue of the most momentous importance, and that is the question of determinism, about which we are to talk tonight. Fortunately, no ambiguities hang about this word or about its opposite, indeterminism. Both designate an outward way in which things may happen. Let us look at the difference between them and see for ourselves.

What does determinism profess? It professes that those parts of the universe already laid down absolutely appoint and decree what the other parts shall be. The future has no ambiguous possibilities hidden in its womb; the part we call the present is compatible with only one totality. Any other future complement than the one fixed from eternity is impossible.

Indeterminism, on the contrary, says that the parts have a certain amount of loose play on one another, so that the laying down of one of them does not necessarily determine what the others shall be. It admits that possibilities may be in excess of actualities, and that things not yet revealed to our knowledge may really in themselves be ambiguous. Of two alternative futures which we conceive, both may now be really possible; and the one becomes impossible only at the very moment when the other excludes it by becoming real itself. Indeterminism thus denies the world to be one unbending unit of fact. It says that there is a certain ultimate pluralism in it; and, so saying, it corroborates our ordinary unsophisticated view of things. To that view, actualities seem to float in a wider sea of possibilities from out of which they are chosen; and, *somewhere,* indeterminism says, such possibilities exist, and form a part of truth.

Determinism, on the contrary, says they exist *nowhere,* and that necessity on the one hand and impossibility on the other are the sole categories of the real. Possibilities that fail to get realized are, for determinism, pure illusions: they never were possibilities at all. There is nothing inchoate, it says, about this universe of ours, all that was or is or shall be actual in it having been from eternity virtually there. The cloud of alternatives our minds escort this mass of actuality withal is a cloud of sheer deceptions, to which "impossibilities" is the only name that rightfully belongs.

The issue, it will be seen, is a perfectly sharp one, which no eulogistic terminology can smear over or wipe out. The truth *must* lie with one side or the other, and its lying with one side makes the other false.

The question relates solely to the existence of possibilities, in the strict sense of the term, as things that may, but need not, be. Both sides admit that a volition, for instance, has occurred. The indeterminists say another volition might have occurred in its place: the determinists swear that nothing could possibly have occurred in its place.

The stronghold of the deterministic sentiment is the antipathy to the idea of chance. As soon as we begin to talk indeterminism to our friends, we find a number of them shaking their heads. This notion of alternative possibility, they say, this admission that any one of several things may come to pass, is, after all, only a roundabout name for chance, and chance is something the notion of which no sane mind can for an instant tolerate in the world.

I wish first of all to show you just what the notion that this is a deterministic world implies. The implications I call your attention to are all bound up with the fact that it is a world in which we constantly have to make what I shall, with your permission, call judgments of regret. Some regrets are pretty obstinate and hard to stifle—regrets for acts of wanton cruelty or treachery, for example, whether performed by others or by ourselves. Hardly any one can remain *entirely* optimistic after reading the confession of the murderer at Brockton the other day: how, to get rid of the wife whose continued existence bored him, he inveigled her into a desert spot, shot her four times, and then, as she lay on the ground and said to him, "You didn't do it on purpose, did you, dear?" replied, "No, I didn't do it on purpose," as he raised a rock and smashed her skull. Such an occurrence, with the mild sentence and self-satisfaction of the prisoner, is a field for a crop of regrets, which one need not take up in detail. We feel that, although a perfect mechanical fit to the rest of the universe, it is a bad moral fit, and that something else would really have been better in its place.

But for the deterministic philosophy the murder, the sentence, and the prisoner's optimism were all necessary from eternity; and nothing else for a moment had a ghost of a chance of being put into their place. To admit such a chance, the determinists tell us, would be to make a suicide of reason; so we must steel our hearts against the thought. And here our plot thickens, for we see the first of those difficult implications of determinism which it is my purpose to make you feel. If this Brockton murder was called for by the rest of the universe, if it had to come at its preappointed hour, and if nothing else would have been consistent with the sense of the whole, what are we to think of the universe? Are we stubbornly to stick to our judgment of regret, and say, though it *couldn't* be, yet it *would* have been a better universe with something different from this Brockton murder in it? That, of course, seems the natural and spontaneous thing for us to do; and yet it is nothing short of deliberately espousing a kind of pessimism. The judgment of regret calls the murder bad. Calling a thing bad means, if it mean anything at all, that the thing ought not to be, that something else ought to be in its stead. Determinism, in denying that anything else can be in its stead, virtually defines the universe as a place in which what ought to be is impossible—in other words, as an organism whose constitution is afflicted with an incurable taint, an irremediable flaw. The pessimism of a Schopenhauer says no more that this —that the murder is a symptom; and that it is a vicious symptom because it belongs to a vicious whole, which can express its nature no otherwise than by bringing forth just such a symptom as that at this particular spot. Regret for the murder must transform itself, if we are determinists and wise, into a larger regret. It is absurd to regret the murder alone. Other things being what they are, *it* could not be different. What we should regret is that whole frame of

things of which the murder is one member. I see no escape whatever from this pessimistic conclusion if, being determinists, our
judgment of regret is to be allowed to stand at all.

The only deterministic escape from pessimism is everywhere to
abandon the judgment of regret. That this can be done, history
shows to be not impossible. On every hand, in a small way, we find
that a certain amount of evil is a condition by which a higher form
of good is brought. There is nothing to prevent anybody from gen-
eralizing this view, and trusting that if we could but see things in
the largest of all ways, even such matters as this Brockton murder
would appear to be paid for by the uses that follow in their train.
An optimism *quand meme,* a systematic and infatuated optimism
like that ridiculed by Voltaire in his *Candide,* is one of the possible
ideal ways in which a man may train himself to look on life. Bereft
of dogmatic hardness and lit up with the expression of a tender and
pathetic hope, such an optimism has been the grace of some of the
most religious characters that ever lived. Even cruelty and treachery may be among the absolutely blessed fruits of time, and to
quarrel with any of their details may be blasphemy. The only real
blasphemy, in short, may be that pessimistic temper of the soul
which lets it give way to such things as regrets, remorse, and grief.
Thus, our deterministic pessimism may become a deterministic
optimism at the price of extinguishing our judgments of regret.

But does not this immediately bring us into a curious logical
predicament? Our determinism leads us to call our judgments of
regret wrong, because they are pessimistic in implying that what is
impossible yet ought to be. But how then about the judgments of
regret themselves? If they are wrong, other judgments, judgments
of approval presumably, ought to be in their place. But as they are
necessitated, nothing else *can* be in their place; and the universe is
just what it was before—namely, a place in which what ought to be
appears impossible. We have got one foot out of the pessimistic
bog, but the other one sinks all the deeper. We have rescued our
actions from the bonds of evil, but our judgments are now held fast.
When murders and treacheries cease to be sins, regrets are theoretic
absurdities and errors. Murder and treachery cannot be good without regret being bad: regret cannot be good without treachery and
murder being bad. Both, however, are supposed to have been foredoomed; so something must be fatally unreasonable, absurd, and

wrong in the world. It must be a place of which either sin or error forms a necessary part. From this dilemma there seems at first sight no escape. Are we then so soon to fall back into the pessimism from which we thought we had emerged? And is there no possible way by which we may, with good intellectual consciences, call the cruelties and the treacheries, the reluctances and the regrets, *all* good together?

Certainly there is such a way, and you are probably most of you ready to formulate it yourselves. The refuge from the quandary lies not far off. The necessary acts we erroneously regret may be good, and yet our error in so regretting them may be also good, on one simple condition; and that condition is this: The world must not be regarded as a machine whose final purpose is the making real of any outward good, but rather as a contrivance for deepening the theoretic consciousness of what goodness and evil in their intrinsic natures are. Not the doing either of good or of evil is what nature cares for, but the knowing of them. Life is one long eating of the fruit of the tree of *knowledge*. I am in the habit, in thinking to myself, of calling this point of view the *gnostical* point of view. But as this term may perhaps lead to some misunderstandings, I will use it as little as possible here, and speak rather of *subjectivism* and the *subjectivistic* point of view.

Subjectivism has three great branches—we may call them scientificism, sentimentalism, and sensualism, respectively. They all agree essentially about the universe, in deeming that what happens there is subsidiary to what we think or feel about it. Crime justifies its criminality by awakening our intelligence of that criminality, and eventually our remorses and regrets; and the error included in remorses and regrets, the error of supposing that the past could have been different, justifies itself by its use. Its use is to quicken our sense of *what* the irretrievably lost is. When we think of it as that which might have been ("the saddest words of tongue or pen"), the quality of its worth speaks to us with a wilder sweetness; and, conversely, the dissatisfaction wherewith we think of what seems to have driven it from its natural place gives us the severer pang.

We have thus clearly revealed to our view what may be called the dilemma of determinism, so far as determinism allows considerations of good and bad to mingle with those of cause and effect in deciding what sort of a universe this may rationally be held to be.

The dilemma of this determinism is one whose left horn is pessimism and whose right horn is subjectivism. In other words, if determinism is to escape pessimism, it must leave off looking at the goods and ills of life in a simple objective way, and regard them as materials, indifferent in themselves, for the production of consciousness, scientific and ethical, in us. To a reader who says he is satisfied with a pessimism, and has no objection to thinking the whole bad, I have no more to say: he makes fewer demands on the world than I, who, making them, wish to look a little further before I give up all hope of having them satisfied.

To escape pessimism is no easy task. If perfection be the principle, how comes there any imperfection here? If God be good, how come he to create—or, if he did not create, how comes he to permit —the devil? The evil facts must be explained as seeming: the devil must be whitewashed, the universe must be disinfected, if neither God's goodness nor his unity and power are to remain impugned. And of all the various ways of operating the disinfection, and making bad seem less bad, the way of subjectivism appears by far the best.

For, after all, is there not something rather absurd in our ordinary notion of external things being good or bad in themselves? But then the moral judgments seem the main thing, and the outward facts mere perishing instruments for their production. This is subjectivism.

The final purpose of our creation seems most plausibly to be the greatest possible enrichment of our ethical consciousness, through the intensest play of contrasts and the widest diversity of characters. This of course obliges some of us to be vessels of wrath, while it calls others to be vessels of honor. But the subjectivist point of view reduces all these outward distinctions to a common denominator. The wretch languishing in the felon's cell may be drinking draughts of the wine of truth that will never pass the lips of the so-called favorite of fortune. And the peculiar consciousness of each of them is an indispensable note in the great ethical concert which the centuries as they roll are grinding out of the living heart of man.

So much for subjectivism! If the dilemma of determinism be to choose between it and pessimism, I see little room for hesitation from the strictly theoretical point of view. Subjectivism seems the more rational scheme. And the world may, possibly, for aught I know, be nothing else. When the healthy love of life is on one, and all its forms and its appetites seem so unutterably real; when the most brutal and the most spiritual things are lit by the same sun, and each is an integral part of the total richness—why, then it seems a grudging and sickly way of meeting so robust a universe to shrink from any of its facts and wish them not to be. Rather take the strictly dramatic point of view, and treat the whole thing as a great unending romance which the spirit of the universe, striving to realize its own content, is eternally thinking out and representing to itself.

No one, I hope, will accuse me, after I have said all this, of underrating the reasons in favor of subjectivism. And now that I proceed to say why those reasons, strong as they are, fail to convince my own mind, I trust the presumption may be that my objections are stronger still.

I frankly confess that they are of a practical order. If we practically take up subjectivism in a sincere and radical manner and follow its consequences, we meet with some that make us pause. Let a subjectivism begin in never so severe and intellectual a way, it is forced by the law of its nature to develop another side of itself and end with the corruptest curiosity. Once dismiss the notion that certain duties are good in themselves, and that we are here to do them, no matter how we feel about them; once consecrate the opposite notion that our performances and our violations of duty are for a common purpose, the attainment of subjective knowledge and feeling, and that the deepening of these is the chief end of our lives—and at what point on the downward slope are we to stop? In theology, subjectivism develops as its "left wing" antinomianism. In literature, its left wing is romanticism. And in practical life it is either a nerveless sentimentality or a sensualism without bounds.

Everywhere it fosters the fatalistic mood of mind. It makes those who are already too inert more passive still; it renders wholly reckless those whose energy is already in excess. All through history we find how subjectivism, as soon as it has a free career, exhausts itself in every sort of spiritual, moral, and practical license. Its optimism turns to an ethical indifference, which infallibly brings dissolution in its train. I have heard a graduate of this very school express in the pulpit his willingness to sin like David, if only he might repent like David. You may tell me he was only sowing his wild or rather his tame, oats; and perhaps he was. But the point is that in the subjectivistic or gnostical philosophy oat-sowing, wild or tame, becomes a systematic necessity and the chief function of life. After the pure and classic truths, the exciting and rancid ones must be experienced; and if the stupid virtues of the philistine herd do not then come in and save society from the influence of the children of light, a sort of inward putrefaction becomes its inevitable doom.

The only escape is by the practical way. But this means a complete rupture with the subjectivist philosophy of things. It says conduct, and not sensibility, is the ultimate fact for our recognition. But this brings us back, to the question of indeterminism and to the conclusion of all I came here to say tonight. For the only consistent way of representing a world whose parts may affect one another through their conduct being either good or bad is the indeterministic way. What interest, zest, or excitement can there be in achieving the right way, unless we are enabled to feel that the wrong way is also a possible and a natural way—nay, more, a menacing and an imminent way? And what sense can there be in condemning ourselves for taking the wrong way, unless we need have done nothing of the sort, unless the right way was open to us as well? I cannot understand the willingness to act, no matter how we feel, without the belief that acts are really good and bad. I cannot understand the belief that an act is bad, without regret at its happening. I cannot understand regret without the admission of real, genuine possibilities in the world. Only *then* is it other than a mockery to feel, after we have failed to do our best, that an irreparable opportunity is gone from the universe, the loss of which it must forever after mourn.

If you insist that this is all superstition, that possibility is in the eye of science and reason impossibility, and that if I act badly 'tis that the universe was foredoomed to suffer this defect, you fall right back into the dilemma, the labyrinth, of pessimism and subjectivism, from out of whose toils we have just wound our way.

Now, we are of course free to fall back, if we please. For my own part, though, whatever difficulties may beset the philosophy of objective right and wrong, and the indeterminism it seems to imply, determinism, with its alternative of pessimism or romanticism, contains difficulties that are greater still. But you will remember that I expressly repudiated awhile ago the pretension to offer any arguments which could be coercive in a so-called scientific fashion in this matter. And I consequently find myself, at the end of this long talk, obliged to state my conclusions in an altogether personal way. This personal method of appeal seems to be among the very conditions of the problem; and the most any one can do is to confess as candidly as he can the grounds for the faith that is in him, and leave his example to work on others as it may.

Let me, then, without circumlocution say just this. The world is enigmatical enough in all conscience, whatever theory we may take up toward it. The indeterminism I defend, the free-will theory of popular sense based on the judgment of regret, represents that world as vulnerable, and liable to be injured by certain of its parts if they act wrong. And it represents their acting wrong as a matter of possibility or accident, neither inevitable nor yet to be infallibly warded off. In all this, it is a theory devoid either of transparency or of stability. It gives us a pluralistic, restless universe, in which no single point of view can ever take in the whole scene; and to a mind possessed of the love of unity at any cost, it will, no doubt, remain forever inacceptable. A friend with such a mind once told me that the thought of my universe made him sick, like the sight of the horrible motion of a mass of maggots in their carrion bed.

But while I freely admit that the pluralism and the restlessness are repugnant and irrational in a certain way, I find that every alternative to them is irrational in a deeper way. The indeterminism with its maggots, if you please to speak so about it, offends only the native absolutism of my intellect—an absolutism which, after all, perhaps, deserves to be snubbed and kept in check. But the determinism with its necessary carrion, to continue the figure of speech, and with no possible maggots to eat the latter up, violates my sense of moral reality through and through. When, for example, I imagine such carrion as the Brockton murder, I cannot conceive it as an act by which the universe, as a whole, logically and necessarily expresses its nature without shrinking from complicity with such a whole. And I deliberately refuse to keep on terms of loyalty with the universe by saying blankly that the murder, since it does flow from the nature of the whole, is not carrion. There are *some* instinctive reactions which I, for one, will not tamper with. The only remaining alternative, the attitude of gnostical romanticism, wrenches my personal instincts in quite as violent a way. It falsifies the simple objectivity of their deliverance. It makes the goose-flesh the murder excites in me a sufficient reason for the perpetration of the crime. It transforms life from a tragic reality into an insincere melo-dramatic exhibition, as foul or as tawdry as any one's diseased curi-osity pleases to carry it out. It leaves me in presence of a sort of subjective carrion considerably more noisome than the objective carrion I called it in to take away. No! better a thousand times, than such systematic corruption of our moral sanity, the plainest pessi-mism, so that it be straightforward; but better far than that the world of chance. Make as great an uproar about chance as you please, I know that chance means pluralism and nothing more. If some of the members of the pluralism are bad, the philosophy of pluralism, whatever broad views it may deny me, permits me, at least, to turn to the other members with a clean breast of affection and an un-sophisticated moral sense. It lets me feel that a world with a *chance* in it of being altogether good, even if the chance never come to pass, is better than a world with no such chance at all. That "chance" whose very notion I am exhorted and conjured to banish from my view of the future as the suicide of reason concerning it, that "chance" is—what? Just this—the chance that in moral respects the future may be other and better than the past has been. This is the only chance we have any motive for supposing to exist. Shame, rather, on its repudiation and its denial! For its presence is the vital air which lets the world live, the salt which keeps it sweet.

And here I might legitimately stop, having expressed all I care to see admitted by others tonight. But I know that if I do stop here, misapprehensions will remain in the minds of some of you, and keep all I have said from having its effect; so I judge it best to add a few more words.

In the first place, in spite of all my explanations, the word "chance" will still be giving trouble. Though you may yourselves be adverse to the deterministic doctrine, you wish a pleasanter word than "chance" to name the opposite doctrine by; and you very likely con-sider my preference for such a word a perverse sort of a partiality on my part. It certainly *is* a bad word to make converts with; and you wish I had not thrust it so butt-foremost at you—you wish to use a milder term.

Well, I admit there may be just a dash of perversity in its choice. The spectacle of the mere word-grabbing game has perhaps driven me too violently the other way; and, rather than be found wrangling for the good words, I am willing to take the first bad one which comes along, provided it be unequivocal. The question is of things, not of eulogistic names for them; and the best word is the one that enables men to know the quickest whether they disagree or not about the things. But the word "chance," with its singular negativity, is just the word for this purpose. Whoever uses it instead of "freedom," squarely and resolutely gives up all pretence to control the things he says are free. For *him,* he confesses that they are no better than mere chance would be. It is a word of *impotence,* and is therefore the only sincere word we can use, if, in granting freedom to certain things, we grant it honestly, and really risk the game. Any other word permits of quibbling, and lets us make a pretence of restoring the caged bird to liberty with one hand, while with the other we anxiously tie a string to its leg to make sure it does not get beyond our sight.

But now you will bring up your final doubt. Does not the admission of such an unguaranteed chance or freedom preclude utterly the notion of a Providence governing the world? Does it not leave the fate of the universe at the mercy of the chance-possibilities, and so far insecure? Does it not, in short, deny the craving of our nature for an ultimate peace behind all tempests, for a blue zenith above all clouds?

To this my answer must be very brief. The belief in free will is not in the least incompatible with the belief in Providence, provided you do not restrict the Providence to fulminating nothing but *fatal* decrees. If you allow him to provide possibilities as well as actualities to the universe, and to carry on his own thinking in those two categories just as we do ours, chances may be there, uncontrolled even by him, and the course of the universe be really ambiguous.

The creator's plan of the universe would thus be left blank as to many of its actual details, but all possibilities would be marked down. The realization of some of these would be left absolutely to chance; that is, would only be determined when the moment of realization came. Other possibilities would be *contingently* determined; that is, their decision would have to wait till it was seen how the matters of absolute chance fell out. So the creator himself would not need to know *all* the details of actuality until they came; and at any time his own view of the world would be a view partly of facts and partly of possibilities, exactly as ours is now.

Now, it is entirely immaterial, in this scheme, whether the creator leave the absolute chance-possibilities to be decided by himself, each when its proper moment arrives, or whether, on the contrary, he alienate this power from himself, and leave the decision out and out to finite creatures such as we men are. The great point is that the possibilities are really *here*. Whether it be we who solve them, or he working through us, at those soul-trying moments when fate's scales seem to quiver, and good snatches the victory from evil or shrinks nerveless from the fight, is of small account, so long as we admit that the issue is decided nowhere else than *here* and *now*. *That* is what gives the palpitating reality to our moral life and makes it tingle, as Mr. Mallock says, with so strange and elaborate an excitement. This reality, this excitement, are what the determinisms suppress by their denial that *anything* is decided here and now, and their dogma that all things were foredoomed and settled long ago. If it be so, may you and I then have been foredoomed to the error of continuing to believe in liberty. It is fortunate for the winding up of controversy that in every discussion with determinism this *argumentum ad hominem* can be its adversary's last word.

"The Dilemma of Determinism," from which the above defence of belief in free will is taken, was published in 1884. Six years later (1890) James published *The Principles of Psychology*. This book embodies one of the great attempts to have Homo sapiens sit for his portrait. It contains interesting and valuable chapters on various aspects of the conscious life of rational animals; among these is the chapter on the Will. Here James touches again on the free will. His remarks are briefer than in the 1884 essay, but the point is repeated that belief in free will is a postulate of moral judgment, and that if this be in contradiction to the postulate of scientific judgment, one must make his choice. This way of putting the matter gives it a certain edge, but it obscures the even more important fact that freedom is a postulate of judgment, whether moral or scientific. The mind which judges the truth of an hypothesis in science is no less the locus of freedom than the mind which judges the rightness of an act.

The question of fact in the free-will controversy is extremely simple. It relates solely to the amount of effort of attention or consent which we can at any time put forth. Are the duration and intensity of this effort fixed functions of the object, or are they not? Now it *seems* as if the effort were an independent variable, as if we might exert more or less of it in any given case.

If it be really indeterminate, our future acts are ambiguous or unpredestinate: in common parlance, *our wills are free.* If the amount of effort be not indeterminate, but be related in a fixed manner to the objects themselves, in such wise that whatever object at any time fills our consciousness was from eternity bound to fill it then and there, and compel from us the exact effort, neither more nor less, which we bestow upon it,—then our wills are not free, and all our acts are foreordained.

When a man has let his thoughts go for days and weeks until at last they culminate in some particularly dirty or cowardly or cruel act, it is hard to persuade him, in the midst of his remorse, that he might not have reined them in; hard to make him believe that this whole goodly universe (which his act so jars upon) required and exacted it of him at that fatal moment, and from eternity made aught else impossible.

My own belief is that the question of free-will is insoluble on strictly psychologic grounds. After a certain amount of effort of attention has been given to an idea, it is manifestly impossible to tell whether either more or less of it *might* have been given or not. To tell that, we should have to ascend to the antecedents of the effort, and defining them with mathematical exactitude, prove, by laws of which we have not at present even an inkling, that the only amount of sequent effort which could *possibly* comport with them was the precise amount which actually came.

The most that any argument can do for determinism is to make it a clear and seductive conception, which a man is foolish not to espouse, so long as he stands by the great scientific postulate that the world must be one unbroken fact, and that prediction of all things without exception must be ideally, even if not actually, possible. It is a *moral* postulate about the Universe, the postulate that *what ought to be can be, and that bad acts cannot be fated, but that good ones must be possible in their place,* which would lead one to espouse the contrary view. But when scientific and moral postulates war thus with each other and objective proof is not to be had, the only course is voluntary choice, for scepticism itself, is systematic, is also voluntary choice. The utmost that a believer in free-will can *ever* do will be to show that the deterministic arguments are not coercive. That they are seductive, I am the last to deny; nor do I deny that effort may be needed to keep the faith in freedom, when they press upon it, upright in the mind.

Genuine determinism affirms not the *impotence* but the *unthinkability* of free-will is what it affirms. It admits something phenomenal *called* free effort, which *seems* to breast the tide, but it claims this as a *portion of the tide*. The variations of the effort cannot be independent, it says; they cannot orginate *ex nihilo,* or come from a fourth dimension; they are mathematically fixed functions of the ideas themselves, which are the tide.

But what, quite as much as the inconceivability of absolutely independent variables, persuades modern men of science that their efforts must be predetermined, is the continuity of the latter with other phenomena whose predetermination no one doubts. Decisions with effort merge so gradually into those without it that it is not easy to say where the limit lies. Decisions without effort merge again into ideo-motor, and these into reflex acts; so that the temptation is almost irresistible to throw the formula which covers so many cases over absolutely all. Where there is effort just as where there is none, the ideas themselves which furnish the matter of deliberation are brought before the mind by the machinery of association. And this machinery is essentially a system of arcs and paths, a reflex system, whether effort be amongst its incidents or not. The reflex way is, after all, the universal way of conceiving the business.

I do not see how anyone can fail to recognize the fascinating simplicity of some such view as this. Nor do I see why *for scientific purposes* one need give it up; science, however, must be constantly reminded that her purposes are not the only purposes, and that the order of uniform causation which she has use for, and is therefore right in postulating, may be enveloped in a wider order, on which she has no claims at all.

Not only our morality but our religion, so far as the latter is deliberate, depend on the effort which we can make. *"Will you or won't you have it so?"* is the most probing question we are ever asked; we are asked it every hour of the day, and about the largest as well as the smallest, the most theoretical as well as the most practical, things. We answer by *consents or non-consents* and not by words. What wonder that these dumb responses should seem our deepest organs of communication with the nature of things! What wonder if the effort demanded by them be the measure of our worth as men! What wonder if the amount which we accord of it be the one strictly underived and original contribution which we make to the world!

Following the 1890 *Principles of Psychology,* James published *Talks to Teachers on Psychology* in 1899. He touched once more on free will, as follows:

If you are asked, *"In what does a moral act consist* when reduced to its elementary form?" you can make only one reply. You can say that *it consists in the effort of attention by which we hold fast to an idea* which but for that effort of attention would be driven out of the mind by the other psychological tendencies that are there.

The duration and amount of this attention *seem* within certain limits indeterminate. We *feel* as if we could make it really more or less, and as if our free action in this regard were a genuine critical point in nature,—a point on which our destiny and that of others might hinge. The whole question of free will concentrates itself, then, at this same small point: "Is or is not the appearance of indetermination at this point an illusion?"

The free-willist believes the appearance to be a reality: the determinist believes that it is an illusion. I myself hold with the free-willists,—not because I cannot conceive the fatalist theory clearly, or because I fail to understand its plausibility, but simply because if free will *were* true, it would be absurd to have the belief in it fatally forced on our acceptance. Considering the inner fitness of things, one would rather think that the very first act of a will endowed with freedom should be to sustain the belief in the freedom itself. I accordingly believe freely in my freedom.[2]

---

[2] From William James, *Talks to Teachers on Psychology,* reprinted by permission of Henry Holt and Company.

QUESTIONS

1. James published an essay "Are We Automata?" in the journal *Mind* for 1879. Changed somewhat, this essay became Chapter 5 of his 1890 *Principles of Psychology*. The essay of 1879 was written with one eye on T. S. Huxley's 1874 paper, "On the Hypothesis That All Animals Are Automata." There is good reading in each of these.

2. How does James get determinism committed to pessimism? Why does he want to do that. If determinism does not object to that, then what?

3. How does he get determinism switched from pessimism to optimism? Having done that, what difficulty does he raise for it?

4. He then offers determinism a third alternative to either pessimism or optimism. Name it. Formulate it. Why would he not commit himself to this third alternative?

5. What does he mean by pluralism and chance? Why do they go together?

6. Why does the question of God come up? How does he deal with it?

7. James calls his paper "The Dilemma of Determinism." What is his point here? Formulate the dilemma in question.

8. Make clear why James does or does not satisfy you in this paper.

3. CRITICAL VS. MECHANICAL

The principle of morality and the freedom of the will are two of the most important matters to be dealt with by a moral philosophy. The one refers to the nature of rightness, the other to the nature of the will which embodies that rightness. Considered as questions, the first asks what fact common to all cases of right action is the reason for calling them cases of right action; the second asks whether criticism of a person for wrongdoing presupposes that he could have done otherwise. The attempt to answer these questions has led to much heated and complicated controversy. For the most part moralists have agreed that there is a principle of morality and that men are free in choosing between right and wrong. But this agreement is by no means universal. As we have seen, one important modern moralist (Nietzsche) enters an emphatic denial on both counts, and he is by no means alone in taking this stand. It is difficult to say that one of these questions is more fundamental than the other. If there is no distinction between right and wrong, why bother to ask whether a person who has done wrong could have done right? And similarly, if a person does not freely choose in doing right or doing wrong, why bother to inquire into the principle upon which this distinction rests?

I propose to conclude this chapter on free will by offering some comments on the denial which seems to me to have the greatest strength and to be the most widely held. It is the denial which rests on the argument that man is a part of nature, that there is no free will in nature, and that therefore there can be no free will in man. This argument denies any final distinction, any ultimate dualism between nature and human nature, between the natural and the human, between "matter" and "mind." I wish to challenge that denial. It is clear of course that making the challenge stick is not equivalent to proving the reality of free will in man. From the fact that there is a dualism between nature and human nature, it does not follow that human nature is the locus of freedom. But one argument against man's freedom will have been met—the argument, namely, that if man is a part of nature and nature has no free will then man can have none either.

My argument for a dualism between nature and human nature asks you to distinguish two types of processes. The first type is illustrated by the process going on in the mind of an astronomer when he is astronomizing about the solar system. The second type is illustrated by the process going on in the solar system about which he is astronomizing. It is not easy to suggest words which in their ordinary usage clearly express this distinction. I propose that we call the first type of process critical and the second mechanical. We can put the matter in the form of questions: Does a critical process differ from a mechanical process? If so, in what ways? When one says that there is no free will in nature, does one mean that all processes in nature are mechanical in the sense set forth below? If so, then either critical processes are mechanical processes, or there is a dualism one term of which falls "outside of nature." Now, my point would be that critical processes are not mechanical processes. Using the two processes mentioned above as examples, I would draw attention to some differences.

The categories needed to describe the first process do not apply to the other process. The properties so described are essential to the first process, whereas they do not occur in the other. You could not characterize the first process unless you made use of the categories I shall suggest; whereas, unless you spoke in metaphor, you could not use these categories to characterize the other process.

(1) The process in the astronomer's mind is purposive. We would need the concept of "purposiveness" to give an account of it. Purpose is what you refer to in one of three uses of the interrogative word "why." You can ask "Why?" meaning "What cause?" as in the question, "Why does steam come out of the kettle spout?" Or you can ask "Why?" meaning "What purpose?" as in the question "Why did you light the gas under the kettle?" Or you can ask "Why?" meaning "What reason?" as in the question "Why do you expect the water to heat if you light the gas under the kettle?" We can ask "Why?" in the second of these senses when we are considering the astronomer's mind. We can ask him why he is investigating the solar system, meaning what purpose does he have in mind. He might answer, "Because I want to find out what laws 'govern' the motion of the planets around the sun. My purpose is to get to know." If he said he had no purpose, we would be somewhat puzzled; whereas we would be puzzled in a different way if he said that he was trying to discover what purpose the *planets* had in going around the sun.

(2) The process in the astronomer's mind is fallible. We would need the concept of "fallibility" to give an account of it. A process is fallible when it can be the locus of error. Fallibility

implies purposiveness. If your purpose is to acquire knowledge, and if also you can fail in this, then you are fallible. Your fallibility would be evidenced if you wound up in either ignorance or error. Either outcome would constitute a failure, provided your purpose had been to acquire knowledge. If the astronomer denied that the process in his mind was fallible, we would be puzzled. Perhaps we could "bring him to his senses," if we asked him whether he included all other astronomers in his denial. On the other hand, if the astronomer complained of the fallibility of the process in the solar system, we would be puzzled in a different way. For him to say that the solar system is fallible would be evidence that he was fallible. This is not to say that the solar system is infallible. It is neither fallible nor infallible. It is neutral to that distinction.

(3) The process in the astronomer's mind can be criticized. It is criticizable. We would need the concept of criticism to give an account of it. To "criticize" is, in one of its meanings, to point out the need for revision. A process which is fallible can become the proper object of criticism. It can become the locus of a condition which needs revision. If the astronomer were to deny that the process in his mind could be criticized, we would be somewhat puzzled. We would suspect him of either excessive pride or excessive humility. On the other hand, if he said that the process in the solar system was the locus of criticism, we would be puzzled in a different way. If he criticized the solar system on the grounds that it made mistakes or if he imagined that the solar system ever criticized him on the grounds that he made mistakes, we would tell him to stop "personifying" the solar system. In using the word "personify" we would indicate that we considered the process in his mind to be different, in important respects, from the process in the solar system.

(4) The process in the astronomer's mind is corrigible. We cannot say that of the process in the solar system. The solar system may indeed be the locus of change, but such change would not be revision. Some changes that occur in the astrono-

mer's mind are, however, instances of revision. For revision to occur a process must be purposive and fallible, and failure, in the sense of error, must have occurred and been detected. It makes sense to say that, if the ways of the solar system undergo change, the beliefs of the astronomer had better undergo revision; but it makes no sense to say that, if the astronomer's hypotheses change, the solar system had better revise its ways.

(5) If you are to give an account of the process in the astronomer's mind, you need the distinction between ends and means. In it, some things occur and function as ends, some as means. This distinction applies because the process is purposive. If the end is "to get to know," some things occur as means to this end. This distinction does not apply to the processes in the solar system. There, so far as we know, nothing occurs and functions as a means to any end. The earth does not turn on its axis as a means, for example, to the end that there be day and night.

(6) The process in the astronomer's mind is the locus of standards, criteria, ideals, principles, norms, rules. In the absence of standards, you could not detect error, and hence could not diagnose fallibility. In the absence of standards, you could not make an error, hence could not be the object of criticism or the locus of revision. Standards, such, for example, as you would find "pervading" the mind of an astronomer, are curious entities. You can ask many difficult questions about them. We speak of "regularities" permeating the processes in the solar system. The word is derived from "regula" meaning "rule." But it would be misleading to compare the "rules" in the solar system with the "rules" in the astronomer's mind. They are dissimilar. If the astronomer has the right "rules" and if he follows them judiciously, he will, in great probability, discover the regularities in the solar system.

(7) The process in the astronomer's mind is the locus of the distinction between the ideal and the actual. Suppose an erroneous hypothesis has taken shape in his mind. It is an actual hypothesis and it is actually there. To propose criticism and revision is to presuppose that much. But, ideally, that hypothesis

ought not to be there: If the astronomer had the right ideal and used it judiciously, it would not be there. This distinction between the actual and the ideal applies to all processes similar to those in the mind of an astronomer, but not to any processes similar to those in the solar system. It is reassuring for an astronomer to say that he is interested only in what is actually going on in the solar system. It would not be reassuring for him to say that he is interested only in what is actually going on in his mind: we want him to be concerned, upon occasion, with what ought to be going on in his mind, where "ought" means "required by the ideal which the actual has violated."

(8) The process in the astronomer's mind is reasoned. This is not to be confused with purposive. There are discriminable elements in that process which are related in an If-then or Since-therefore way. If you disentangle an hypothesis from the process going on in his mind and ask "Why?" in the sense of "For what reason?" you would expect to get an answer. A reason operates to justify. The process in the astronomer's mind is the locus of beliefs, and it makes sense to say that there are reasons for those beliefs and that the reasons justify them. When a process is purposive, it can also be reasoned: if, for example, a man's purpose is to acquire knowledge and he presents you with some of his acquisitions, you can ask him his reasons for accepting them as instances of knowledge. In this sense you might speak of man as a rational animal, an animal that deals in reasons. In a quite different sense the astronomer might speak of the solar system as a rational order. The sense in which the solar system is a rational order is quite different from the sense in which the astronomer is a rational animal: he deals in reason; it does not. For the process in his mind, you can demand justification; for the process in the solar system, you cannot. When you speak of the solar system as a "rational" order, you mean that a reasoning animal can investigate it and give reasons for the conclusions which he arrives at. We would be puzzled if the astronomer said that there were no reasons for the processes going on in his mind; and we would be puz-

zled in a different way if he said that there were reasons for what
went on in the solar system.

(9) The process in the astronomer's mind is the locus of possible alternatives between or among which a choice must be
made. It may be this in several ways, but it is most clearly this
in the case where the astronomer finds himself confronted with
rival hypotheses. Here he is confronted with possible alternatives. He must choose between or among them. He must then
proceed to justify, find reasons for his choice. If he is unable to
do this, he begins to suspect that he chose mistakenly. If the
astronomer denied that possible alternatives ever occur in, or,
as we say, "to," his mind, he would mark himself down as an
unimaginative fellow. If he denied that he ever chose between
or among such alternatives, we would, I think, be entitled to
ask him," Why don't you?" It is not clear what he could use for
an answer. If he denied that he ever chose the wrong alternative, relinquished it, and tried another, we would suspect him
of being either unusually astute or unusually pigheaded. If he
denied that, having chosen, he ever set himself to justify his
choice, we would, I think, write him off as lacking in self-
knowledge. What else is an astronomer for, it might be asked,
if not to find reasons for chosen hypotheses about the solar system? We need the related notions of "possible alternatives"
and "choice among them" to give an account of the process in
the mind of the astronomer, whereas we do not need these notions to give an account of the solar system. The process in the
solar system is not the locus of possible alternatives or of any
choosing on its part between or among such possible alternatives. The lady in Tennyson's poem whispers that the stars run
blindly. This would seem to be a metaphorical way of stating
that they are not confronted with possible alternatives between
or among which they choose. Tennyson's lady may be right
about the stars; but, if she said it about the process in the mind
of the astronomer, we would accuse her of ignorance or obscurantism.

(10) The process in the astronomer's mind is the locus of

responsibility. To say that the astronomer is "responsible" for what he does is to say, literally, that he is able to "answer for" what he does. When he cannot do this, we say that his thinking is irresponsible. That is a damaging criticism. We think that a mind ought to be able to answer for what goes on in it. That is a primary demand. We would be puzzled by the astronomer who denied any responsibility for what went on in his mind. We would be equally puzzled, but in another way, by the astronomer who affirmed that the solar system was, in a similar sense, responsible for what goes on in it. The solar system is neither responsible nor irresponsible. It is neutral to that distinction.

(11) The process in the astronomer's mind is the locus of presuppositions. They are present in any mind intent upon knowing. If an astronomer denied that there were any presuppositions, we would describe him as naive, lacking in self-knowledge. We would say to him "*Nosce te ipsum,*" and expect him to take the hint. It makes sense to say of an astronomer's generalizations that they presuppose the principle of induction, the principle of parsimony, the principle of limited independent variety and so on. It makes no sense to say that processes in the solar system have presuppositions. The solar system has no presuppositions. It has none for the reason that it makes none.

(12) The process in the astronomer's mind is the locus of meaning. There is an ambiguity here: in one sense you can say that the solar system is the locus of meaning, as, for example, in the statement, "That cloud means rain." But I am referring to meaning as you have it in such statements as "He means what he says," "His meaning was clear by the time he finished speaking," "It is meaningless to say that the square root of minus one is round and green," "If you mean that Caesar was not assassinated, you are mistaken." In the sense in which the word, or its derivatives, is used in those statements, you can say that the astronomer's mind is the locus of meaning. We would be scandalized by an astronomer who denied that what went on in his mind had, in that sense, any meaning. We would be equally scan-

dalized if he affirmed that what went on in the solar system had, in that same sense, any meaning.

(13) The process in the astronomer's mind is educable, can be educated. This fact is related to but not identical with the fact that it is purposive, fallible, criticizable, corrigible, pervaded by standards, reasoned, responsible, meaningful. To say that it can be educated is not the same thing as to say that it can be conditioned. The "response" of a mind that has been educated is not the same thing as the "reaction" of a mind that has been conditioned. I do not propose here to inquire into the difficulties and delicacies that mark the attempt to educate. My point is merely that you can educate the astronomer but you cannot educate the solar system. It is conceivable that you could modify the behavior of the solar system, provided you had access to sufficient physical power. It is not clear what would be meant by educating or re-educating the solar system.

(14) I come now to a point which it is impossible to state, given only one astronomer and the solar system. It requires at least two astronomers and the solar system. The minds of the astronomers are the locus of community. Between them there is an I-Thou relation. You can say of this notion of community what Saint Augustine said of time: you know what it is until some one asks you about it. It is not enough to say that the astronomer's minds have something in common. The question is, What do they have in common, by virtue of which they are the locus of community? I do not know any clear and simple answer. I have mentioned the I-Thou relation, but if you understand that, you understand community. It is, I believe, the function of standards to disclose an area of community. I know that when community is there you can, as we say, communicate; and that when it is not there you cannot. Community is a presupposition of communication. One astronomer can "commune" with another astronomer, but he cannot "commune" with the solar system; between him and it there is no I-Thou relation. No planet in the solar system can "commune" with any other planet, because, while they have things in common, they are

not the required things. Whatever these required things are, you can say that astronomers have them in common, that astronomers and planets do not have them in common, and that planets and planets do not have them in common. If an astronomer denied this fact of community between himself and others, it is difficult to see how or why he would try to convince us of the tenability of his denial. On the other hand, if he affirmed this fact of community between himself and the solar system, we would, as earlier, tell him to stop "personifying" the solar system; and the word would indicate that we considered the process in his mind to be different in important respects from the process in the solar system.

(15) I have mentioned a number of features which characterize the processes in the astronomer's mind and distinguish it from the process in the solar system. I want to add a last item which applies to all these others, they are "subjective," meaning that they occur in or characterize a "subject," in this case the astronomer. This does not mean that they are either idiosyncratic or inaccessible or "merely a matter of opinion," but that they characterize subjects. This is a term which you would never apply to the solar system nor to any property of the solar system. There is nothing subjective about the process in the solar system. To encounter the subjective you must go among subjects, not among objects.

I have mentioned ways in which the process in the mind of an astronomer differs from the process in the solar system. It also differs in those ways from the processes in his brain and nervous system. These are not the only differences. They may not be the most important differences; but they are differences. None of these features which characterize the one process characterize the other process. I have proposed that we call the one process "critical" and the other "mechanical." I can then say that a critical process differs from a mechanical process in at least those ways. In what remains I propose to speak in general about critical processes and mechanical processes, confining myself to four remarks.

(1) To begin with, cognizing (the knowing activity) is not the only instance of a critical process. The features which mark the process in the mind of the astronomer mark, *mutatis mutandis,* the process going on in the mind of a poet endeavoring to express or objectify an emotion within the limits imposed by rhyme, rhythm, conventional linguistic usage, and so forth. His relation to his feeling is not the same as the astronomer's relation to the solar system, but the process in his mind is characterized by the same features that you find in the process in the astronomer's mind. You can say of the process in the poet's mind that it is purposive, fallible, criticizable, corrigible, educable, and reasoned; that it is the locus of standards, alternatives, responsibility, the ideal and the actual, presuppositions, meanings, and community. It is not his feeling but his effort to express his feeling which is the locus of those features. The same can be said of the processes in the minds of practitioners of the other arts. The same features are present in the process in the mind of a man who knows what duty requires and is endeavoring to detect its presence in a specific situation and embody those requirements in his actions. Other examples could be added. The point is merely that the effort to acquire knowledge, the the cognition drive, is not the only instance of critical processes. These three instances (astronomer, poet, good man) differ interestingly and importantly among themselves, but they have features in common by virtue of which all are critical, and these they do not share with any mechanical process whatever.

(2) The critical process in the astronomer's mind is related to two mechanical processes: one in the solar system and one in his brain and nervous system. Its relations to these two mechanical processes is not the same. Its relation to the processes in the solar system could be called the cognition relation. Its relation to the process in his brain and nervous system could not be called the cognition relation. *Qua* astronomer he is not cognizing the process in his brain and nervous system. The distinction between the critical process in his mind and the mechanical process in his brain and nervous system enables you to

pose a nice speculative question: what is the relation between them? No answer is suggested here. To leave the question unanswered, however, is not to repudiate the distinction which enabled you to raise it.

(3) Critical processes are rule-guided. I am not sure whether "rule-guided" means the same as "goal-guided." I incline to think that the two ideas are not the same but are closely related. In any case, the notion of rule-guided leads to the distinction between a critical rule and a descriptive rule. We are perhaps most familiar with the notion of critical rules as they function in the mind's attempts to acquire knowledge of the external world. I take this to be a mark of the fact that such knowledge has enormous utility in the conduct of life. We have meditated upon the rules which, if acted upon, will enable one to acquire such knowledge. If you do not follow these rules you will land in ignorance or error; that is, if knowledge is your purpose, you will land in failure. Critical rules define the possibility of success or failure. Critical rules are capable of violation. Critical rules define the possibility of criticism and revision. Critical rules function only in what I have called critical processes, but they function in all such processes.

They are sharply distinguishable from mechanical rules. A mechanical rule is one which describes a mechanical process. It is what most people mean by a law of nature or a scientific law. Where such rules tell you the whole story of a process, that process is predictable but not corrigible. If you know the right critical rules, and if you follow them judiciously, you will in great probability get to know some mechanical rules. A knowledge of mechanical rules presupposes a knowledge of some critical rules and the ability to observe them. A knowledge of mechanical rules is come at inductively, whereas it is not clear that the same thing can be said of the critical rules which guide your efforts to make the induction. Mechanical rules define the possibility of apparent exceptions. If you know the mechanical rule which "governs," say, the formation of rain clouds, you are in a position to detect an apparent exception. The point is that you will not, in connection with mechanical rules, admit the possibility of a real exception. You will endeavor to understand the event in question in such a manner as an "exception" will be seen to have been apparent only, not genuine. If you fail in your attempts to do this you will abandon the rule and go in search of another which will include the event as an instance and not leave it as an exception. Mechanical rules must be sacrificed if they do not enable you to account for all relevant cases. So long as mechanical rules are genuine, they preclude the possibility of exceptions which are genuine. The concept of an exception is not the same as the concept of a violation: the one is diagnostic of mechanical rules and defines the basis of their collapse; the other is diagnostic of critical rules and defines the basis of their power. If you come upon an exception to a mechanical rule, you have ruined the rule; if you come upon a violation of a critical rule, you have not ruined the rule. There is a relation between critical rules and mechanical rules which can be indicated by means of a slang metaphor: critical rules "go bail" for mechanical rules. We use critical rules to get at mechanical rules. The sun cannot discover the mechanical rules which describe or "govern" the behavior of its planets because, among other reasons, the sun is not the locus of those critical rules which you must know and follow if you are to perform reliable inductions. If you threaten the integrity, the reality, the validity, of critical rules, you cut yourself off from a knowledge of mechanical rules. It would be a matter of some irony to become so enamoured of mechanical rules that you forgot this fact about critical rules. No one ever does that; but some people think they do. The matter can be put this way: mechanical rules require the existence of critical rules for their disclosure. When you say that, you are not far from Descartes' "*Cogito ergo sum*," because to say "I think; therefore, I am," is to say "I am the locus of critical rules; therefore I am the locus of existence." And you are not far from Socrates' "*Nosce te ipsum*," because to know your "self" is to know where critical rules are to be encountered.

(4) Mention of Socrates and Descartes suggests also Kant. Like them he is alert to the distinction between the critical and the mechanical and particularly to the distinction between critical rules and mechanical rules. His writings celebrate the systematic character of this distinction. It is diagnostic for him of the status of mind in the world order and of will in the moral order. Now, a distinction which reaches from Socrates to Descartes and Kant has something radical about it, something which goes to the "root" of philosophy. I am convinced that this is so in the case of the distinction between the critical and the mechanical, and particularly so, if you think of philosophy as the theory of criticism. I would like to elaborate that point by way of conclusion. I can think of no distinction which is more diagnostic of the modern mind. The modern mind prides itself upon being critical: it would, I think, rather be critical than right; even though it should insist that its reason for being critical is that that is the surest way to be right. And the modern mind prides itself upon having used its critical powers to discover the ways in which and the extent to which its environment is mechanical. To be critical and to discover that its environment is mechanical would seem to be, in large part, the destiny of the modern mind. As matters stand today, I see no other destiny which is regarded as having greater prestige. Other destinies may be more wished for, but none are more sought after. You have in the critical and mechanical a distinction to which the modern mind cannot profess indifference. If you can relate philosophy to that distinction, you have guaranteed it a place in the modern world. Now it seems to me that philosophy's job is not the exploration of the mechanical. A philosopher who proposes discourse on the mechanical is inviting competition which he cannot meet. The scientists have that claim staked out and have been mining it so efficiently that they are entitled to say, "No philosopher need apply." To the extent that a process is mechanical, you had better be scientific about it. However, the surer you are of the existence of mechanical processes, the surer you had better be of the existence of

critical processes. In that sense the reality of the mechanical guarantees the reality of the critical.

We were led to propose this account of critical processes by the argument which says that since man is part of nature, and nature contains no free will, so man also does not. If the points to which attention has been drawn are admitted, then we have to do one of two things: either extend the term nature to include critical processes as distinct from and not reducible to mechanical processes, or admit that critical processes fall "outside of nature." In either case we have a radical dualism. In the first case the dualism falls inside of nature but retains its reality. In the second case the dualism includes nature as one term and (say) mind as its second term. Either way will suffice to deal with the argument about nature and man. This way of dealing with that argument does not prove free will in man. It merely secures a dualism, one term of which can be the locus of his freedom.

QUESTIONS

1. You can describe what a thing does and what a person does. It is doubtful that you would criticize a thing for what it does; but it is not doubtful that you might criticize a person for what he does. Why is this? What are the postulates or presuppositions of description? Of criticism? Do these sets ever conflict? What then?

2. Select any four of the terms said to apply to the process in the astronomer's mind. Show why you would not apply them to the process in the solar system.

3. "You cannot propose criticism where you cannot diagnose purpose." What does that mean? Do you agree? If not, why not?

4. If the clouds in the sky were blown by the wind into the shape "2 + 2 = 5," would you say that they were in error? If a tape-recording, when played over, announces that 2 + 2 = 5, would you say that it had made a mistake?

5. If to educate a person in regard to a certain subject-matter (for example, arithmetic) is to make him into a potential critic in regard to that field, able to detect and revise error, would you say that educating is the same as conditioning?

6. Distinguish between descriptive rules and critical rules. Which does a natural science seek to discover? If psychology is a natural science, would it be fair to say that it has nothing to tell us about the critical rules which it uses, nor about mental processes to the extent that they are critical processes?

7. Would you get a bigger jolt from discovering that none of your behavior is purposive, or from discovering that some of it is? Why?

8. What is the difference between a Watsonian behaviorist investigating a logician, and a logician investigating a Watsonian behaviorist?

9. If you personify a thing, you give rise to metaphor. If you "thingify" a person, do you also give rise to metaphor?

10. Can any natural scientist, speaking strictly *as* natural scientist, say anything wise?

V. *Legislative Definition*

1. THE STATE AND LAW

Ethics and Morals. There is a difference between reflecting upon the nature of rightness and doing an act because you believe it to be right. The former is sustained by the desire to arrive at a clear and distinct idea of the nature of rightness, of what makes an act right; the latter, by the desire to actualize rightness in conduct. The former eventuates in ethical theory; the latter in moral action, or morality. An act is moral if done because believed to be right. If you believe that a certain principle defines rightness, you have an ethical theory. If you do an act because you believe it to be right, you have morality.

We have been concerned with ethical theory, with the desire to possess a clear and distinct idea of the nature of right and wrong. Our first three authors (Paley, Bentham, Kant) shared that desire, but arrived at different ethical theories. Our second three authors (Nietzsche, Dewey, Ayer) did not share that desire. They rejected the notion of an ethical theory, and therefore did not attempt to formulate one. They propounded theories about ethical theories, but they did not propound ethical theories. We return in the present chapter to a consideration of ethical theories and their embodiment in action. If the reader has become convinced that having an ethical theory and embodying it in action is a misguided idea, he may find little to justify this concluding chapter. On the other hand, if he is still convinced that acts are right because they embody a certain principle, and desires to embody that principle in his actions, there remain some matters for him to think about.

If a person knows or believes he knows what is right and tries to embody that knowledge in his action, he is a person of conscience: he acts by means of (*con*) his knowledge (*scientia*) in matters of right and wrong. While the idea of knowledge is built into the word "conscience," the word is normally used to emphasize the desire that rightness shall be embodied in conduct. To "have a conscience" is thus to be sensitive to the demand that rightness shall be embodied in action. To be "conscientious" is to respect that demand, to feel concern that one's actions shall be right. This sensitivity, this concern, can dominate a person's life, can energize his will. When this is the case, you have moral passion, the drive to do always and only what you believe to be right. A man of strong moral conviction is one who strives to do what he believes to be right. You thus need an ethical theory, a theory about the nature of rightness, to define moral conviction. To the person who takes morality seriously, who desires that his conduct shall conform to what he believes to be right, an ethical theory is exceedingly important. It is not merely a guide to action, but a guide to the most important thing about action, namely its rightness. Its embodiment is the most important demand made upon his will as expressed in action.

Good Society. We are concerned, in the present chapter, with the notion of a good society. We can begin by noting that a good society is one which expresses the wills of good men. No other definition seems to get at the heart of the matter. This definition presupposes the notion of "good man." We can begin here by noting that a good man is one who tries always to do what is right and avoid doing what is wrong. This presupposes the notions of right and wrong; that is, it presupposes an ethical theory. You therefore need an ethical theory if you are to define the good man and through him the good society. Thus Paley or Bentham or Kant could define the good man and through him the good society. Their definitions would differ because their theories differ. Paley's good man would be one who tried always to conform his actions to the will of God; and his good society would be one which expressed the wills of such men. Bentham's good man would be one who tried always to maximize human happiness; and his good society would be one which expressed the wills of such men. Kant's good man would be one who tried always to act on a maxim which he could will to become a universal law, and his good society would be one which expressed the wills of such men.

The claim that a good society is one which expresses the wills of good men raises the question, How does it do so? How would a good society express the wills of good men? You get a large part of the answer if you say "By its laws and institutions." If a society's laws and institutions require what, left to themselves, good men would do anyway, then they can be said to express the wills of good men. If, however, they require what, left to themselves, good men would not do, then they cannot be said to express the wills of good men. Thus, if a law requires that men pay their debts, and if, left to themselves, good men would do that anyway, then that law can be said to express the wills of good men. Again, if an institution (say, marriage) requires that a man support the mother of his children, and if, left to themselves, good men would do that anyway, then that institution can be said to express the wills of good men.

A good society, then, is one which expresses the wills of good men; and it does this, in great part, through its laws and institutions. To a man of good will, therefore, laws and institutions are exceedingly important. Pressure will be brought to bear upon him to see that he obeys them. If they require wrong action of him, they place him in a dilemma: he must either refuse to obey them or refuse to do what is right. There are times when this is not an easy choice. Suppose the law requires that before taking public office a man must take oath ("so help me God") that he will fulfill the duties of his office. Suppose the man does not believe that God exists, or believes that knowledge of Him is so slight and vague that it should not be made essential to pledging his word. To take oath under those circumstances would seem to be a wrong act. To refuse to do so would be to bar oneself from taking public office. Suppose the law requires a woman to pledge herself to obey the man she desires to have as her husband. Suppose she cannot see her way clear to make such a pledge. What is she to do? Agree, and keep her fingers crossed? Refuse, and remain unmarried? Suppose the law requires a heavy income tax at a time when government is corrupt, when public moneys are wasted or used for evil ends. Under those circumstances a taxpayer is subsidizing a wrong action. If he is a man of good will, he is faced with a hard decision. Suppose the law permits human slavery. Suppose a man who believes that slavery is wrong, is himself a slave. He has no recourse against the law, since slaves have no political status. If he submits, he subjects himself to wrongdoing and perpetuates the evil pattern. If he rebels, he will be imprisoned or executed. He is faced with a law-made difficult decision. These cases illustrate the fact that persons of good will can find themselves at loggerheads with the laws and institutions of their time and place.

There is of course another side to this picture. A good man's concern with the law does not always, nor indeed usually, arise out of a conflict between the goodness of his will and the evil of what the law requires. He may, and for the most part perhaps does, find that what is good in his will is caught up and expressed in the law's demand. This point need not be taken for granted. Consider the laws and institutions of your time and place. How many of them require of you what, as a person of good will, you would do or want to do, anyway? It is not necessary to read the law books to find answers to your question. The intent of the laws is all around you. You can get at it this way: What are the actions that, under assignable circumstances, you consider it wrong to do? Which of these actions will the laws try to prevent you from doing? What are the actions that, under assignable circumstances, you consider it right to do? Which of these actions will the laws try to see that you do? What wrongs in your society need righting? Could laws right those wrongs? If not, they are irrelevant to the present discussion. If so, they testify to the law's power to bring about what, as good man, you want done. Where good men have successfully devised laws to express good will, a good man sees in their work an extension of his own will. His conformity to these laws does not violate his conscience. Their enforcement does not confront him with the hard demand that he do what is wrong or take the consequences.   ..

The good man's stake in laws and institutions is twofold. To the degree that they require action from him, he wants it to be right action, wants it to be what, left to himself, he would do anyway. To the degree that they claim to be *his* laws, devised in his name by persons authorized by him, he wants them to prescribe right action because through them he will be prescribing action for others, and no good man wants to prescribe wrong action for others. To the degree that he finds it necessary to prescribe thus indirectly for others, he wants to prescribe right action, action which those others, in so far as they are good men, would do anyway. As good man he is under obligation to respect goodness in them.

Ethics and Politics. Since a good society is one which expresses the wills of good men, and does this via its laws and institutions, it behooves us to look more closely into the structures and processes which these and related expressions refer to. The embodiment of an ethical theory in a politically organized community is a slow and complex process. The detailed analysis of these matters is not the task of ethics. As Aristotle long ago remarked, ethics leads you into politics; ethical theory leads you into political theory. However, some remarks on a few of the major terms may help us to think about ethical theory in terms of political embodiment.

State. Let us make a beginning with the term *state*. A state is a community of persons organized to make law possible. It is no doubt more than that, but it is at least that. What is a person? What do persons have in common, enabling them to constitute a community, when they are thought of as organized to make law possible? What is a law? What conditions make law possible? How would the absence of those conditions make law impossible? What things do laws make possible? How would the absence of law make those things impossible? Where a community is organized to make law possible, let us speak of the *legislative way of life.* Where a community's institutions are created or shaped by law, let us speak of the *legislative definition* of those institutions. If there is to be significant and enduring embodiment of ethical theory, it will be, in great part, because human affairs are amenable to the legislative way of life and to the legislative definition of institutions. An ethical theory which cannot be translated into the laws and institutions of a politically organized community has a remote and tenuous hold on human life. Its embodiment in human affairs will be relatively slight. Its embodiment shows, better than anything else, what the theory concretely means. Such embodiment is its fruit, and by its fruit it is finally known. To agree in ethics with Paley or Bentham or Kant or any other moralist, is to endorse the laws and institutions which would give adequate embodiment to the ethical theory in question.

The notion of a state, or political order, may be made clearer if contrasted with the notion of an economy or economic order. The one is a community of persons organized to make law possible. The other is a community of persons organized to make possible production by division of labor and, as a consequence, distribution by some form of exchange. To the degree that a community is aware of itself as a state, aware of the powers and aims which make it a state, it can set itself to give legislative definition to its economy. To the degree that in doing this it expresses the wills of good men, it will give its economy a claim on the wills of good men. If you have an ethical theory, along what lines would it gain embodiment in the transactions and arrangements of an economic order? To what degree would this embodiment require the action of a community organized to make law possible? Your answer to that question shows the extent to which the embodiment of your ethical theory, in respect to economic life, requires enactment by the state.

We are concerned with the notion of laws and institutions as embodiments of ethical theory, as attempts on the part of communities or their legislating bodies to devise laws, and through them to define institutions which shall embody their understanding of the nature of rightness. If they succeed in doing this, their laws and institutions will express the wills of good men, will require of all what, left to himself, a good man would require of himself. If they succeed in doing this, embodying their ethical theory in their laws and institutions, they will constitute a good society.

In a modern self-governing state, this legislative defining or redefining of major institutions is largely the task of elected representatives. It is their responsibility: they must "answer for" the legislative shaping or reshaping of the institutions. In a self-governing state they must answer to those who live under the institutions as legislatively defined. The laws whereby the institution is defined are "laid down"; they are legislative theses. The question is, what are their hypo-theses? If their hypotheses are ethical principles, then to the degree that they successfully embody these principles they can say: "Behave this way in respect to so and so and you will be doing what is right."

Law. A state, we have suggested, is a community of persons organized to make law possible. How, then, are we to conceive of law? The notion of law can be illustrated by reference to particular pieces of legislation, but that is not to the point here. What *is* a law? Why is law necessary? Wherein does a law formulated by a legislator differ from a law formulated by a scientist? When an ethical theory is embodied in law, what *sort* of thing has it been embodied in?

A law is a requirement made by a state upon its members. It is thought of as mandatory upon all, or upon all who make up a class which it defines. It has, potentially, the weight of the community back of it. Unlike a law of nature, it can be violated.

Its violator commits a "crime," and may be visited with punishment, that is, pain inflicted for wrongdoing. Law occurs at two levels, either defining the conditions under which particular proposals can become laws (laws about laws) or enacting particular proposals. An example of second-level law is the rule that persons shall pay taxes proportioned to their incomes. An example of first-level law is the rule that a proposal cannot be come a law unless voted in by a majority of the legislators.

It is sometimes said that a law formulated by a legislator differs essentially from a law formulated by a scientist. Thus the legislator's law is prescriptive and the scientist's law is descriptive. Again, they can be contrasted in respect to the notion of violation. You can violate a legislator's law, whereas you cannot violate a scientist's law. A legislator's law is not nullified when violated; it is simply violated, disobeyed. On the other hand, a scientist's law is nullified if a "violation" in the sense of an exception occurs. The legislator can acknowledge the occurrence of a violation of his law without being thereby called upon to revise his law so that the violation is included as a case of obedience. The scientist is differently placed in respect to his law. If a "violation" in the sense of an exception occurs, he must revise his law so that the exception will be included as a case of the revised law. The legislator can acknowledge the criminal. The scientist cannot acknowledge the exception. The legislator need not come to terms with the criminal. The scientist must come to terms with the exception. It is not demanded of a legislator's law that it enable you to predict; whereas that is an essential demand upon the scientist's law. It need not be a criticism of a legislator's law that men disobey it; whereas it is an essential criticism of a scientist's law that events do not "obey" it. It is an essential criticism of a legislator's law to say that it is unjust; whereas it is an essential criticism of a scientist's law to say that it is inaccurate.

There is, then, an important difference between a law formulated by a legislator and a law formulated by a scientist. But there is an equally important similarity. Each may be regarded as hypotheses calling for verification. In the case of the scientist, this is obvious. He formulates, say, a law of falling bodies or expanding gasses. He offers these as hypotheses. They can be tested by reference to those matters. Positive instances confirm his hypotheses; negative instances disconfirm them, enabling him to revise his formulations, bringing them more closely into line with the behaviors of falling bodies or expanding gasses. His thinking is highly purposive: he intends an accurate description; and he may also intend it as a usable and reliable basis for action. In seeking to carry out this purpose he may encounter failure: he may come out in ignorance or in error. Because he knows what he is about, and can detect failure, when it occurs, and institute revision, his behavior can be called self-critical. Now the same thing can be said of the activity of the legislator: it too is self-critical. To the degree that he knows what he is about, he can detect failure when it occurs and institute revision. In this sense his law is as hypothetical, as much an hypothesis, as the law of the scientist; and as open, in principle, to testing, confirming, and disconfirming. If he offers his law as a method for bringing about a certain result, he offers it as an hypothesis. If he offers his law as embodying a certain principle, he offers it as an hypothesis. If he offers his law as requiring what, left to themselves, good men would do anyway, he offers it as an hypothesis. If he offers his law as conforming to the will of God, he offers it as an hypothesis. In each of these cases, his formulation may fail to be what it purports to be. Experience may bring this fact to light. He can thereupon revise his law. He is no more infallible than the scientist, and, in principle, need be no less self-critical of his offerings. His fallibility requires that he be self-critical.

A law may be objected to. The objection may be that it is too costly to administer; or that it is too difficult to enforce; or that it deals with matters which should not be made the subject of legislation; or that it protects the interests of some special group; or that its enactment involved a violation of first-level laws; or that people do not want the results which it will produce; or that it violates some people's rights; or that it is, for some other reason, unjust. These are representative objections. The list is not exhaustive: there are no doubt other grounds upon which laws have been objected to. Nor are the items exclusive: it may be that they overlap. The question for our consideration is this: which objections would be dictated by an ethical theory? If a man says, "My objection to this law is that it costs too much to administer. Another law could be devised to produce the same results at less cost," he does not appear to be making a moral judgment. If questioned, however, he might defend his objection by a line of argument that would lead to moral judgment. Thus he might go on to say, "To do something one way, when you could do it another and less costly way, is wasteful, and waste is wrong." Or he might go on to say, "To use more of the public money when you might use less violates a tacit agreement between legislators and those whom they represent, and violating agreements is wrong." In these cases his initial objection would have been traced back to something which he regarded as "wrongdoing." At that point he could be asked to formulate the ethical theory required to diagnose the action as wrongdoing. The law would be such that its enactment would be wrongdoing on his part. He would be saying, "A good man would not enact this law. This law would not express the will of good men. This law, if enforced, would require good men to do what, left to themselves, they would refrain from doing." If the argument reached this point, it would be clear that the original objection was in fact a moral one, did involve an ethical theory. Here is a question: Are there any objections that might be made to a law or group of laws which would not, in the last analysis, turn out to be moral objections, objections resting upon an ethical theory? If so, what are those objections? What is there about them which prevents them from being traced back to an ethical theory? If the reader will take this assignment seriously he will begin to detect the social significance of his ethical theory.

Law pervades the life of society in more ways than one might suspect. How much of what you do depends on the presence of law in your community? What functions in public life would disappear if your community abandoned the legislative way of life? That second question provides a good lead: What social functions are required by the legislative way of life? In a community which lives the legislative way of life there will, of course, be (1) legislators and (2) subjects: persons whose primary job is to devise and revise the laws, and persons whose primary job is to obey the law. These are at opposite ends of the scale.

(3) But the picture is not so simple as that. If legislators are to devise and revise laws, they must have access to information which outruns their personal knowledge. The legislative way of life involves here a group whose primary job is to make such information available, and to make sure that it is reliable. Let a measure be proposed requiring labor unions to incorporate and to make public the amount, the sources, and the disposition of their funds. What information would a legislator want before voting for or against such a proposal?

(4) Legislators subject to first-level laws cannot always be sure that their second-level laws do not conflict with the first-level laws. If such conflict occurs, their work will be, as they say, "unconstitutional." The legislative way of life involves here a group whose primary job is to provide expert judgment on this point. If legislators could have this question settled in advance, they would be saved the job of undoing their work later. If they cannot or will not settle this question in advance, they must have access to informed criticism which will subsequently point out their error.

(5) Legislators can devise and revise laws. They cannot go much beyond that. Laws must be administered. A law requiring, for instance, marriage licenses or driver's licenses can be placed on the books, but cannot be left at that. It must be carried out. The legislative way of life needs a group here whose primary job is to administer the law, to see to it that the

law gets known and that arrangements exist for conforming to its demands.

(6) Legislators cannot directly enforce their laws. Administering should be distinguished from enforcing. If a law requiring licenses is known, if arrangements exist for conforming to its demands, and if a person simply refuses to secure a license, this is not a problem of administration. The law must be enforced. The legislative way of life needs a group here whose primary job is to uncover violations of the law, apprehend violators, try them, and punish them.

(7) Law enforcement is essential to the legislative way of life, but it is not infallible. Mistakes can occur. A person can be unjustly accused. He may not know how to handle his case before the law. The legislative way of life depends at this point on the existence of a group whose primary task is not to legislate nor to inform legislators, nor to criticize legislators, nor to administer or enforce the laws. Their job is to know the law, to make this knowledge available to persons who have dealings with the law, and to see that they receive just treatment within the scope of the law.

(8) Legislators must somehow be secured. In a community where they are elected by those for whom they are to devise and revise laws, the legislative way of life depends on a group whose primary job is to vote in the legislators and hold them responsible. Such persons are traditionally called citizens. They choose those who are to devise and revise the law. They may also choose those who are to fulfill other functions connected with the legislative way of life. Election of legislators by citizens is one way of attempting to ensure that those who legislate are answerable to those for whom they legislate.

(9) In contrast to the citizen stands the rebel. His function should not be misunderstood nor its value underestimated. The rebel can be a symbol of the legislative way of life. His proper task can be seen if he is contrasted with the legislator, the administrator, the judge, the policeman, the attorney, and the

criminal. In essence he is not any of these. His diagnostic act is not theirs. He is the man who uses force against government. His action can be honorable and of good intent. His function can be made clear via the notion of justifiable punishment. The legislative way of life sometimes requires punishment, the use of force, in dealing with persons of bad will who refuse to conform to the law's demands. Government denied the right to punish, to use force, in the name of the law, would, on many occasions, be placed in an unmanageable position. Bad will in men under the law is neither so rare nor so weak that government can be rightfully denied the use of force or punishment. Now, revolution is the citizen's ultimate recourse against bad will in government. The line of argument which entitles government to punish subjects, will, *mutatis mutandis*, entitle citizens to revolt against government. The rebel is the person who expresses this ultimate right of men of good will to use force upon government. Revolution is for the citizen what punishment is for the legislator: a last resort against men of bad will, who cannot be argued with and must therefore be "dealt" with. Above all, the rebel should not be confused with either the criminal or the anarchist. The criminal may not want the law changed; he may simply want to be an exception to its demands. He may not object to its enforcement upon others, so long as it leaves him free. The anarchist, if there be such a person, is the man who objects to law in principle, who would do away with all laws, or do away with all forms of force used to impose laws. The rebel does not, like the criminal, intend his action to be an exception to existing law; nor does he propose that laws be abolished. His point is that government—those whose job it is to devise, revise, administer and enforce the law—must be dealt with forcibly. If government has gotten into the hands of men of bad will, and only the use of force can get it into the hands of men of good will, then the rebel's case for revolution is comparable to a government's case for punishing criminals. A government producing bad law is inimical to the legislative way of life, more so perhaps than the criminal violating good law. The rebel's justification must be that he proposes to reinstate conditions under which government expresses the wills of good men. Unless he can say this of himself, he is not a rebel but an enemy. Most of the great rebels of history have had to risk their lives, or give their lives, to prove that they were rebels, not enemies.

Law is necessary to civilized living—necessary in order that action may be calculated. If nature's laws were suspended, human action could not be planned. Human affairs being what they are, this amounts to saying that human life could not be lived. Nature is that order, not of their own making, which men can get to know and can then presuppose in their actions. If no law could be discovered in the matter of water boiling or water freezing, these two processes could not enter into plans. When men turn from nature to human nature their task is in part to devise an order. A social order, structured by legislation, is something you can get to know about and can then presuppose in your actions. But, to a degree, such an order must be created by legislative action. A usable social order is not entirely the work of legislation. Instinct and custom would no doubt provide a crude nucleus. But the results would fall short of the demands made by civilized living in great modern societies. Ignorance, indifference, and bad will would take too great a toll. Legislation, legislative definition of major institutions—in short, the legislative way of life—is man's characteristic method of creating a usable and defensible social order.

Primary and Secondary. The thought underlying this chapter is something like this: A state is a community of persons organized to make law possible. It is the primary institution. Through the instrumentality of law a state can provide legislative definition for its secondary institutions—property, marriage, and so on. The distinction here between primary and secondary is not the distinction between more and less important, but between that which provides and that which receives legislative definition. The state provides or can provide legislative definition of other institutions; they do not provide legislative definition of it. For that reason it is here called primary. In contrast, such institutions as marriage and property receive legislative definition. For that reason they are here called secondary. The point is not that the primary institution is more important than the secondary ones, the state more important than marriage or property; the point is that it provides legislative definition and they receive it.

For Example, Property. The notion of a secondary institution may be illustrated with reference to property. This institution, the phrase says, receives or can receive legislative definition. A state can specify, by means of law, what citizens may and may not do in the matter of property. Of property in land, it may say, for example, that it may or may not be bequeathed; that it must be bequeathed en bloc or may be divided up before the owner's death; that it must be bequeathed to the eldest son or may be divided among all members of the family; that it is subject to an annual tax, a death tax, church, education, and sales or other taxes; that it may or may not be held by women; that it does or does not entitle the owner to a vote; and so on. It would require a volume to set forth the ways in which the institution of property has been or might be shaped or defined through the instrumentality of law. Our business here is not to inquire into those details, but to recall a few of them to illustrate the notion of the legislative definition of the institution in question. The legislative definition of an institution may differ from one age to another, and from one people to another. Once defined it may have to be redefined, either because the original job was poorly done or because conditions which justified the original definition have meanwhile changed. Defined one way in England, it may be differently defined in France or America or Russia. The institution will have one legislated "shape" in a competitive economy and another in a socialist economy. At one time the definition of an institution may be largely the work of custom, only slightly the work of legislation. Later, law may step in and fix or revise the work of custom. The laws governing the conduct of life in respect to an institution—what, under the law, you may or must do or refrain from doing—form the legislative definition of that institution.

Other Secondary Institutions. Property is not the only secondary institution. The press, the school, the church, marriage, and the family are also secondary institutions. Of them you can say: they are form or organization proposed for or imposed upon certain needs and desires. Let us take as an example our need and desire for news about what is going on in the world. How are these needs and desires to be dealt with? Which of them are we entitled to have satisfied? Who shall do it? What control have we over who does it and how he does it? Most people need and desire news, but some few need and desire to be in the news. How are these complementary needs and desires (news and publicity, to know about and to be known about) to be brought together? The answer to these and many other questions is "the press." It is form or organization proposed for or imposed on the needs and desires in question. A community requires some patterned, organized, acknowledged, way of dealing with its need and desire for news and publicity. The press, considered as an institution, is one way of doing this. As an institution, it must have legislative definition: what, under law, may and may not be done in this matter of news and publicity?

We need and desire various kinds of knowledge and skill which, left to ourselves, we could not obtain. This need and desire is wide and deep in human affairs. A person's needs and desires here outrun his individual capacities and resources to deal with them. He cannot secure these knowledges and skills for himself or for those dependent on him. What is required here is an institution to organize these matters, give them form, deal with them. It must serve as keeper, transmitter, and extender of useful and desirable knowledges and skills. It must bring together those who have the needs and those who can deal with the needs. The institution here is the school. Like the press, it must have legislative definition: what, under law, may and may not be done in this matter of educating each generation?

No society can afford to leave its major institutions wholly without legislative definition and redefinition. The stakes are too high. Needs and desires which are strong enough and important enough to become "institutionalized," to require and secure some patterned, organized, acknowledged way of being dealt with, are going to be the locus of tensions and conflicts, claims and counterclaims, which cannot be left wholly to custom or private judgment.

No one who cares whether his own and other peoples' actions are right or wrong, and who has a theoretical understanding of the nature of right and wrong in action, will profess indifference to the legislative definition of the major institutions of his society. To the degree that law prescribes and prohibits actions, to the degree that a people is law-abiding—to that degree the legislative definition of their major institutions fixes for them complex and far-reaching patterns of action. If it is right that one person buy and sell other persons, have them and use them as property, and the law prohibits this, then it prohibits a person from doing what is right. Such a law could not be looked upon as embodying an ethical theory, if slavery is right. If it is wrong for married women to own property, and the law permits them to own property, then the law is protecting them in wrongdoing. Such a law could not be looked upon as embodying an ethical theory, if it is wrong for married women to own property. In short, the idea of every man his own moralist must finally show what stuff it is made of by confronting this equally important idea of the legislative way of life.

QUESTIONS

This portion of Chapter V is built around the following definitions, generalizations, and distinctions. Be prepared to explain and illustrate each. Be prepared to criticize or defend each.

1. An act is moral if done because believed to be right.

2. A good man is one who tries always to do what is right and avoid doing what is wrong.

3. A good society is one that expresses the wills of good men.

4. You need an ethical theory (i.e., a theory of right and wrong) to define the good man and (through him) the good society.

5. If laws and institutions require what, left to themselves, good men would do anyway, then they express the wills of good men.

6. A state is a community of persons organized to make law possible.

7. If there is to be significant and enduring embodiment of ethical theory, it will be, in great part, because human affairs are amenable to the legislative way of life and to the legislative definition of institutions.

8. An economy is a community of persons organized to make possible production by division of labor and (therefore) distribution by exchange.

9. Punishment is pain inflicted for wrongdoing.

10. A law formulated by a legislator differs in many essential ways from a law formulated by a scientist.

11. Both legislators' laws and scientists' laws may be regarded as hypotheses calling for verification.

12. Are there any objections that might be made to a law which would not in the last analysis turn out to be objections resting on an ethical theory?

13. Distinction: First-level laws and second-level laws.

14. Government denied the right to punish and to use force in the name of the law would, on many occasions, be placed in an unmanageable position.

15. The rebel can be a symbol of the legislative way of life.

16. Nature is that order, not of their own making, which men can get to know and can then presuppose in their actions.

17. Distinction: primary institutions and secondary institutions.

18. An institution is form or organization proposed for certain human needs and desires; examples—property, or the press.

19. An educational system is a keeper, transmitter, and extender of useful and desirable skills and knowledges.

20. The idea of every man his own moralist must be confronted with the idea of the legislative way of life.

2. MARRIAGE AS AN INSTITUTION

By way of conclusion it is suggested that the reader set him-self to propose legislative definition for one of mankind's major secondary institutions, the institution of marriage. Let the reader imagine that he is a conscientious member of a lawmak-ing body, elected to office by a community organized to make law possible. The task before him and his fellow members is to provide legislative definition or redefinition of the institution of marriage. What permissions, prescriptions, and prohibitions will he make mandatory upon all members of his community in the matter of marriage? The assumption here is that he intends, as far as possible, to give this institution the legislative shape required to express the wills of good men, to form part of a good society.

At this point the reader might say: "If I were a conscientious elected lawmaker charged with the responsibility of providing legislative definition for the institution of marriage, I would try to find out what my community or the majority in my com-munity want in the way of marriage legislation and give it to them. My responsibility would not go beyond that. It would not be my job to figure out what ways of acting are right and then embody these in legislation. As legislator I have no re-sponsibility for the rightness or wrongness of the actions per-mitted, prescribed, or prohibited by the laws which I devise or revise. My job is to give the people what they want, not what I think they ought to want." If the reader says this, he will side-step the problem proposed in the remainder of this chap-ter. He will pass on to the community itself the responsibility of deciding what ought, in all conscience, to be permitted, pre-scribed, or prohibited by law in the matter of marriage.

To reinstate our problem we would then approach the reader in his capacity of law-abiding, tax-paying private citizen. He would then acquire the responsibility in a new form. Speaking now as a man of good will, as a member of a good society, how does he want this institution defined? The legislator is waiting to carry out his (the citizen's) will in a set of laws governing the conduct of life in respect to marriage. What are his instructions to the legislator? The question is posed on the assumption that in answering, the reader (now a citizen) will speak only as good man, concerned that his society shall express the wills of good men, and concerned therefore that this institution shall receive such legislative definition as will fit it to express the wills of good men. Whether the reader agrees to be a legislator or insists upon being only a citizen, we have our proposed problem.

Suppose the reader agrees to be a legislator. What does he want to know? How might he make a beginning? He might do worse than ask himself what needs and desires are the matter for which the institution of marriage provides the form. A precise answer may be difficult to arrive at. But one cannot reasonably propose legislative definition (or redefinition) of the institution, if one neither knows nor cares what needs and desires will thereby receive form or organization. Before asking "What form shall the institution provide?" let us ask "What needs and desires does it provide *for?*" Some suggestions may be in order:

(1) In the first place, for all but a few persons, might be put the desire for sexual satisfaction, at least at the time when marriage is being contemplated. To mention this desire first is not to assign it a pre-eminence; but given men and women in whom this desire was initially or permanently absent, or noticeably less than it is, the institution of marriage would be something quite other than it is.

(2) In the second place, one might put the desire for intimate companionship, the desire to be more than a friend or an acquaintance. This notion may be vague. Perhaps it can be gotten at by way of contrast. The relation in question is not normally the relation which obtains between colleagues in a university, nor between teacher and student, nor between doctor and patient, nor between landlady and roomer, nor between brother and sister, nor even between parent and child. In each

of these relations there is a limit to the degree of personal close-
ness that is possible or even desired. But, somehow, somewhere
we do desire to reduce to a minimum those subtle formalities
and barriers which constitute us the isolated atoms we generally
find ourselves to be. We do desire that the "inner me" shall be
known and delighted in for precisely what it is. This desire,
differing perhaps in intensity from person to person, is as real
and imperious as the desire for sexual satisfaction.

(3) In the third place, one might put the desire for emotional
stability, the desire to put an end to focussing our emotions now
here, now there. There are, in the early peregrinations of the
human soul, a certain charm and stimulation in exploring another's emotional possibilities. But the charm tends to wear off,
if the experience is too often repeated. A sense of emotional
disarrangement sets in, a sense of being torn up by the roots, a
sense of lost labor and wasted effort, a sense of belonging
finally in no one's settled pattern. This brings with it a kind of
casualness and cynicism which, I believe, we deeply desire to
be free from.

(4) In the fourth place, one might put the desire to share
values and ideals. This is not the same as the three points mentioned already. All four may occur together; but they do not
always do so. The strength of this desire is sometimes ignored
or denied by the cynics and the worldly-wise. It would seem,
however, that their belittling attitude involves some self-decep-
tion. We do discover in ourselves loyalties to various values and
ideals. These loyalties may vary in strength. They may be false
or misleading. But we do have them, and we do desire, with a
great hunger, to share them and pursue them with someone
else. Deprive men or women of the satisfaction of this desire,
and they will experience a genuine loss.

(5) In the fifth place, one might put the desire for children.
This is distinct from the others already suggested. It has seemed
to me that this is often a desire that grows *with* marriage,
rather than a desire that leads *to* marriage. It is not easy to be
sure on this point. It is one thing to be delighted with the

thought of having children—and this does often incline persons to marriage—but it is another thing to desire children. In any case, however, it is a matter to be kept in mind by our hypothetical legislator.

These five needs or desires clamour for satisfaction in the young and nubile soul. There are no doubt others. But young men and women do find themselves aware of these needs; and marriage, as an institution, is proposed for them. These, along with others, are the matter; the institution proposes the form. These are the drives seeking satisfaction; marriage is the proffered arrangement.

A man who is going to propose legislative definition or redefinition of an institution should have some knowledge of it as now constituted. He is not going to start from scratch. There is an institution of marriage, now in existence. Its shape is not clearly defined. Such shape as it has is the work partly of custom, partly of legislation. It is not uniform throughout the country, nor from one country to another. As in the case of property, it would take a volume to review in detail what has been and might be done to give shape and variety to the institution of marriage. In this matter we must not let the trees prevent us from seeing the woods. We must ask for a generally recognizable picture of the institution as at present shaped by custom and law. We can say some things without getting lost in differences or details:

(1) We can say that as it now stands the institution proposes monogamy; that is, marriage between one man and one woman. When divorce and remarriage occur this is altered to what might be called consecutive polygamy. (2) The institution proposes that marriage be permanent, dissoluble only by death. Elaborate exceptions may be provided by law or custom, but the point to note is that they are exceptions. It would be misleading to say that for the institution as it now exists, impermanence is as regulative an idea as permanence. The rule is: "Stay married if you can." The exception is: "Break it up if you must." (3) The institution proposes what might be called exclusive-

ness; that is, the rights and privileges which marriage brings are expected to be enjoyed only within the confines of marriage, not before marriage, and not during marriage with any third party. Whatever the practice, this is the proposed rule. (4) The institution is offered as the basis for family life; that is, it is the bridge which leads over from youthful amorousness to those peculiar affections and ties which mark off the family from other associations into which persons may enter. This is certainly the general practice, by either law or custom. Most families are built around a marriage. The number of exceptions is unimportant. (5) The institution proposes that marriage be heterosexual; that is, it neither makes nor allows any provision for marriage between persons of the same sex. Men cannot marry men, nor women, women. The reason is not that such unions do not, because they cannot, eventuate in families—the intention to marry does not of necessity carry with it the intention to have children—it is simply because marriage as now instituted is not for persons of the same sex. (6) The institution permits, though does not actually require, in both parties, a profound ignorance of each other and of marriage itself. It makes no provision for learning what the other party is "really" like; nor what marriage is like, except by observing the marriages of others. It also permits, though does not actually require, in both parties, a state of emotional excitement such as attends few other steps which either will be called upon to take. (7) The institution does not assume that a woman will become (or continue to be) "self-supporting" after marriage. The point here is hedged around by qualifications and exceptions. Many women are "self-supporting" wives. Some men are not even "self-supporting" husbands. Moreover, being a good wife and mother is itself a full-time job. If being a wife and mother carried a salary, and women had to earn it or quit, it would be obvious that most wives are "self-supporting." But, after all qualifications and exceptions are noted, there is still a point here. As now defined, marriage is for most women an alternative to a "job"; and, for most men, something which they must be able to "afford." (8) The institution often claims divine sanction for itself, and has very considerable social and legal sanction; that is, the limitations which it imposes are backed up by some of the strongest and subtlest pressures to be met with anywhere in a modern community.

A man who is going to propose legislative definition or re-definition of an institution should have some familiarity with the controversies which it has stirred up. Back of these may lie complaints based on genuine hardships. He should become familiar with persistent and widespread criticism. It is the function of criticism to point out the need for revision. If the criticism is valid, there is a case for revision. A legislator who does not know what criticisms his institution has drawn down upon itself is not only ignorant, he is dangerously ignorant. His ignorance may threaten the execution of his avowed purposes. He wants to know how, in all conscience, his institution should be legislatively defined or redefined. If, as it stands, it outrages the consciences of normal men and women, then their indigna-tion is righteous, and relevant to his purposes. A legislator should have access to all kinds of factual, statistical, and tech-nical literature bearing on his institution. He should know what government documents and the investigations of sociologists and psychologists and psychoanalysts can tell him. But these are not, by intention at least, vehicles of criticism and protest. He should read and ponder such items as Bertrand Russell's *Marriage and Morals,* Bernard Shaw's *Getting Married,* Pius XI's *Christian Marriage,* and G. K. Chesterton's *Superstition of Divorce.*

Indeed, he could make a good beginning with Pius XI's *Christian Marriage,* an encyclical letter addressed by the Pope to his hierarchy, and through them to Catholic Christians all over the world. This little book (40-some pages), read carefully and reflectively, will enable you to clarify to yourself what you know or don't know, what you think or don't think, what you care or don't care, what you presuppose or don't presuppose, about the institution of marriage. It was written, the author says, "in view of the present conditions, needs, errors and views that affect the family and society." It is not easy reading, but it forces a person to clarify his own mind on a wide range of questions pertaining to the institution of marriage. Mr. Chesterton said of one of Mr. Shaw's prefaces, that he could write a paragraph on every sentence which he accepted and a chapter on every sentence which he rejected. In its own way, *Christian Marriage* is that sort of book. It approaches its subject from four sides, beginning with a description of the origin, the nature, and the purpose of Christian marriage. It then sets forth the blessings of Christian marriage, followed by a review of ten or a dozen beliefs and practices which deviate from the Christian conception of marriage. To a Christian, these would be what the author calls "fallacies." It concludes with some proposals for reinstating the Christian conception of marriage in the minds and hearts and wills of men and women in the modern world. The little book has a certain bearing on the legislative definition or redefinition of the institution of marriage. This relevance rests on the fact, which you can gather as you go along, that the author would not protest if lawmakers in modern states took his book as providing a blueprint for their legislative endeavors. If our hypothetical legislator forced himself to figure out where he would go along with this papal encyclical, and where he would not; forced himself also to figure out his reasons for going along or not going along, he would, in respect to theses and hypo-theses, get to know his own mind on the subject of the legislative definition or redefinition of his institution. It would force him to search his own mind for his answer to this question: "What permissions, prescriptions, and prohibitions are you, in the name of conscience, in the name of right and wrong, prepared to make mandatory upon all members of your community in the matter of marriage?" And to this further question: "If your mandates are theses, what are your hypo-theses?" If he bogs down en route, Mr. Russell and Mr. Shaw are there to goad him into renewed efforts.

We have been urging our legislator to become familiar with his institution in respect to its matter, its form, and the criticisms which demand its reform. As this inventory proceeds, he will see that he is getting at three groups of questions: (a) questions having to do with entering marriage; (b) questions having to do with actions in marriage; (c) questions having to do with getting out of marriage. There are probably other groups of questions, but these are certainly representative and central.

Thus, under group (a) he would have the general question of who shall and who shall not be permitted to marry. This will break down into a number of separate questions. In each case our legislator is concerned to prescribe, or at least not to prohibit, ways of acting which are right. This may not be the only condition which justifies legislative action. But, for the purposes of this chapter, his question is: "Where do you come out if you seek to make your legislative definition embody only your ethical theory?" Thus, if there is nothing wrong in a marriage between persons of different religions, he will not propose legislation against it. On the other hand, if it is wrong for a brother to marry his sister, he (our legislator) will propose a law forbidding it. What will he say about interracial marriage? About remarriage, after the death of one party, by the surviving party? About age limit? About age differences? About parental consent? About mental health? About physical health? About nationality? About presumed sterility? About education? About earning power? About bigamy? About homosexuals? About mutual consent? About a criminal record? About social equality? These questions suggest others, but they are suffcient to indicate what group (a) includes.

In group (b) he is faced with questions of conduct in marriage. Once people are married, would our legislator regulate their actions? Will he legislate against two-timing? Against wife-beating? Against shrewishness? Against birth control? Against sterilization? Against abortion? Against refusal to bear children? What actions on the part of married people toward each other or toward a third party—where the relation involves their married status—are right or wrong? There is a common-sense point in much of this which, for the moment, we are side-stepping. Our legislator might say "There are some actions, for example, wife-beating, which are wrong, but which I would not propose legislation against. And there are other actions which are right but which I would not require by law." We cannot let him say this. We want to know what the institution would look like if it were an embodiment of ethical theory and nothing else. If he says, "But it would be wrong to legislate against this wrong action," he is shifting his assignment. We did not ask for a legislative definition of legislative definition but for a legislative definition of marriage. His point, of course, is exceedingly important and could not be indefinitely postponed. It raises these questions: When is it wrong for law to prescribe action even though the action itself would be right? When is it wrong for law to prohibit action even though the action itself would be wrong?

In group (c) his central question is the condition for getting out of marriage. This will break down into distinct but related questions. If he says "It is everywhere and always wrong for any-one to step out of any marriage, no matter what the circumstances may be," he simplifies his thesis, but probably at the cost of considerably complicating his hypo-theses. The same would hold if he went to the opposite extreme and said: "It is every-where and always right for anyone to step out of any marriage no matter what the circumstances may be." The chances are he will stop short of both extremes. Then he must make clear what exceptions he will allow, and how his hypo-theses will permit these and no others. Does he distinguish among these three: annulment, separation, divorce? And between divorce with and without permission to remarry? His difficulties become manifold if he proposes to recognize divorce. He must then indicate the conditions under which divorce is right.

QUESTIONS

There is only one question for this section; namely, what legislative definition of the institution of marriage would the reader propose? The section does not answer this question; but it does what it can to put the question before the reader, by directing his attention to a number of points which it would be well for him to have in mind before tackling the assignment.

3. J. S. MILL: A PLEA FOR LIBERALISM

The preceding section asked the reader to imagine himself a member of a lawmaking group charged with the responsibility of providing legislative definition or redefinition of one of society's major secondary institutions, marriage. "How," the reader was asked, "how would you handle such an assignment? Along what lines would you propose legislative definitions for this institution? What do's and don't's connected with this institution would you make mandatory upon all who would participate in the institution, placing the full weight of the law back of these demands?" A reader so circumstanced would be in a position to wield considerable power. As modern communities go, few persons have more power over others than those who devise or revise the laws. To an increasing degree, as legislators decide, the members of a community act or refrain from acting. Such power is not absolute, but it is unquestionably great. To wield such power is to be responsible for much; responsible, through one's use of such power, for what others do or refrain from doing, as a consequence of one's use of that power.

A slight familiarity with the history of legislative social reform shows that legislative power may be misused in either (or both) of two ways: (1) It may be used to require people to do what is wrong. That is not frequent, but it is by no means impossible. If a certain way of acting is wrong, and a law is passed requiring people to act in that way, then, to the degree that people are law-abiding, they are being required to do what is wrong. No conscientious legislator would want to be responsible for that state of affairs. (2) It may be used to require people to do what should be left up to them to do or leave undone. Here the rightness or wrongness of the way of acting is not in question; the point is that it is a way of acting which law should say nothing about. An instance might be found in what is called "breach of promise," in the sense of promise to marry. If a man engages to marry a woman, he should, as we say, "live up to his promise." But do we want the law to force him to do so? If a woman engages to marry a man, she should live up to her promise. But do we want the law to force her to do so? If we hesitate, or say "no" at this point, it is not that we regard such promises lightly, nor that we feel that it is right to break them; it is rather that we regard such matters as better left up to individuals to settle for themselves. A man does right, often, in sending his sons to college; but do we want a law requiring him to do so? A man does wrong if he deliberately destroys a masterpiece of painting which he has bought and paid for; but do we want a law forbidding him to do so? A man does wrong to be mean to his friends or miserly or wasteful with his money; but do we want a law forbidding him to be so? There are an indefinite number of ways in which a man of good will would act, but we would not want bad men forced by law to act in these ways. There are matters which we want people "left alone" about, left legally free to do them or not do them, regardless of what good men would do. In some matters we want people left legally free to do what is foolish; in some matters, to do what is wrong. In other words, we don't want the law to force men to do what is wrong; but we also don't want the law to prohibit them in all instances from doing what is wrong nor force them in all instances to do what is right. These are reflections that might well occur to a person possessing the power to devise and revise a community's laws. In proportion as you possess the power to force people to act or refrain from acting in a certain way, you might well ask whether, in regard to a particular matter, you should use or refrain from using that power.

The balance of this section contains a long selection from John Stuart Mill's 1859 publication, *On Liberty*. The selection is from Chapters I and IV. In this book, Mill was concerned to defend the right of the individual to think and act for himself. This right meant a great deal to the author. He believed that societies and governments frequently intrude where they have no right to do so. He wrote his book to point out this fact and to protest against it. His book is Western man's finest handling of the theme. It became the testament of liberalism. I can think of no bettter sequel to the assignment made in the preceding section. If its presence here inclines you to secure the complete book (*On Liberty* by John Stuart Mill) and give it a full-length reading, its presence will have been justified.

The subject of this Essay is not the so-called Liberty of the Will . . . but Civil, or Social Liberty: the nature and limits of the power which can be legitimately exercised by society over the individual. A question seldom stated, and hardly ever discussed, in general terms, but which profoundly influences the practical controversies of the age by its latent presence, and is likely soon to make itself recognized as the vital question of the future. It is so far from being new, that, in a certain sense, it has divided mankind, almost from the remotest ages; but in the stage of progress into which the more civilized portions of the species have now entered, it presents itself under new conditions, and requires a different and more fundamental treatment.

The struggle between Liberty and Authority is the most conspicuous feature in the portions of history with which we are earliest familiar. . . . But in old times this contest was between subjects. or some classes of subjects, and the Government. By liberty, was meant protection against the tyranny of the political rulers. The rulers were conceived . . . as in a necessarily antagonistic position to the people whom they ruled. They consisted of a governing One, or a governing tribe or caste, who derived their authority from inheritance or conquest, who, at all events, did not hold it at the pleasure of the governed, and whose supremacy men did not venture, perhaps did not desire, to contest, whatever precautions might be taken against its oppressive exercise. Their power was regarded as necessary, but also as highly dangerous; as a weapon which they would attempt to use against their subjects, no less than against external enemies. . . . The aim, therefore, of patriots was to set limits to the power which the ruler should be suffered to exercise over the community; and this limitation was what they meant by liberty. It was attempted in two ways. First, by obtaining a recognition of certain immunities, called political liberties or rights, which it was to be regarded as a breach of duty in the ruler to infringe, and which, if he did infringe, specific resistance, or general rebellion, was held to be justifiable. A second, and generally a later expedient, was the establishment of constitutional checks, by which the consent of the community, or of a body of some sort, supposed to represent its interests, was made a necessary condition to some of the more important acts of the governing power. . . . A time, however, came, in the progress of human affairs, when men ceased to think it a necessity of nature that their governors should be an independent power, opposed in interest to themselves. It appeared to them much better that the various magistrates of the State should be their tenants or delegates, revocable at their pleasure. In that way alone, it seemed, could they have complete security that the powers of government would never be abused to their disadvantage. By degrees this new demand for elective and temporary rulers became the prominent object of the exertions of the popular party, wherever any such party existed; and superseded, to a considerable extent, the previous efforts to limit the power of rulers.

As the struggle proceeded for making the ruling power emanate from the periodical choice of the ruled, some persons began to think that too much importance had been attached to the limitation of the power itself. *That* (it might seem) was a resource against rulers whose interests were habitually opposed to those of the people. What was now wanted was, that the rulers should be identified with the people; that their interest and will should be the interest and will of the nation. The nation did not need to be protected against its own will. There was no fear of its tyrannizing over itself. Let the rulers be effectually responsible to it, promptly removable by it, and it could afford to trust them with power of which it could itself dictate the use to be made. Their power was but the nation's own power, concentrated, and in a form convenient for exercise. . . .

But, in political and philosophical theories, as well as in persons, success discloses faults and infirmities which failure might have concealed from observation. The notion, that the people have no need to limit their power over themselves, might seem axiomatic, when popular government was a thing only dreamed about, or read of as having existed at some distant period of the past. . . . In time, however, a democratic republic came to occupy a large portion of the earth's surface, and made itself felt as one of the most powerful members of the community of nations; and elective and responsible government became subject to the observations and criticisms which wait upon a great existing fact. It was now perceived that such phrases as "self-government," and "the power of the people over themselves," do not express the true state of the case. The "people" who exercise the power are not always the same people with those over whom it is exercised; and the "self-government" spoken of is not the government of each by himself, but of each by all the rest. The will of the people, moreover, practically means the will of the most numerous or the most active *part* of the people; the majority, or those who succeed in making themselves accepted as the majority; the people, consequently, *may* desire to oppress a part of their number; and precautions are as much needed against this as against any other abuse of power. The limitation, therefore, of the power of government over individuals loses none of its importance when the holders of power are regularly accountable to the community, that is, to the strongest party therein. . . . Like other tyrannies, the tyranny of the majority was at first, and is still vulgarly, held in dread, chiefly as operating through the acts of the public authorities. But reflecting persons perceived that when society is itself the tyrant—society collectively, over the separate individuals who compose it—its means of tyrannizing are not restricted to the acts which it may do by the hands of its political functionaries. Society can and does execute its own mandates: and if it issues wrong mandates instead of right, or any mandates at all in things with which it ought not to meddle, it practices a social tyranny more formidable than many kinds of political oppression, since, though not usually upheld by such extreme penalties, it leaves fewer means of escape, penetrating much more deeply into the details of life, and enslaving the soul itself. Protection, therefore, against the tyranny of the magistrate is not enough: there needs protection also against the tyranny of the prevailing opinion and feeling; against the tendency of society to impose, by other means than civil penalties, its own ideas and practices as rules of conduct on those who dissent from them; to fetter the development, and, if possible, prevent the formation, of any individuality not in harmony with its ways, and compel all characters to fashion themselves upon the model of its own. There is a limit to the legitimate interference of collective opinion with individual independence: and to find that limit, and maintain it against encroachment, is as indispensable to a good condition of human affairs, as protection against political despotism.

But though this proposition is not likely to be contested in general terms, the practical question, where to place the limit—how to make the fitting adjustment between individual independence and social control—is a subject on which nearly everything remains to be done. All that makes existence valuable to any one, depends on the enforcement of restraints upon the actions of other people. Some rules of conduct, therefore, must be imposed, by law in the first place, and by opinion on many things which are not fit subjects for the operation of law. What these rules should be, is the principal question in human affairs; but if we except a few of the most obvious cases, it is one of those which least progress has been made in resolving. No two ages, and scarcely any two countries, have decided it alike; and the decision of one age or country is a wonder to another. Yet the people of any given age and country no more suspect any difficulty in it, than if it were a subject on which mankind had always been agreed. The rules which obtain among themselves appear to them self-evident and self-justifying. This all but universal illusion is one of the examples of the magical influence of custom, which is not only, as the proverb says, a second nature, but is continually mistaken for the first. The effect of custom, in preventing any misgiving respecting the rules of conduct which mankind impose on one another, is all the more complete because the subject is one on which it is not generally considered necessary that reasons should be given, either by one person to others, or by each to himself. People are accustomed to believe, and have been encouraged in the belief by some who aspire to the character of philosophers, that their feelings, on subjects of this nature, are better than reasons, and render reasons unnecessary. The practical principle which guides them to their opinions on the regulation of human conduct, is the feeling in each person's mind that everybody should be required to act as he, and those with whom he sympathizes, would like them to act. No one, indeed, acknowledges to himself that his standard of judgment is his own liking; but an opinion on a point of conduct, not supported by reasons, can only count as one person's preference; and if the reasons, when given are a mere appeal to a similar preference felt by other people, it is still only many people's liking instead of one. To an ordinary man, however, his own preference, thus supported, is not only a perfectly satisfactory reason, but the only one he generally has for any of his notions of morality, taste, or propriety, which are not expressly written in his religious creed; and his chief guide in the interpretation even of that. Men's opinions, accordingly, on what is laudable or blameable, are affected by all the multifarious causes which influence their wishes in regard to the conduct of others, and which are as numerous as those which determine their wishes on any other subject. Sometimes their reason—at other times their prejudices or superstitions: often their social affections, not seldom their antisocial ones, their envy or jealousy, their arrogance or contemptuousness: but most commonly, their desires or fears for themselves— their legitimate or illegitimate self-interest. . . . The likings and dislikings of society, or of some powerful portion of it, are thus the main thing which has practically determined the rules laid down for general observance, under the penalties of law or opinion. And in general, those who have been in advance of society in thought and feeling, have left this condition of things unassailed in principle, however they may have come into conflict with it in some of its details. They have occupied themselves rather in inquiring what things society ought to like or dislike, than in questioning whether its likings or dislikings should be a law to individuals. They preferred endeavoring to alter the feelings of mankind on the particular points on which they were themselves heretical, rather than make common cause in defense of freedom, with heretics generally. The only case in which the higher ground has been taken on principle and maintained with consistency, by any but an individual here and there, is that of religous belief: a case instructive in many ways, and not least so as forming a most striking instance of the fallibility of what is called the moral sense: for the *odium theologicum*, in a sincere bigot, is one of the most unequivocal cases of moral feeling. Those who first broke the yoke of what called itself the Universal Church, were in general as little willing to permit difference of religious opinion as that church itself. But when the heat of the conflict was over, without giving a complete victory to any party, and each church or sect was reduced to limit its hopes to retaining possession of the ground it already occupied; minorities, seeing that they had no chance of becoming majorities, were under the necessity of pleading to those whom they could not convert, for permission to differ. It is accordingly on this battle-field, almost solely, that the rights of the individual against society have been asserted on broad grounds of principle, and the claim of society to exercise authority over dissentients, openly controverted. The great writers to whom the world owes what religious liberty it possesses, have mostly asserted freedom of conscience as an indefeasible right, and denied absolutely that a human being is accountable to others for his religious belief. Yet so natural to mankind is intolerance in whatever they really care about, that religious freedom has hardly anywhere been practically realized, except where religious indifference, which dislikes to have its peace disturbed by theological quarrels, has added its weight to the scale. In the minds of almost all religious persons, even in the most tolerant countries, the duty of toleration is admitted with tacit reserves. One person will bear with dissent in matters of church government, but not of dogma; another can tolerate everybody, short of a Papist or a Unitarian; another, every one who believes in revealed religion; a few extend their charity a little further, but stop at the belief in a God and in a future state. Wherever the sentiment of the majority is still genuine and intense, it is found to have abated little of its claim to be obeyed. . . .

The object of this Essay is to assert one very simple principle, as entitled to govern absolutely the dealings of society with the individual in the way of compulsion and control, whether the means used be physical force in the form of legal penalties, or the moral coercion of public opinion. That principle is, that the sole end for which mankind are warranted, individually or collectively, in interfering with the liberty of action of any of their number, is self-protection. That the only purpose for which power can be rightfully exercised over any member of a civilized community, against his will, is to prevent harm to others. His own good, either physical or moral, is not a sufficient warrant. He cannot rightfully be compelled to do or forbear because it will be better for him to do so, because it will make him happier, because, in the opinions of others, to do so would be wise, or even right. These are good reasons for remonstrating with him, or reasoning with him, or persuading him, or entreating him, but not for compelling him, or visiting him with any evil in case he do otherwise. To justify that, the conduct from which it is desired to deter him, must be calculated to produce evil to some one else. The only part of the conduct of any one, for which he is amendable to society, is that which concerns others. In the part which merely concerns himself, his independence is, of right, absolute. Over himself, over his own body and mind, the individual is sovereign.

It is, perhaps, hardly necessary to say that this doctrine is meant to apply only to human beings in the maturity of their faculties. We are not speaking of children, or of young persons below the age which the law may fix as that of manhood or womanhood. Those who are still in a state to require being taken care of by others, must be protected against their own actions as well as against external injury. For the same reason, we may leave out of consideration those backward states of society in which the race itself may be considered as in its nonage. . . .

It is proper to state that I forgo any advantage which could be derived to my argument from the idea of abstract right, as a thing independent of utility. I regard utility as the ultimate appeal on all ethical questions; but it must be utility in the largest sense, grounded on the permanent interests of man as a progressive being. . . . No society in which these liberties are not, on the whole, respected, is free, whatever may be its form of government; and none is completely free in which they do not exist absolute and unqualified. The only freedom which deserves the name, is that of pursuing our own good in our own way, so long as we do not attempt to deprive others of theirs, or impede their efforts to obtain it. Each is the proper guardian of his own health, whether bodily, or mental and spiritual. Mankind are greater gainers by suffering each other to live as seems good to themselves, than by compelling each to live as seems good to the rest.

Though this doctrine is anything but new, and, to some persons, may have the air of a truism, there is no doctrine which stands more directly opposed to the general tendency of existing opinion and practice. Society has expended fully as much effort in the attempt (according to its lights) to compel people to conform to its notions of personal, as of social excellence. The ancient commonwealths thought themselves entitled to practice, and the ancient philosophers countenanced, the regulation of every part of private conduct by public authority, on the ground that the State had a deep interest in the whole bodily and mental discipline of every one of its citizens; a mode of thinking which may have been admissible in small republics surrounded by powerful enemies, in constant peril of being subverted by foreign attack or internal commotion, and to which even a short interval of relaxed energy and self-command might so easily be fatal, that they could not afford to wait for the salutary permanent effects of freedom. In the modern world, the greater size of political communities, and, above all, the separation between spiritual and temporal authority (which placed the direction of men's consciences in other hands than those which controlled their worldly affairs), prevented so great an interference by law in the details of private life; but the engines of moral repression have been wielded more strenuously against divergence from the reigning opinion in self-regarding, than even in social matters; religion, the most powerful of the elements which have entered into the formation of moral feeling, having almost always been governed either by the ambition of a hierarchy, seeking control over every department of human conduct, or by the spirit of Puritanism. And some of those modern reformers who have placed themselves in strongest opposition to the religions of the past, have been no way behind either churches or sects in their assertion of the right of spiritual domination. . . .

Apart from the peculiar tenets of individual thinkers, there is also in the world at large an increasing inclination to stretch unduly the powers of society over the individual, both by the force of opinion and even by that of legislation: and as the tendency of all the changes taking place in the world is to strengthen society, and diminish the power of the individual, this encroachment is not one of the evils which tend spontaneously to disappear, but, on the contrary, to grow more and more formidable. The disposition of mankind, whether as rulers or as fellow citizens, to impose their own opinions and inclinations as a rule of conduct on others, is so energetically supported by some of the best and by some of the worst feelings incident to human nature, that it is hardly ever kept under restraint by anything but want of power; and as the power is not declining, but growing, unless a strong barrier of moral conviction can be raised against the mischief, we must expect, in the present circumstances of the world, to see it increase. . . .

The strongest of all the arguments against the interference of the public with purely personal conduct, is that when it does interfere, the odds are that it interferes wrongly, and in the wrong place. On questions of social morality, of duty to others, the opinion of the public, that is, of an overruling majority, though often wrong, is likely to be still oftener right; because of such questions they are only required to judge of their own interests; of the manner in which some mode of conduct, if allowed to be practiced, would affect themselves. But the opinion of a similar majority, imposed as a law on the minority, on questions of self-regarding conduct, is quite as likely to be wrong as right; for in these cases public opinion means, at the best, some people's opinion of what is good or bad for other people; while very often it does not even mean that; the public, with the most perfect indifference, passing over the pleasure or convenience of those whose conduct they censure, and considering only their own preference. There are many who consider as an injury to themselves any conduct which they have a distaste for, and resent it as an outrage to their feeling; as a religious bigot, when charged with disregarding the religious feelings of others, has been known to retort that they disregard his feeling, by persisting in their abominable worship or creed. But there is no parity between the feeling of a person for his own opinion, and the feeling of another who is offended at his holding it; no more than between the desire of a thief to take a purse, and the desire of the right owner to keep it. And a person's taste is as much his own peculiar concern as his opinion or his purse. It is easy for any one to imagine an ideal public, which leaves the freedom and choice of individuals in all uncertain matters undisturbed, and only requires them to abstain from modes of conduct which universal experience has condemned. But where has there been seen a public which set any such limit to its censorship? or when does the public trouble itself about universal experience? In its interferences with personal conduct it is seldom thinking of anything but the enormity of acting or feeling differently from itself; and this standard of judgment, thinly disguised, is held up to mankind as the dictate of religion and philosophy, by nine-tenths of all moralists and speculative writers. These teach that things are right because they are right; because we feel them to be so. They tell us to search in our own minds and hearts for laws of conduct binding on ourselves and on all others. What can the poor public do but apply these instructions, and make their own personal feelings of good and evil, if they are tolerably unanimous in them, obligatory on all the world?

The evil here pointed out is not one which exists only in theory; and it may perhaps be expected that I should specify the instances in which the public of this age and country improperly invests its own preferences with the character of moral laws. I am not writing an essay on the aberrations of existing moral feeling. That is too weighty a subject to be discussed parenthetically, and by way of illustration. Yet examples are necessary, to show that the principle I maintain is of serious and practical moment, and that I am not endeavoring to erect a barrier against imaginary evils. And it is not difficult to show, by abundant instances, that to extend the bounds of what may be called moral police, until it encroaches on the most unquestionably legitimate liberty of the individual, is one of the most universal of all human propensities.

As a first instance, consider the antipathies which men cherish on no better grounds than that persons whose religious opinions are different from theirs, do not practice their religious observances, especially their religious abstinences. To cite a rather trivial example, nothing in the creed or practice of Christians does more to envenom the hatred of Mohammedans against them, than the fact of their eating pork. There are few acts which Christians and Europeans regard with more unaffected disgust, than Mussulmans regard this particular mode of satisfying hunger. It is, in the first place an offense against their religion; but this circumstance by no means explains either the degree or the kind of their repugnance; for wine also is forbidden by their religion, and to partake of it is by all Mussulmans accounted wrong, but not disgusting. Their aversion to the flesh of the "unclean beast" is, on the contrary, of that peculiar character, resembling an instinctive antipathy, which the idea of uncleanness, when once it thoroughly sinks into the feelings, seems always to excite even in those whose personal habits are anything but scrupulously cleanly, and of which the sentiment of religious impurity, so intense in the Hindoos, is a remarkable example. Suppose now that in a people, of whom the majority were Mussulmans, that majority should insist upon not permitting pork to be eaten within the limits of the country. This would be nothing new in Mohammedan countries. Would it be a legitimate exercise of the moral authority of public opinion? and if not, why not? The practice is really revolting to such a public. They also sincerely think that is is forbidden and abhorred by the Deity. Neither could the prohibition be censured as religious persecution. It might be religious in its origin, but it would not be persecution for religion, since nobody's religion makes it a duty to eat pork. The only tenable ground of condemnation would be, that with the personal tastes and self-regarding concerns of individuals the public has no business to interfere.

To come somewhat nearer home: the majority of Spaniards consider it a gross impiety, offensive in the highest degree to the Supreme Being, to worship him in any other manner than the Roman Catholic; and no other public worship is lawful on Spanish soil. The people of all Southern Europe look upon a married clergy as not only irreligious, but unchaste, indecent, gross, disgusting. What do Protestants think of these perfectly sincere feelings, and of the attempt to enforce them against non-Catholics? Yet, if mankind are justified in interfering with each other's liberty in things which do not concern the interests of others, on what principle is it possible consistently to exclude these cases? or who can blame people for desiring to suppress what they regard as a scandal in the sight of God and man? No stronger case can be shown for prohibiting anything which is regarded as a personal immorality, than is made out for suppressing these practices in the eyes of those who regard them as impieties; and unless we are willing to adopt the logic of persecutors, and to say that we may persecute others because we are right, and that they must not persecute us because they are wrong, we must beware of admitting a principle of which we should resent as a gross injustice the application to ourselves.

The preceding instances may be objected to, although unreasonably, as drawn from contingencies impossible among us: opinion, in this country, not being likely to enforce abstinence from meats, or to interfere with people for worshiping, and for either marrying or not marrying, according to their creed or inclination. The next example, however, shall be taken from an interference with liberty which we have by no means passed all danger of. Wherever the

Puritans have been sufficiently powerful, as in New England, and in Great Britain at the time of the Commonwealth, they have endeavored, with considerable success, to put down all public, and nearly all private, amusements: especially music, dancing, public games, or other assemblages for purposes of diversion, and the theater. There are still in this country large bodies of persons by whose notions of morality and religion these recreations are condemned; and those persons belonging chiefly to the middle class, who are the ascendant power in the present social and political condition of the kingdom, it is by no means impossible that persons of these sentiments may at some time or other command a majority in Parliament. How will the remaining portion of the community like to have the amusements that shall be permitted to them regulated by the religious and moral sentiments of the stricter Calvinists and Methodists? Would they not, with considerable peremptoriness, desire these intrusively pious members of society to mind their own business? This is precisely what should be said to every government and every public, who have the pretension that no person shall enjoy any pleasure which they think wrong. But if the principle of the pretension be admitted, no one can reasonably object to its being acted on in the sense of the majority, or other preponderating power in the country; and all persons must be ready to conform to the idea of a Christian commonwealth, as understood by the early settlers in New England, if a religious profession similar to theirs should ever succeed in regaining its lost ground, as religions supposed to be declining have so often been known to do.

To imagine another contingency, perhaps more likely to be realized than the one last mentioned. There is confessedly a strong tendency in the modern world towards a democratic constitution of society, accompanied or not by popular political institutions. It is affirmed that in the country where this tendency is most completely realized—where both society and the government are most democratic—the United States—the feeling of the majority, to whom any appearance of a more showy or costly style of living than they can hope to rival is disagreeable, operates as a tolerably effectual sumptuary law, and that in many parts of the Union it is really difficult for a person possessing a very large income, to find any mode of spending it, which will not incur popular disapprobation. Though such statements as these are doubtless much exaggerated as a representation of existing facts, the state of things they describe is not only a conceivable and possible, but a probable result of democratic feeling, combined with the notion that the public has a right to a veto on the manner in which individuals shall spend their incomes. We have only further to suppose a considerable diffusion of Socialist opinions, and it may become infamous in the eyes of the majority to possess more property than some very small amount, or any income not earned by manual labor. Opinions similar in principle to these, already prevail widely among the artisan class, and weigh oppressively on those who are amenable to the opinion chiefly of that class, namely, its own members. It is known that the bad workmen who form the majority of the operatives in many branches of industry, are decidedly of opinion that bad workmen ought to receive the same wages as good, and that no one ought to be allowed, through piecework or otherwise, to earn by superior skill or industry more than others can without it. And they employ a moral police, which occasionally becomes a physical one, to deter skillful workmen from receiving, and employers from giving, a larger remuneration for a more useful service. If the public have any jurisdiction over private concerns, I cannot see that these people are in fault, or that any individual's particular public can be blamed for asserting the same authority over his individual conduct, which the general public asserts over people in general.

But, without dwelling upon suppositious cases, there are, in our own day, gross usurpations upon the liberty of private life actually practiced, and still greater ones threatened with some expectation of success, and opinions propounded which assert an unlimited right in the public not only to prohibit by law everything which it thinks wrong, but in order to get at what it thinks wrong, to prohibit any number of things which it admits to be innocent.

Under the name of preventing intemperance, the people of one English colony, and of nearly half the United States, have been interdicted by law from making any use whatever of fermented drinks, except for medical purposes: for prohibition of their sale is in fact, as it is intended to be, prohibition of their use. And though the impracticability of executing the law has caused its repeal in several of the States which had adopted it . . . an attempt has notwithstanding been commenced, and is prosecuted with considerable zeal by many of the professed philanthropists, to agitate for a similar law in this country. The association, or "Alliance" as it terms itself, which has been formed for this purpose, has acquired some notoriety through the publicity given to a correspondence between its Secretary and one of the very few English public men who hold that a politician's opinions ought to be founded on principles. . . . The organ of the Alliance, who would "deeply deplore the recognition of any principle which could be wrested to justify bigotry and persecution," undertakes to point out the "broad and impassable barrier" which divides such principles from those of the association. "All matters relating to thought, opinion, conscience, appear to me," he says, "to be without the sphere of legislation; all pertaining to social act, habit, relation, subject only to a discretionary power vested in the State itself, and not in the individual, to be within it." No mention is made of a third class, different from either of these, viz. acts and habits which are not social, but individual; although it is to this class, surely, that the act of drinking fermented liquors belongs. Selling fermented liquors, however, is trading, and trading is a social act. But the infringement complained of is not on the liberty of the seller, but on that of the buyer and consumer; since the State might just as well forbid him to drink wine, as purposely make it impossible for him to obtain it. The Secretary, however, says, "I claim, as a citizen, a right to legislate whenever my social rights are invaded by the social act of another." And now for the definition of these "social rights." "If anything invades my social rights, certainly the traffic in strong drink does. It destroys my primary right of security, by constantly creating and stimulating social disorder. It invades my right of equality, by deriving a profit from the creation of a misery I am taxed to support. It impedes my right to free moral and intellectual development, by surrounding my path with dangers, and by weakening and demoralizing society, from which I have a right to claim mutual aid and intercourse." A theory of "social rights," the like of which probably never before found its way into distinct language: being nothing short of this—that it is the absolute social right of every individual, that every other individual shall act in every respect exactly as he ought; that whosoever fails thereof in the smallest particular, violates my social right, and entitles me to demand from the legislature the removal of the grievance. So monstrous a principle is far more dangerous than any single interference with liberty; there is no violation of liberty which it would not justify; it acknowledges no right to any freedom whatever, except perhaps to that of holding opinions in secret, without ever disclosing them: for, the moment an opinion which I consider noxious passes any one's lips, it invades all the "social rights" attributed to me by the Alliance. The doctrine ascribes to all mankind a vested interest in each other's moral, intellectual, and even physical per-- fection, to be defined by each claimant according to his own standard.

Another important example of illegitimate interference with the rightful liberty of the individual, not simply threatened, but long since carried into triumphant effect, is Sabbatarian legislation. Without doubt, abstinence on one day in the week, so far as the exigencies of life permit, from the usual daily occupation, though in no respect religiously binding on any except Jews, is a highly beneficial custom. And inasmuch as this custom cannot be observed without a general consent to that effect among the industrious classes, therefore, in so far as some persons by working may impose the same necessity in others, it may be allowable and right that the law should guarantee to each the observance by others of the custom, by suspending the greater operations of industry on a particular day. But this justification, grounded on the direct interest which others have in each individual's observance of the practice, does not apply to the self-chosen occupations in which a person may think fit to employ his leisure; nor does it hold good, in the smallest degree, for legal restrictions on amusements. It is true that the amusement of some is the day's work of others; but the pleasure, not to say the useful recreation, of many, is worth the labor of a few, provided the occupation is freely chosen, and can be freely resigned. The operatives are perfectly right in thinking that if all worked on Sunday, seven days' work would have to be given for six days' wages: but so long as the great mass of employments are suspended, the small number who for the enjoyment of others must still work, obtain a proportional increase of earnings; and they are not obliged to follow those occupations, if they prefer leisure to emolument. If a further remedy is sought, it might be found in the establishment by custom of a holiday on some other day of the week for those particular classes of persons. The only ground, therefore, on which restrictions on Sunday amusements can be defended, must be that they are religiously wrong; a motive of legislation which never can be too earnestly protested against. "Deorum injuriae Diis curae." It remains to be proved that society or any of its officers holds a commission from on high to avenge any supposed offense to Omnipotence, which is not also a wrong to our fellow creatures. The notion that it is one man's duty that another should be religious, was the foundation of all the religious persecutions ever perpetrated, and if admitted, would fully justify them. Though the feeling which breaks out in the repeated attempts to stop railway traveling on Sunday, in the resistance to the opening of Museums, and the like, has not the cruelty of the old persecutors, the state of mind indicated by it is fundamentally the same. It is a determination not to tolerate others in doing what is permitted by their religion, because it is not permitted by the persecutor's religion. It is a belief that God not only abominates the act of the misbeliever, but will not hold us guiltless if we leave him unmolested.

I cannot refrain from adding to these examples of the little account commonly made of human liberty, the language of downright persecution which breaks out from the press of this country, whenever it feels called on to notice the remarkable phenomenon of Mormonism. Much might be said on the unexpected and instructive fact, that an alleged new revelation, and a religion founded on it, the product of palpable imposture, not even supported by the *prestige* of extraordinary qualities in its founder, is believed by hundreds of thousands, and has been made the foundation of a society, in the age of newspapers, railways, and the electric telegraph. What here concerns us is, that this religion, like other and better religions, has its martyrs; that its prophet and founder was, for his teaching, put to death by a mob; that others of its adherents lost their lives by the same lawless violence; that they were forcibly expelled, in a body, from the country in which they first grew up; while, now that they have been chased into a solitary recess in the midst of a desert, many in this country openly declare that it would be right (only that it is not convenient) to send an expedition against them, and compel them by force to conform to the opinions of other people. The article of the Mormonite doctrine which is the chief provocative to the antipathy which thus breaks through the ordinary restraints of religious tolerance, is its sanction of polygamy; which, though permitted to Mohammedans, and Hindoos, and Chinese, seems to excite unquenchable animosity when practiced by persons who speak English, and profess to be a kind of Christians. No one has a deeper disapprobation than I have of this Mormon institution; both for other reasons, and because, far from being in any way countenanced by the principle of liberty, it is a direct infraction of that principle, being a mere riveting of the chains of one-half of the community, and an emancipation of the other from reciprocity of obligation towards them. Still, it must be remembered that this relation is as much voluntary on the part of the women concerned in it, and who may be deemed the sufferers by it, as is the case with any other form of the marriage institution; and however surprising this fact may appear, it has its explanation in the common ideas and customs of the world, which teaching women to think marriage the one thing needful, make it intelligible that many a woman should prefer being one of several wives, to not being a wife at all. Other countries are not asked to recognize such unions, or release any portion of their inhabitants from their own laws on the score of Mormonite opinions. But when the dissentients have conceded to the hostile sentiments of others, far more than could justly be demanded; when they have left the countries to which their doctrines were unacceptable, and established themselves in a remote corner of the earth, which they have been the first to render habitable to human beings; it is difficult to see on what principles but those of tyranny they can be prevented from living there under what laws they please, provided they commit no aggression on other nations, and allow perfect freedom of departure to those who are dissatisfied with their ways. A recent writer, in some respects of considerable merit, proposes (to use his own words) not a crusade, but a *civilizade*, against this polygamous community, to put an end to what seems to him a retrograde step in civilization. It also appears so to me, but I am not aware that any community has a right to force another to be civilized. So long as the sufferers by the bad law do not invoke assistance from other communities, I cannot admit that persons entirely unconnected with them ought to step in and require that a condition of things with which all who are directly interested appear to be satisfied, should be put an end to because it is a scandal to persons some thousands of miles distant, who have no part or concern in it. Let them send missionaries, if they please, to preach against it; and let them, by any fair means (of which silencing the teachers is not one), oppose the progress of similar doctrines among their own people. If civilization has got the better of barbarism when barbarism had the world to itself, it is too much to profess to be afraid lest barbarism, after having been fairly got under, should revive and conquer civilization. A civilization that can thus succumb to its vanquished enemy, must first have become so degenerate that neither its appointed priests and teachers, nor anybody else, has the capacity, or will take the trouble, to stand up for it. If this be so, the sooner such a civilization receives notice to quit, the better. It can only go on from bad to worse, until destroyed and regenerated (like the Western [Roman] Empire) by energetic barbarians.

QUESTIONS

Following are some general statements which occur in the selection from Mill. Consider them in reference to such questions as the following: What do they mean? Are they true? Re what point do they occur in the essay? Does he give any reasons? Or examples?

1. "The nature and limits of the power which can be legitimately exercised by society over the individual . . . is . . . the vital question of the future."

2. "The limitation of the power of government over individuals loses none of its importance when the holders of power are regularly accountable to the community."

3. "All that makes existence valuable to anyone depends on the enforcements of restraints upon the actions of other people."

4. "Some rules are necessary. What rules, is the principal question in human affairs. Little progress has been made here."

5. "Wherever there is an ascendent class, a large portion of the morality of the country emanates from its class interests."

6. ". . . religious freedom has hardly anywhere been practically realized, except where religious indifference . . . has added its weight. . . ."

7. "The only part of the conduct of anyone, for which he is answerable to society, is that which concerns others."

8. "Despotism is legimate in dealing with barbarians provided the end be their improvement and the means effective to that end."

9. "I regard utility as the ultimate appeal on all ethical questions."

10. "To make anyone answerable for doing evil to others is the rule;

to make him answerable for not preventing evil is . . . the exception."

11. "Mankind are greater gainers by allowing each other to live as seems good to themselves, than by compelling each to live as seems good to the rest."

12. "The only freedom which deserves the name, is that of pursuing our own good in our own way. . . . "

13. ". . . religion [is] the most powerful of the elements which have entered into the formation of moral feeling. . . ."

14. ". . . religion . . . [has] almost always been governed either by the ambition of a hierarchy, seeking control over every department of human conduct, or by the spirit of Puritanism."

15. ". . . the tendency of all the changes taking place in the world is to strengthen society, and diminish the power of the individual. . . . "

16. "The disposition of mankind, whether as rulers or as fellow-citizens, to impose their opinions and inclinations as a rule of conduct upon others, . . . is hardly ever kept under restraint by anything but want of power. . . . "

INDEX

Index